Language Assessment and Programme Evaluation

Edinburgh Textbooks in Applied Linguistics

Edinburgh Textbooks in Applied Linguistics

Series Editors: Alan Davies and Keith Mitchell

Language Assessment and Programme Evaluation

Brian K. Lynch

Edinburgh University Press

For my two most beloved ones, Buni and Sam

© Brian K. Lynch, 2003

Edinburgh University Press Ltd
22 George Square, Edinburgh

Typeset in Garamond
by Norman Tilley Graphics, Northampton,
and printed and bound in Great Britain
by Antony Rowe Ltd, Chippenham

A CIP record for this book is available from
the British Library

ISBN 0 7486 1562 8 (paperback)

Contents

Series Editors' Preface

This new series of single-author volumes published by Edinburgh University Press takes a contemporary view of applied linguistics. The intention is to make provision for the wide range of interests in contemporary applied linguistics which are provided for at the Master's level.

The expansion of Master's postgraduate courses in recent years has had two effects:

1. What began almost half a century ago as a wholly cross-disciplinary subject has found a measure of coherence so that now most training courses in Applied Linguistics have similar core content.
2. At the same time the range of specialisms has grown, as in any developing discipline. Training courses (and professional needs) vary in the extent to which these specialisms are included and taught.

Some volumes in the series will address the first development noted above, while the others will explore the second. It is hoped that the series as a whole will provide students beginning postgraduate courses in Applied Linguistics, as well as language teachers and other professionals wishing to become acquainted with the subject, with a sufficient introduction for them to develop their own thinking in applied linguistics and to build further into specialist areas of their own choosing.

The view taken of applied linguistics in the Edinburgh Textbooks in Applied Linguistics Series is that of a theorising approach to practical experience in the language professions, notably, but not exclusively, those concerned with language learning and teaching. It is concerned with the problems, the processes, the mechanisms and the purposes of language in use.

Like any other applied discipline, applied linguistics draws on theories from related disciplines with which it explores the professional experience of its practitioners and which in turn are themselves illuminated by that experience. This two-way relationship between theory and practice is what we mean by a theorising discipline.

The volumes in the series are all premised on this view of Applied Linguistics as a theorising discipline which is developing its own coherence. At the same time, in order to present as complete a contemporary view of applied linguistics as possible other approaches will occasionally be expressed.

Each volume presents its author's own view of the state of the art in his or her topic. Volumes will be similar in length and in format, and, as is usual in a textbook series, each will contain exercise material for use in class or in private study.

Alan Davies
W. Keith Mitchell

Preface

This book attempts to present the range of paradigms, perspectives, designs, purposes, methods, analyses and approaches to validity and ethics that currently define language assessment and programme evaluation. In order to navigate through these topics, the reader needs to be aware of the guiding structure. I begin with the topic of paradigms and purposes for doing both assessment and evaluation. This, I believe, is a necessary starting point, but one that is the most complex of all topics handled in the book. The understandings developed for paradigms and purposes continue to be discussed and elaborated in the following chapters, however. Chapter 2 demonstrates how a consideration of paradigm, purpose, audiences, goals and context can lead to the design of an assessment procedure or programme evaluation: a design, in this case, being the means for organising the data-gathering and analysis that will serve the assessment and evaluation goals and purposes. Chapters 3 and 4 focus on quantitative methods for gathering and analysing assessment and evaluation data; Chapters 5 and 6 focus on qualitative methodology. The final chapter considers the fundamental issues of validity and ethics, and their interrelationship, in the practice of assessment and evaluation, and how these differ between the two major paradigms presented in Chapter 1. Each chapter ends with a set of exercises designed to have the reader think through the content in more detail, and to apply it, where appropriate, to familiar contexts. There is also a set of suggested readings for further exploration of each chapter's main topics.

It perhaps would have been wiser to stake out one paradigmatic perspective and focus on the issues, techniques and guidance that it could give us concerning the difficult problems of assessment and evaluation. I hope that my decision to present a fuller range of options will provide benefits that outweigh the potential for being overwhelmed. I recall a criticism of one of my first published articles on evaluation: it was said that so many methods were presented, it made it difficult to see the forest for the trees. My goal here was to allow you to see both the forest and the trees. Of course, in choosing to present paradigm differences as important first points of departure, the problem is complicated further. There is no one forest to be seen.

My choice to present the paradigm issue in dichotomous terms – 'positivism' versus 'interpretivism' – was made for the sake of focusing on what I see as the major differences between groups of approaches that cluster around either label. This made my job of portraying different approaches to design, information collection and analysis easier, but ran the risk of oversimplifying the nature of both clusters, as well as losing certain differences within clusters. For example, there are important distinctions that can be made between critical theory, critical applied linguistics and constructivism. Focusing on these distinctions did not seem to further the goal of presenting alternatives for a coherent practice of assessment and evaluation. So, I use the positivist–interpretivist distinction to help provide some coherence, but I have also attempted to provide reference to different perspectives within these paradigm clusters (such as the critical-testing perspective within interpretivism, and the critical-realist perspective within positivism).

Although my training was grounded in the positivist paradigm, I have come to appreciate and use interpretivism more and more during the last ten years of my professional life. Part of what I find attractive and useful about the interpretivist perspective is that it makes sense in terms of my worldview as it extends beyond my professional life as well. Since reading John K. Smith's (1988) article titled 'The evaluator/researcher as person vs. the person as evaluator/researcher', I have been intrigued by the idea that our professional views of the world can, or perhaps should, be integral with our personal views of the world. If we believe that our personal relationships are co-constructed, if we believe that our experience of the world is relative to our particular time, place, history and culture, rather than these things being independently existing truths, then why would we opt for a different paradigmatic perspective when approaching our professional work? Some will answer this question by citing the need to keep the professional and the personal (or individual) separate. In the words of a dear friend and colleague, 'I hope I do my professional work better than I manage my personal life!' There is also a clear and understandable need for certainty. In the past, more of us were able to find that certainty in religion or other socio-cultural institutions, perhaps. With the advent of the postmodern world, these traditional sources of certainty are in doubt for many. So, it is not surprising that we turn to our professional lives to find some semblance of order, of truth, of ethical coherence.

At the Language Assessment Ethics Conference, organised by Antony Kunnan and the Charter College of Education, California State University, Los Angeles, in May 2002, the task of creating a code of practice for the International Language Testing Association (ILTA) was central to many of the discussions. By the end of the conference, the general mood was that this may be an impossible task, given the international nature of the association. The principles articulated in the Code of Ethics (ILTA 2000) seemed reasonable, but necessarily too general to translate easily into a code of practice that would be relevant and acceptable to all cultures, countries and language-assessment contexts represented by ILTA. In fact, some participants wondered if the most ethical response to the problem might not be to abandon these somewhat philosophical discussions and concentrate our efforts on the problems of designing better tests.

I would like to suggest that we consider the time and effort spent on discussing the ethics of language assessment and programme evaluation are directly relevant to making better forms of assessment and better approaches to evaluation. The time and effort spent by the participants of the Los Angeles conference on ethics in assessment brought a connection between our profession and our humanity. It suggested to me that, although we need to be cautious about codifying such things as ethics, we should perhaps strive to let our personal and professional worldviews achieve a coherence that can guide ethical decisions. Language assessment and programme evaluation are inherently social and political activities. Our professional codes need to recognise this, rather than attempting to portray a false sense of neutrality and objectivity. This may argue against having universal codes for the profession, or it may argue for articulating codes as dynamic sites of struggle, where the central issues of validity and ethics, of selecting designs and methods of analysis for our practice, are presented not as rules or principles, but as activities in need of constant debate and reconstruction.

Acknowledgements

AUTHOR'S ACKNOWLEGEMENTS

This book represents the synthesis of research, practice, teaching, learning, conversations, reading and observation over a variety of contexts. I remain grateful to my early mentors in assessment and evaluation: J. D. Brown, Frances Butler, James Popham, Harold Levine and the late Leigh Burstein. What I have managed to learn over the years has also been the result of working with excellent colleagues, students and friends in the ESL Service Courses and the Department of TESL and Applied Linguistics at UCLA, and in the Centre for Communication Skills and the Department of Linguistics and Applied Linguistics at the University of Melbourne. I want to give particular thanks to my colleagues in the Department of Applied Linguistics at Portland State University: Kim Brown, Tucker Childs, Susan Conrad, Jan DeCarrico, Tom Dieterich, Lynn Santelmann, Marge Terdal, and especially Kathy Harris and Steve Reder. Thanks also to Betsy Kraft, Kristen Setzler, Erik Simensen, Sharon Canada, Reika Okumura, Karin Tittelbach and the students in my TESOL Methods, Research Design and Language Testing classes. Without the supportive environment that these people have shared with me, the book would not have been completed. I want to acknowledge a few people who have inspired me with their own work as well as their friendship: Russ Campbell, Fred Davidson, Liz Hamp-Lyons, Thom Hudson, Alastair Pennycook, Peter Shaw, Elana Shohamy, Neomy Storch, and, most importantly, Tim McNamara. It is also important to acknowledge the invaluable assistance of Sarah Edwards, the series co-editors Alan Davies and Keith Mitchell, and the entire Edinburgh University Press staff. I owe a great debt to Alan Davies, in particular, for his encouragement and support of this project. Finally, I offer a special thanks to my brother, Dennis, and my mom, Margaret, for their constant love and inspiration, and to my wife Buni and son Sam for letting me all but disappear from their lives during the writing of this book.

Chapter 1

Introduction: paradigms and purposes

1.1 INTRODUCTION

This book examines the overlapping areas of evaluation and assessment. As I will be using the term, language assessment is defined as the range of procedures used to investigate aspects of individual language learning and ability, including the measurement of proficiency, diagnosis of needs, determination of achievement in relation to syllabus objectives and analysis of ability to perform specific tasks. I define programme evaluation as the systematic inquiry into instructional sequences for the purpose of making decisions or providing opportunity for reflection and action. These two areas overlap in the sense that programme evaluation often makes use of data from language assessment, along with non-assessment data, to arrive at its conclusions. It should also be pointed out that assessment is used as a superordinate term to testing; that is, assessment includes, but is not limited to, measurement procedures generally referred to as tests.

In this way of conceptualising the areas, all testing is seen as a form of assessment which relies on quantification or measurement in order to arrive at its assessment interpretation. Assessment can also make use of forms that do not require quantification, such as portfolio assessment, in which the results are reported as qualitative profiles for each individual learner rather than a score or set of scores. The overlap between evaluation and assessment indicates that the former can include the latter, in the sense that evaluation decisions, judgements, reflections and actions will often be made based on assessment data. The reverse can also be true: assessment interpretations (for example, diagnosis of learner needs, determination of achievement) can be made using data originally gathered for evaluation purposes. However, evaluation will also make use of data and procedures falling outside the realm of assessment (for example, the analysis of programme documentation and observational notes from staff meetings) and assessment can be independent of any programme evaluation goal per se (for example, a decision or judgement concerning the programme).

For each of the topics that this book will address, there are necessarily separate treatments for assessment and evaluation. However, their overlap and interaction will also become apparent. Most importantly, I aim to set both assessment and evaluation within the context of audiences and problems typically encountered by applied-linguistics theoreticians and practitioners. In the spirit of this series, which sees applied linguistics as a 'theorising discipline', and Alan Davies' suggestion for a 'theorising approach' (2000: 142), I view theory and practice as mutually informing domains.

Underlying all attempts to assess individual language ability and evaluate language programmes, there is a set of assumptions about the nature of what is being assessed or evaluated. These assumptions have to do with the nature of reality, or what we believe we can know about it; the ways in which we should position ourselves in relation to that reality, or how we can establish knowledge; and the methods that we should employ in pursuing knowledge. Using these three levels of consideration, we can define the 'paradigm', or approach to research and practice (see Lincoln and Guba 2000).

Assessment and evaluation are also driven by specific purposes. These can involve getting answers to particular questions:

- Is this student ready for the next level of instruction?
- Is this programme achieving its objectives?

There can also be more general purposes that assessment and evaluation attempt to inform:

- What can we say about this student's proficiency in language?
- What links can be discovered between the processes of this programme and the achievement of its students?

In the sections that follow, the notion of approach will be presented for assessment in terms of the distinction between mainstream testing and alternative assessment, which follow from different research paradigms. For evaluation, approach will similarly be distinguished in terms of different research paradigms and strategies. The relationship between approach and paradigm will be explored further in the chapter on designing assessment and evaluation (Chapter 2), as well as in relation to validity (Chapter 7).

Following the discussion of paradigms and approaches, ways of thinking about assessment and evaluation in terms of purposes will be presented. These discussions provide the general backdrop against which to develop a more detailed consideration of assessment and evaluation theory and practice.

1.2 PARADIGMS

A paradigm, as the term will be used in this book, can be thought of as a lens through which we view the world. Different lenses can be used that imply different assumptions about the nature of the world and the ways in which we should attempt to understand it. There are many different lenses that exist for viewing and understanding the world, and a complete treatment of the notion of paradigm would take this book too far off its proposed track. However, some discussion and presentation of paradigms is essential for understanding the various approaches to assessment and evaluation that exist. What follows, then, will be a necessary simplification of a complex and constantly shifting set of boundaries that define the current paradigms, or lenses, that are being used to view and understand the world of language ability and language programmes.

One way in which the distinction between major paradigms has been discussed is in terms of 'quantitative' versus 'qualitative'. Ultimately these labels are unsatisfactory for signalling paradigm differences because they focus on the methodological level only. That is, they are descriptive of different types of data and data analysis, but do not adequately capture the different assumptions about the nature of reality or the relationship between the researcher and that reality. For example, whether we gather quantitative data or qualitative data (or a combination of the two), we may have very different assumptions about what it is we are trying to know, and how we can pursue that knowledge. One set of assumptions could be that reality is independent of the researchers (assessors, evaluators) and their attempts to know it; that in order to capture that reality as it 'really is', we need to be objective and approach it from the perspective of the distanced observer. This is a characterisation, somewhat over-simplified for the limited purposes of the introduction that I am attempting here, of the research paradigm that I believe is currently dominant in the field of applied linguistics. Another set of assumptions could be that reality is dependent on our attempts to know it, that it is a social construction and must be understood subjectively (and intersubjectively) through the interaction of participants in the research process. This would be a somewhat simplified characterisation of various paradigms and perspectives that currently provide an alternative to the dominant approach to research in our field. We could be guided by either set of assumptions, regardless of whether we were using quantitative or qualitative data and analytic techniques.

One way that I have attempted to present the paradigm distinction is through the use of the labels 'positivistic' and 'naturalistic' (Lynch 1996). However, like the quantitative–qualitative distinction, these terms are ultimately unsuccessful as well. Most researchers, and certainly philosophers of science, would maintain that positivism is dead and that it is too general a term to be useful in characterising current approaches to research. The term naturalistic gets confused with naturalism in the physical sciences and thus loses its ability to represent a set of assumptions that are in contrast to those of the physical science model. Even in attempting to discuss the failure of previous dichotomous labels, I have used the terms 'dominant' versus 'alternative'. This distinction fails to capture the fact that within the dominant paradigm there are ongoing and transforming debates, and the use of 'alternative' sets this paradigmatic perspective in opposition to the dominant paradigm only, rather than communicating an independent position.

Perhaps trying to dichotomise something that is, in fact, much more complicated than a two-category system is the wrong way to conceptualise paradigms. Unfortunately, the alternative leads us to a potentially never ending list of paradigms and perspectives within paradigms. Despite the diversity and overlap between the views, there are certain distinctions between the currently dominant paradigm based on the physical sciences and alternative paradigms such as constructivism, interpretivism, critical theory and phenomenology (see, for example, Kincheloe and McLaren 2000; Lynch 2001b; Pennycook 2001; Schwandt 2000). For want of better terms, I will use 'positivist' to describe what I see as the cluster of perspectives forming the currently dominant paradigm in applied linguistics, and 'interpretivist' to describe the cluster of perspectives that differ from that dominant paradigm in essential ways (Schwandt 2000).

I have chosen not to use the term 'postpositivist' (see Lincoln and Guba 2000) to represent the current, modified versions of positivism because of its tendency to be confused with postmodernism, poststructuralism, and postcolonialism (see Pennycook 2001). Similarly, I use 'interpretivism' instead of 'constructivism' (see Lincoln 1990; Lincoln and Guba 2000) because of the latter's tendency to be confused with constructivist and social constructionist learning theory (Pearce 1995).

One characteristic, already briefly introduced, that distinguishes these two paradigm clusters is the difference between seeing language ability and language programmes as parallel to objects and phenomena of the physical world, and viewing them as part of the social world, which is seen as essentially different from the physical world. This distinction acknowledges that there are valid ways of pursuing knowledge about language, ways that can even claim the mantle of social 'science', that do not follow the model of the physical (or natural) sciences. It also leads to another distinction in how the researcher pursues knowledge, in our case, in relation to language ability and language programmes.

The positivist view sees objectivity as a guiding principle, with the researcher required to stay neutral and disinterested in relation to what is being researched. This perspective sees a meaningful and important distinction between 'facts' – the elements of knowledge we are after – and 'values' – subjective biases which can potentially distort our ability to know the facts. In addition to objectivity as a guiding principle, this approach gives primacy to the discovery of causal relationships, which are seen to be key to our knowledge, and to the goal of generalising from the particular results of our research to larger populations of people.

The interpretivist view finds it impossible to separate facts from values and accepts the inherent subjectivity in any research conducted in relation to people, to the social world. Because knowledge is seen as something that is socially constructed, rather than the discovery of an independently existing reality, the notion of causality plays a different and less central role. Causal relationships are simply another, possible construction or explanation for certain aspects of the social world that we are researching. They are not taken to be universal laws that govern people and their actions, including the acquisition and use of language. Rather than strict causality – one variable preceding and causing another – this approach tends to see relationships as more complex and fluid, with directions of influence being mutual and shifting rather than unidirectional and fixed. In any event, the relationships involved with aspects of the social world such as language are not seen to be external and independent of our attempts to understand them. Instead of attempting to achieve a true match between our research observations and reality, this approach understands reality as being constructed in and through our observations and pursuit of knowledge.

In the following section, I will examine what different approaches to assessment and evaluation might be like, with different underlying assumptions along the lines that have been outlined above. By 'approach', I mean a combination of paradigm and strategy for designing and carrying out the activities of assessment and evaluation. Here the discussion will centre on paradigmatic assumptions; later (Chapter 2) there will be a discussion of the strategies for design and implementation.

1.3 ASSESSMENT

As previously mentioned, assessment can be seen to encompass measurement and non-measurement approaches to collecting the information necessary for decisions about individual language ability and achievement. The measurement approaches, including testing, are the ongoing tradition of psychometrics and the basis for mainstream language-testing research and practice. This psychometric basis can be seen as aligned with the paradigm that was discussed in the preceding section variously as 'quantitative', 'positivist', 'dominant' (based on the physical sciences model). Non-measurement approaches are also used within the dominant paradigm of language-testing (for example, the use of conversation analysis to investigate interlocutor and examinee behaviour in oral interview testing). However, non-measurement approaches can also be used within a different paradigm of research and practice, such as the one discussed above as 'qualitative', 'naturalistic', 'alternative'. The research and practice within this paradigm has sometimes been referred to as 'alternative assessment.'

Alternative assessment, often associated with educational reform, assumes a different paradigm or different 'culture' than testing or the more traditional approaches to assessment. This culture has been defined as distinct from the culture of testing by researchers such as Wolf et al. (1991) and Birenbaum (1996) and includes the following characteristics:

- assessment practices are considered as integral to teaching;
- students are made active participants in the process of developing assessment procedures, including the criteria and standards by which performances are judged;
- both the process and the product of the assessment are evaluated;
- the reporting of assessment results is done in the form of a qualitative profile rather than a single score or other quantification.

Although at first glance these characteristics may not seem radically different from traditional testing, they do call into question the key, paradigmatic assumptions underlying the mainstream approach. Language testing assumes that the aspects of language ability that we are interested in are things that can be measured, however imperfectly. It furthermore assumes a reality – in our case the social reality of language and language use – that exists independently from our attempts to understand it. As discussed in the previous section, this reality is conceived as an objective entity that can be captured with the proper tools and procedures. Alternative assessment is based on a different set of assumptions. It views language ability and use as a reality (or realities) that do not exist independently of our attempts to know them. With this approach to assessment, then, our judgements or decisions cannot be accomplished as a measurement task; there is no 'true score' representing the reality of the individual's language ability 'out there', waiting to be approximated. This view of alternative assessment assumes a sense of language ability that is created, interpreted or constructed, in the act of our attempts to assess and understand it. This construction includes a variety of perspectives – examinee, teacher, test administrator, test developer – and requires an approach to validity that shares this relativistic sense of the reality, or realities, we are assessing. The relationship between approach (positivist, mainstream versus interpretivist, alternative) and validity will be discussed further in Chapter 7. For now, let me re-emphasise that this dichotomy – mainstream versus alternative – is being used to introduce the notion of differing paradigms. In the fullness of language-assessment thought and practice, many different strains and varieties are being developed, some that attempt to combine elements of both paradigms. For example, Douglas' work on the testing of language for specific purposes acknowledges the need to understand language ability:

> from the perspective of the language user ... to interpret test performance from the point of view of language users in the specific situation of interest ... [it is] an exercise rooted in an understanding of human activity from the point of view of the participants in the activity.
>
> (Douglas 2000: 10)

1.4 EVALUATION APPROACHES

Like assessment, evaluation approaches can also be distinguished based on differences in research paradigms. This has been discussed in the literature on programme evaluation as the 'quantitative–qualitative debate' and, more generally, in the educational research literature as the 'paradigm dialog' (Guba 1990). On the one hand, there are approaches that are aligned with what I've referred to as the dominant research paradigm, positivism, also known in its current version as 'postpositivism' (Phillips 1990). These approaches make use of experimental and quasi-experimental designs, in which a comparison is made between outcome measures (usually end of programme achievement or proficiency tests) given to the programme group and some sort of comparison group. Sometimes, the quantitative results are interpreted with the help of qualitative data and analysis (usually interviews with programme participants or observations of programme events). On the other hand, there is the position that approaches evaluation with non-positivist research paradigms such as interpretivism, constructivism or critical theory. These approaches tend to adopt non-experimental designs, where the programme setting is not manipulated or controlled. Instead, the design of the evaluation emerges and evolves (rather than being fixed in advance), and the data and analysis tend to be exclusively qualitative with the goals of describing and interpreting the programme as a dynamic process.

As with assessment approaches, the more fundamental differences in assumptions between paradigms go beyond methodology. The approaches to evaluation that use the positivist paradigm see the programme as an objective reality that exists externally to the evaluator and evaluation. With a disinterested stance by the evaluator in relation to the programme, and with a distinction between facts and values in relation to the programme, this objective reality can be captured, or at least reasonably approximated in the data-gathering and analysis. The approaches that are parallel to interpretivist assessment see the programme as a socially interpreted and constructed reality, one that the evaluator must directly engage with in order to understand. Furthermore, this understanding will be one of many possible under-standings, all of them 'interested' (see, for example, Pennycook 1989) and value-laden, reflecting the paradigm's view that realities are multiple, and understood only in the context, and act, of studying them. This distinction becomes most important when deciding on how to provide evidence for the validity of evaluation findings (and will be discussed in Chapters 2 and 7).

1.5 PURPOSES

Within the different approaches to assessment and evaluation there are a range of motivations, or purposes, for assessing and evaluating. At times, these purposes will determine, at least in part, the approach that we choose. At other times, the purposes can be pursued within either of the two major approaches outlined in the preceding section, and aspects of the assessment or evaluation context (such as specific questions to be answered, specific requirements for the type of evidence that will be accepted by those requesting the assessment or evaluation) will influence the choice of approach.

Purposes for assessment are generally discussed using different terms and typologies than those used for describing evaluation purposes. However, as pointed out by Cohen (1994; also see Jacobs et al. 1981), they both have two general types of motivation: administrative and instructional. Administrative purposes include making decisions about how to select or place individuals within language pro-grammes and how to organise or develop those programmes. Instructional purposes include decisions about what individuals have achieved, as well as what they still need to learn, and how well components of the language programme are working. A distinction that is sometimes made along these lines is the difference between 'summative' and 'formative' evaluation or assessment (Scriven 1967). In general, summative can be seen to correspond to administrative purposes. It is concerned with decisions about whether an individual student is ready for a particular level of a programme (or ready for entry or exemption) or not, whether the programme is successful or not. Formative refers to decisions about assessing the progress and ongoing needs of individuals in a language programme or the ongoing nature of the programme (which components are working, which need to be changed). Of course, summative and formative overlap, as do administrative and instructional: when we assess an individual's ability for placement or selection (summative, administrative), we are able to make decisions about their ongoing needs (formative, instructional); when we gather evidence to decide whether a programme is successful or not (summative, administrative), we are usually interested in the possibility of making changes to improve it (formative, instructional). There are times, however, when one decision type or the other is the focus and the primary motivation for our evaluation or assessment efforts.

1.5.1 Assessment purposes

The categorisation of tests and assessment procedures by purpose is generally done with relatively familiar labels such as 'proficiency', 'selection/exemption', 'placement', 'achievement', and 'diagnostic'. Cohen (1994) sees proficiency and achievement testing as serving a variety of purposes, rather than being purposes in themselves. Basically, proficiency testing matches the administrative purposes discussed in the preceding section, and achievement testing matches instructional purposes. Within these two categories – proficiency/administrative and achievement/instructional – more specific purposes for assessment can be defined.

With proficiency/administrative testing, we are addressing the need to know someone's general ability or level of knowledge without reference to a particular instructional sequence. That is, we are interested in what they know, what they can do, not what they have learned. The reference point is some sort of ability or set of skills that exist outside of any particular curriculum. Most often, this reference point is a context or situation in a particular institution or industry. Note that this institution may be a school or university, but the individual is being tested or assessed not in relation to their achievement of particular objectives in the curricula of those institutions but in relation to their general preparedness to enter those settings and succeed. An example of a proficiency test is the Test of English as a Foreign Language (TOEFL) or the International English Language Testing System (IELTS).

The information from a proficiency test can serve many specific purposes. In addition to an understanding of the individual's general ability or level of knowledge, we can make decisions about whether they should be selected or exempted from a particular job or course of study. Depending on the degree to which our proficiency test specifically matches the requirements or objectives of the workplace or curriculum of study, the proficiency test can also be used to make decisions about placement (into a particular area of work, or a particular level of a course).

To assess or test for achievement is to determine the degree to which an individual has learned a set of pre-specified objectives or curricular material. This purpose for assessment typically occurs at the end of an instructional sequence, such as at the end of an academic term, or at the end of a particular teaching and learning unit within that term. Individual students are being assessed in relation to the goals for that instructional sequence: how well did they learn the material that was presented and practised in class? Examples of achievement tests are the typical midterm and final examinations given in many language classrooms. However, within the achievement/ instructional category of assessment, other forms appear, along with a variety of specific purposes.

For example, along with providing evidence of individual student progress, achievement assessment can be used for diagnostic purposes. This is usually done in a situation where there are specific objectives to be learned or carried out, such as an instructional curriculum or workplace setting. Has the individual mastered these objectives? In what areas does the individual need further instruction? There can also be a proficiency/administrative aspect to this purpose, however, since the individual is not expected to have already mastered everything being assessed, and the need can be for information about how to place the individual into the instructional curriculum (or workplace training).

In addition to formal tests, achievement assessment may be carried out with non-testing procedures where the purpose is observation and the provision of feedback to the individual learner. This purpose for assessment can be seen as part of 'assessment for learning' described by Rea-Dickins (2001). This view, aligned with the culture of alternative assessment, sees assessment as being embedded within instruction, with a focus on facilitating learning, rather than measuring learning. Its goal is to encourage the learner to 'think evaluatively' and to self-assess. Assessment activities are designed to provide feedback to students and to enhance their awareness of and reflection on their language learning. They also provide the teacher with progress and diagnostic information about the individual students, and this information can ultimately be used for more formal, even summative, reporting purposes.

Another way of viewing purpose is by 'decision type'. Since all assessment and almost all testing is about making decisions, we can think of the types of decisions we are called upon to make as being either 'relative' or 'absolute'. Absolute is used here, not in the sense of perfect, but in terms of assessing the individual against a criterion; we want know whether they do or do not meet the requirements of the criterion. The criterion, in this case, is not a specified score level of performance or achievement, but the language ability, skills or knowledge that is being assessed. Relative decisions are ones that we make when assessing the individual against other individuals. We want to know how their ability, skill or knowledge relates to others taking the test or assessment procedure. This difference in decision type is also related to the distinction between 'criterion-referenced' and 'norm-referenced' measurement (the former being concerned with absolute decisions and the latter with relative decisions). I will offer a closer look at this distinction in Chapters 2 and 4. In the meantime, it should be pointed out that Brindley (1989, 1998) has argued for criterion-referenced assessment as being able to serve both the major types of purposes discussed here: summative (administrative, proficiency) and formative (instructional, achievement).

1.5.2 Evaluation purposes

The distinction in evaluation between summative and formative was introduced by Scriven (1967). Formative evaluation occurs while the programme is being implemented and developed. The goal is to recommend changes for improving it, and, towards this end, it focuses on programme processes. Typically the outcome of a formative evaluation is numerous small-scale recommendations for change. Summative evaluation occurs at the end of a programme's natural term or cycle. The goal is to make an ultimate judgement about the programme's worth, whether it has succeeded in meeting its objectives or not. Typically the outcome of a summative evaluation is a formal report to be used in large-scale decisions such as whether to continue funding the programme or not.

Most people involved in language programme administration and evaluation (see, for example, Brown 1989) would say that few, if any, programmes are ever entirely completed in terms of development, making summative evaluation difficult in its extreme form. In fact, most evaluations represent a combination of formative and summative. If we are interested in judging the ultimate worth of a programme, we are usually open to explanations of why it is or is not working, and recommendations for improvement. Rea-Dickins and Germaine (1992) also discuss this formative versus summative distinction as 'confirming' versus 'innovating'; that is, sometimes our motivation for evaluation is to decide whether or not our current practice (programme) is doing what it should; at other times our motivation is to bring about innovation or change in those practices.

When a strict summative evaluation is called for, Brown (1989) points out it is best to avoid doing it in 'crisis mode'. One way around this problem is to make formative evaluation an ongoing part of programme process, so that the necessary information and procedures for gathering it are available without disruption (or at least with minimal disruption) to the normal running of the programme. This leads to another way of looking at evaluation purposes: responding to external mandates and demands versus internal motivations for evaluation.

Often, the purpose of an externally motivated evaluation is to arrive at a summative or combined summative-and-formative judgement of the programme by looking at material indicators, for example, the programme's resources (books, media, professional credentials of staff, classroom space) as the primary indicators of its worth. This is a familiar scenario for evaluations done by 'outside experts', or the 'Jet-In-Jet-Out' experts – 'JI-JOEs' (Alderson and Scott 1992) – that are recruited to do external reviews.

Besides looking at the material indicators, or other programme 'products' (such as achievement test scores), another purpose for evaluation is to examine how the materials are used and the products achieved. The major purpose here is to understand programme process, and several models for doing this type of evaluation have been proposed (and will be discussed in Chapter 2).

Elsewhere (Lynch 1996) I have discussed evaluation purposes as the interaction between audience and goals, with the following as the key questions:

- Who is requesting the evaluation?
- Who will be affected by the evaluation?

The people identified by these questions are usually referred to as the 'stakeholders.' They are the ones who are most centrally concerned with what the evaluation will be able to say about the programme. Particular evaluation stakeholders, or audiences, tend to have particular evaluation goals, or purposes, which can be ascertained with the following questions:

- Why is the evaluation being conducted?
- What information is being requested and why?

With different audiences for the same evaluation context, there will be the possibility of different, and even conflicting, goals. Sometimes evaluation purposes are communicated at the beginning of the evaluation process and remain fairly constant; at other times they evolve and change over the course and, as a result of, the evaluation. The relationship between audience and evaluation purposes will be given more detail in the next chapter.

1.6 THE RELATIONSHIP OF ASSESSMENT TO EVALUATION

Using the definitions of assessment and evaluation presented earlier in this chapter, it is clear that the former focuses on decisions about individuals and the latter on ones concerning entire language programmes of study. As a result, assessment focuses on the teaching and learning process, as it affects individual learners, as well as issues involving selection or entry to that process, promotion within it, and certification of completion or mastery. Evaluation focuses primarily on institutional issues (institution being defined broadly as everything from the classroom, to the school and the society in which they are located) and, in particular, is motivated to a large extent by accountability requirements (for example, society's taxpayers demanding evidence that state school funding is being used efficiently and wisely).

This is not to say that assessment and evaluation are completely separate activities. Evaluation uses information from assessment, among other types of information, to arrive at its decisions in relation to educational institutions and their programmes. Over the past two decades, assessment, primarily in the form of tests, has been at the centre of much of the accountability debate. And assessment information can sometimes be better understood within the larger frame of programme evaluation. Certain individual assessment performances may be more fully explained as a result of interaction with particular programme or institutional factors. Programme evaluation information may provide a description of programme characteristics that are associated with higher (group) performance on the assessment procedures. This type of information may help explain individual assessment performance, depending on the relationship between the programme and the assessment procedure. For example, it may be that the assessment procedure is focused on an aspect of language ability that has not been emphasised in the programme, or has been taught in a way that is not captured by the assessment procedure. Perhaps the programme has emphasised reading skills such as skimming for the main idea or scanning for specific information, but the assessment procedure requires a more extensive reading approach. This, of course, raises issues of validity for the assessment procedure: is it assessing what it claims to be assessing? This also has implications for the validity of the programme evaluation: has it chosen the appropriate assessment procedures for investigating the programme's effectiveness? But it also points out the interaction between assessment and evaluation: each provides information that needs to be interpreted in light of the other. Validity in assessment and evaluation, as well as the choice of assessment procedures for evaluation, will be discussed further in the following chapters.

This relationship of assessment to evaluation can also be seen as dependent on the research paradigm within which the assessment and/or the evaluation is taking place. For example, the use of language test data will be required or preferred within the positivist paradigm, since it is designed to provide an objective measure of individual language ability, and this can also be used for evaluation purposes as the measure of the programme's effect. If an interpretivist research paradigm is chosen, then language ability will be conceptualised in a different way; it will not be seen as an objective, measurable characteristic of the individual, but as something that needs to be understood through a process of interpretation and dialogue between assessor and participants. For programme evaluation, the programme will be understood in the same way, as something that is interpreted and constructed through the interaction of evaluator and participants.

It may be possible to use assessment information gathered within an interpretivist paradigm in a programme evaluation that is being carried out within a positivist paradigm. In most cases, this would be done as part of a multiple strategies approach, and there would still be the need for some sort of measurement data on programme effectiveness. The interpretivist assessment information would be used as complementary to the positivist test data for making decisions about the programme. It may also be possible to use positivist test data within an interpretivist research approach to programme evaluation. The language test data, in this case, will need to be interpreted within the dialogue between evaluator and participants and become part of the reconstruction of the programme's meaning from those perspectives. That is, individual assessment will not be seen as an independent measure of the programme's effect. This will be discussed further in the next chapter.

Another way of thinking about the relationship of assessment to evaluation has been suggested by Brindley (1998). He points out that evaluation often needs to respond to the requirements of large-scale comparability (for example, comparing individual and school performances across a nation). This is most often the case when responding to the accountability issues mentioned above. Parents (and tax-paying non-parents) want to know how individual student performance (and group performance) relates to standards, and those standards are generally in reference to comparisons with a larger population: how is student X doing, compared with the average for her school, her area, her country, other countries? Brindley goes on to elaborate the dilemma that this large-scale comparability can be difficult to reconcile with the notion of assessment as being focused on teaching and learning. As mentioned earlier in this chapter, his solution to this dilemma is to use criterion-referenced assessment procedures, as well as a range of interpretivist, alternative assessment approaches, for both teaching/learning purposes and large-scale accountability.

In order to carry out Brindley's solution, however, there needs to be an acceptance of the interpretivist research paradigm for both assessment and evaluation. Without this acceptance, the large-scale comparability and accountability audience will expect standardised, traditional language test data as the requisite evidence for individual language achievement and programme effectiveness. The traditional expectations for evidence will also mandate the use of general proficiency tests over tests that are designed to measure the specific objectives of the language programme. The reason for using general proficiency tests has to do with the purpose and audience for the accountability issue within programme evaluation. The purpose tends to be summative – is the programme worth the funding that is provided? – and the ultimate audience is the taxpaying public. This requires evidence that the people responsible for making the decisions (educational administrators and government officials) are capable of understanding and communicating to the public. Usually the preferred information would be quantitative, presented in summary form (for example, group averages on tests), with the appearance of scientific analysis (for objective credibility). On the other hand, those responsible for assisting in the collection of the assessment information and, more importantly, those responsible for providing the programme's curriculum (educators) will be interested in more detailed and complex information about individual student learning and its interaction with the language programme; that is, they will have a more formative purpose. This audience will be less satisfied with the standardised test information, reduced to numerical averages, that might serve the large-scale accountability audience and purpose. Brindley's solution, then, needs to span the gap between those two general audiences and purposes and offer detailed information about learning achievements and programme processes that can also be summarised in a less complex fashion with a rationale for its credibility. These issues will underlie the discussion of designs (Chapter 2), measures (Chapter 3), and interpretivist assessment procedures (Chapter 5).

EXERCISES

1. Locate recent issues of applied linguistics journals such as *Language Learning*, *Applied Linguistics*, *TESOL Quarterly*, *Studies in Second Language Acquisition*, and *Language Testing*. Choose several articles that are of interest to you, and try to determine the paradigm, as discussed in this chapter, that best fits the research.

2. Create a list with two columns: assessment and evaluation. Under each, write examples of the sorts of activities you have participated in, conducted, or witnessed that seem to be one or the other. Are there any activities that you've experienced that seem to be both assessment and evaluation?

3. Using the list of assessment and evaluation activities from Exercise 2, above, try

to identify the *purpose(s)* for each. Do the activities suggest one paradigm or the other? Why or why not?

SUGGESTIONS FOR FURTHER READING

1. Lincoln, Y. S. and E. G. Guba (2000), 'Paradigmatic controversies, contradictions, and emerging confluences', in N. K. Denzin and Y. S. Lincoln (eds), *The Handbook of Qualitative Research* (2nd edn), Thousand Oaks, CA: PineForge (Sage), pp. 163–88.

This chapter represents an updating of Guba and Lincoln's (1989) original work defining research paradigms in the context of programme evaluation. Rather than arguing for strict differences between paradigms, the authors show how boundaries are beginning to blur. At the same time they articulate important considerations that underlie different approaches to research.

2. Schwandt, T. D. (2000), 'Three epistemological stances for qualitative inquiry: Interpretivism, hermeneutics, and social constructionism', in N. K. Denzin and Y. S. Lincoln (eds), *The Handbook of Qualitative Research* (2nd edn), Thousand Oaks, CA: PineForge (Sage), pp. 189–213.

This chapter provides a comprehensive explanation of interpretivism, which I am using as a general label that includes several related paradigms. Schwandt's discussion focuses on two of those paradigms: hermeneutics and constructivism.

3. Phillips, D. C. (1990), 'Postpositivistic science: myths and realities', in E. G. Guba (ed.), *The Paradigm Dialog*, Newbury Park, CA: Sage, pp. 31–45.

This chapter presents a thorough treatment of the current state of the positivist paradigm, which Phillips refers to as 'postpositivism'. The author responds to many of the criticisms of various versions of positivism, arguing for objectivity as a 'regulative ideal' rather than an epistemological absolute.

Chapter 2

Designing assessment and evaluation

2.1 INTRODUCTION

In the preceding chapter I discussed paradigms and purposes in ways that were primarily independent of particular assessment and evaluation contexts. This chapter will emphasise context, demonstrating the connection between research paradigm, assessment and evaluation purposes and designs for carrying out those purposes. I will conceptualise the design of assessment and evaluation as a series of steps that begins with the identification of audience and goals, moves to an inventory of the particular context and its predominant themes, and then decides on a paradigm and design that matches the combination of audience, goals and context. This discussion will draw upon previous work: the context-adaptive model for programme evaluation (Lynch 1996), and the concept of the mandate in relation to test development (Davidson and Lynch 2002). The particular audiences and goals that motivate assessment and evaluation are necessary and useful starting points for deciding upon a design. Here, design refers to a systematic approach to gathering the information necessary to accomplish the assessment or evaluation goals; that is, it specifies how to get the information necessary to make decisions or judgements about individuals or programmes. Throughout the rest of the book, I will tend to refer to the individuals responsible for designing and conducting the assessment or evaluation as the 'assessment or evaluation teams'. This will be done for convenience sake, acknowledging the fact that at times the assessment or evaluation will be done by individuals rather than teams of individuals.

2.2 AUDIENCES AND GOALS

Both assessment and evaluation have multiple potential audiences, also referred to as 'stakeholders'. The term stakeholder, broken down, reveals the notion of people who hold some sort of stake in the assessment or evaluation judgement or decision. Of course, there are various levels of stakes that various people will hold. A primary level of stakeholder, those for whom the stakes are highest, would obviously include those being assessed or evaluated. In the case of assessment, students or other learners are primary stakeholders, as are their teachers and, in most cases, their families. In the case of evaluation, it is the programme, not the participants, for which a judgement or decision is being made. Those responsible for the programme – sponsors, funders, administrators – become the primary stakeholders and audience for the evaluation. However, in most contexts, teachers also feel responsible for the programme that they work within, and it would be a mistake not to include them in the primary-stakeholder level. Similarly, although I have in the past characterised students as secondary stakeholders in programme evaluations (Lynch 1996: 168), it seems important to include them at the primary level. Even though individual students are transitory participants in a programme, any cohort represents a constant and essential set of stakeholders and deserves to be included in the primary stakeholder level.

The reason for distinguishing the primary level of stakeholders from other levels is to determine the audiences that should legitimately have a voice in determining the goals for assessment and evaluation. These are also the persons who will receive a reporting of the results of the assessment or evaluation process.

Secondary stakeholders include those persons who are not directly involved or responsible for the immediate assessment or evaluation context, but who have occasional contact with the context or who work in settings that are in close proximity. This audience will be interested in the outcomes of the assessment or evaluation in terms of its ability to inform their own practice or experience. Examples of this level of stakeholder include administrators, teachers, students (and their families) and community organisations (formal and informal) that are involved with similar assessment and evaluation judgements and decisions in other contexts (such as schools in adjacent communities). They will not normally have a voice in setting goals, but they may participate in review or information sessions associated with the particular assessment or evaluation, and be able to request or access results through published reports.

A final, tertiary level of stakeholders exists, and it is composed of interested administrators, teachers, students (and their families), community organisations, and language testers and programme evaluators who have little or no contact with the particular assessment or evaluation context. These people will interact with the assessment and evaluation results through the published literature.

These different audiences (levels and particular cases within levels) will have potentially different goals or purposes in mind for the assessment or evaluation. Purposes for assessment and evaluation were discussed in the previous chapter. Here they are associated with particular audiences in particular contexts. For example, in the context of a language programme that receives its funding from the government, a key member of the primary audience will be the government agency that oversees programme funding. The goal of the evaluation in this case will tend to be what was described as a summative judgement in the previous chapter; that is, a decision may be required about whether or not to continue (or cut, or augment) the programme's funding. This type of evaluation goal is linked to the accountability issue, also discussed in the previous chapter; politicians and the taxpaying public they represent want to know whether or not the programme is working in order to assure themselves that money is being spent wisely. Another audience, such as the teachers within the programme may have a very different purpose in mind for the evaluation. They may want detailed, descriptive information about how the curriculum goals are being realised in the classroom so that they can make informed decisions about the need for changes in the programme.

Since the answers to the summative type of evaluation questions usually require quantitative evidence, this type of evaluation context will influence assessment contexts as well. For example, school teachers who want to make decisions about the language ability of their individual students will need to be aware of the type of tests the students will ultimately be judged against. In another assessment context, however, a teacher may have particular goals that do not relate to these larger evaluation and accountability issues. These goals may include diagnosing particular strengths and weaknesses of individual students in relation to a particular curriculum or instructional module.

Some of the frustration that teachers may feel with the larger evaluation context comes from the difficulty in connecting these classroom judgements and the information that such assessments give them with the standardised tests that typically define accountability evaluation efforts. They may feel they have been given an assessment mandate (Davidson and Lynch 2002) or, rather, had one imposed upon them from forces external to their teaching context. The goals, or objectives, for such assessment mandates have recently come to be referred to as 'content standards' resulting in 'standards-based assessment', especially in the United States (Brandt 1998: 5). Trying to integrate this type of mandate into their classroom practice may be difficult or impossible for teachers to achieve. However, it may also allow them to sharpen their sense of what it is that they are trying to assess, that they should be assessing, in relation to their particular learners and the curriculum designed for them, by viewing their current practice through the lens of the assessment goals expressed by the mandate. The outcome of this process can be a moulding, or perhaps a subversion of the original mandate into a new articulation of assessment purpose and goals.

2.3 CONTEXT AND THEMES

The preliminary understanding of audiences and goals is further elaborated during the next phase of assessment and evaluation design process: the taking of an inventory of the assessment or evaluation context and the formulation of the dominant themes and major issues that emerge from that context. This phase will be more time consuming when the assessment or evaluation is being designed by individuals or teams who do not normally work or participate in the context. Outsider assessment and evaluation experts are typically called upon in order to provide a fresh perspective or, perhaps, an objective and neutral view of the context (and the presence or absence of this motivation will help to determine the most appropriate design, as I will discuss in the next section). However, even when the assessment or evaluation is being designed and conducted by an individual or team that are active participants in the context, an inventory and elaboration of themes needs to be explicitly catalogued. When the project is a single classroom assessment, designed by the classroom teacher, this phase will not need to be as lengthy or as elaborate, perhaps, as when conducted by outsiders. It is important that the assessment or evaluation team, even when working on a small-scale project in a familiar context, gives some thought to how the context interacts with their goals and other potential audiences, and to articulate the important issues that exist in relation to these goals and audiences.

A context inventory will include a variety of dimensions (see, for example, Lynch 1996: 5–6) that detail the resources available for the assessment or evaluation, the time requirements, features of the language classroom or programme, characteristics of the language learner or programme participants, theoretical and philosophical influences, and socio-political and cultural issues. For example, in an assessment context, the following types of questions should guide the development of the inventory (this is an exemplary, not exhaustive, list):

- Are there instruments that already exist and are capable of being used or modified for the assessment goals?
- Are there other individuals that can assist in the development and/or administration of the assessment procedures?
- Are there individuals that can provide the statistical analysis that may be necessary for answering the assessment questions?
- Are there individuals that can provide guidance for handling psychological problems associated with the assessment?
- Are there individuals that can provide expertise for working with particular types of individuals (for example, young children, individuals with learning disabilities, gifted individuals)?
- When do the assessments need to be given (month, day and time of day)?
- How much time will be available for the assessments?
- Will it be possible to assess students one-on-one, or will the assessment need to be done in groups?
- Are there particular individuals or subgroups that need to be assessed, or will the assessment be carried out with an entire class, school or district?
- What are the native language and cultural backgrounds of the individuals to be assessed?
- What are the previous educational experiences of the individuals to be assessed?
- What is the relationship of this assessment to previous assessment and/or teaching activities?
- What are the beliefs and theories of language and language learning that motivate the teaching and assessment?
- What is the attitude of individual learners towards assessment?
- What is the relationship between teacher/assessor and learners?
- Who decides on teaching and assessment goals?
- How are assessment results typically used and by whom?

- How are the assessment results typically reported?
- Are there perceptions of bias or unfair treatment of individuals or subgroups in the assessment context or larger community?
- What are the major social and political goals and agendas that exist surrounding the assessment context?

In an evaluation context, many of these same questions will need to be asked in order to develop the context inventory. There are also questions that are more specific to evaluation audiences and goals:

- Is there a group of learners that can serve as a comparison for the programme being evaluated?
- How were the learners selected for the programme (and for the comparison group, if one exists)?
- What are the professional backgrounds and experience of the programme staff?
- To what extent will the programme participants (administrators, students, teachers, others) be available for information-gathering (including administering evaluation procedures and participating in data-gathering such as interviews)?
- What understandings do the programme participants have of the evaluation goals?
- What are the attitudes of the programme participants towards evaluation in general, and the proposed evaluation in particular?
- Will there be particular types of evaluation expertise available (such as ethnographers, classroom discourse analysts, multivariate statistical analysts)?
- What is the size and scheduling of the programme and its classes?
- What are the instructional materials, including electronic media, available to the programme?
- Are there particular social, political or cultural issues that have motivated the evaluation?
- Are there particular social, political or cultural issues – both within the programme and in the community surrounding it – that are likely to affect the interpretation of evaluation results?

In the course of compiling the context inventory, major themes that relate to or even help clarify the assessment or evaluation goals will begin to surface. At this stage, it is a good idea to make a preliminary listing of these themes, with the understanding that others may emerge and existing themes may change as the assessment or evaluation proceeds. The following are some examples (again, illustrative, not exhaustive) of general themes and issues that can arise (some will be more relevant to assessment and some to evaluation, but all have the potential to be relevant to either context). These are the general expressions; in particular contexts they will have more specific articulations:

- conflicts between teaching philosophy/theory and learner expectations;
- support for programme from larger administrative units;

- the relationship between governmental agendas and assessment practices;
- personality and management-style conflicts;
- the match between teaching activities and assessment procedures;
- student motivation and attitudes towards teachers and programme;
- test anxiety;
- mixed levels of language proficiency;
- separate skills versus integrated skills teaching and assessment;
- the role and status of the language programme within a larger administrative unit;
- teacher autonomy and programme coherence;
- the role and status of teachers and students in curriculum decisions;
- social justice concerns;
- the role and status of the language in the community.

The context and themes identified in this phase of the assessment or evaluation project will continue to be drawn upon throughout its design and implementation. This information helps the assessment or evaluation team determine the limits and constraints of the project, in order to decide upon the most feasible and appropriate design. As the assessment or evaluation is carried out, new information will become available concerning the context and important new themes will emerge. In this sense, the phases outlined in this chapter need to be viewed as iterative rather than linear.

2.4 SELECTING AN APPROACH/DECIDING ON PARADIGMS

In order to select a particular design for carrying out the assessment or evaluation, some preliminary judgements need to be made, coordinating the information from audiences, goals, context and themes, concerning which paradigm should inform the design. The basic question becomes: what type of evidence is required to make a convincing assessment or evaluation argument? This ultimately relates to validity, which I will discuss in Chapter 7. For example, suppose the audience and goals include government-funding agencies and an explicit request for statistical evidence in the form of test scores and a comparison with a rival programme. This sort of evidence implies a particular view of what is being assessed or evaluated, one that is primarily associated with the positivist paradigm. The assessment or evaluation individuals or teams may need to modify their preferred research paradigm, in order to provide their audiences with information and interpretations of that information that are convincing. Of course, this may result in a serious conflict for assessors or evaluators. If my understanding of the type of language ability that is being assessed or is at the core of the language programme being evaluated leads me to believe that an interpretivist approach is called for, but the primary audience (or a part of it) is demanding a positivist approach, I may need to decline to participate in the project. I use the first person here consciously, in order not to sound as if I am preaching to the reader ('You may have to do this; you should do that …'). What I want to call attention to is that assessment and evaluation, like teaching, is inherently political. We (and here I consciously include myself and the reader as potential assessors and evaluators) are forced to make decisions that involve our research philosophy and our social and political beliefs. This does not mean that our personal research preferences or political beliefs should necessarily be used as the basis for making decisions about professional conduct in assessment and evaluation. It is something that needs to be seriously considered, however, before making a commitment to any project.

In the discussion of context and themes, I mentioned that outsider experts will often be selected in order to provide an objective view. This motivation for an assessment or evaluation project immediately implicates a paradigm that is essentially positivist (and I do not intend this, here as elsewhere, to be seen as inherently good or evil), believing in the possibility and desirability of an objective stance towards the thing we are assessing or evaluating. Assuming the assessment or evaluation team is confident that such a paradigm can be appropriate for answering the assessment or evaluation questions, then this initial requirement – an external expert – will suggest a positivist paradigmatic stance that will lead to particular design options, to be discussed in the next section.

It may be that an external expert is hired to begin the assessment or evaluation project, but that the audience and goals, along with the particular context and themes, suggest a view of language ability as something that is co-constructed and that needs to be understood through a dialogic, co-constructed inquiry. This means that the assessment or evaluation needs to be carried out as an active dialogue between the assessment or evaluation teams and the participants in the assessment or evaluation context. In this case, an interpretivist paradigm is implicated and will lead to a different set of options for designing the assessment or evaluation. Or, conversely, an internally motivated and conducted assessment or evaluation – one that assumes the necessity of local knowledge as essential for designing, implementing and interpreting the results – may arrive at an understanding of the goals, context and themes that suggests the need for measuring aspects of language ability. This orientation, in turn, will implicate a positivist paradigm. Finally, particular audience–goals–context–themes combinations may result in a dialogue between paradigms and possibly lead to the attempt at using both (the possibility and associated difficulties with combining paradigms in 'mixed designs' will be discussed later in this chapter).

In addition to whether the assessment or evaluation is internally or externally motivated and conducted, particular goals and themes will suggest a preference for one paradigm or the other to guide selection of the design. I have already mentioned that summative goals – needing to decide whether the individual has or does not have a particular ability, whether the programme is worth the resources needed to keep it going – will tend to be pursued within a positivist paradigm. This is not to say that the interpretivist paradigm is incapable of providing summative information; rather, the types of audiences and goals that require summative judgements are typically looking for scientific (in the traditional, experimental method sense of the term), quantitatively-based information that the positivist paradigm is designed to provide. This is the kind of evidence that is generally required at the levels of policy formulation and decisions about educational funding. As mentioned in the previous chapter, there are proposals for combining this type of evidence and reporting with the kind of evidence about detailed descriptions of language achievement and learning process that the interpretivist paradigm works towards (for example, Brindley 1998).

The basic concepts that determine the link between evidence required and research paradigm to follow, then, include the notion of objectivity and the requirement for and ability to measure the language ability we are interested in; the need for a comparison or control group (or norm-group statistics) in order to make valid claims about language ability and acquisition (see, for example, Doughty 1991; Fotos 1994; Gregg 1984; Gregg et al. 1997; Long 1984, 1998). These concepts lead towards the positivist paradigm. Other basic concepts include the intersubjectivity and socially constructed nature of language, language learning and knowledge (see, for example, Auerbach 1994; Block 1996; Kramsch 2000; Pavlenko and Lantolf 2000; Pennycook 2001; Rampton 1995; Swain 2000). These concepts lead towards the interpretivist paradigm.

2.5 SELECTING A DESIGN

Once the assessment or evaluation team has considered the paradigm question, choices for particular designs must be made, and these are guided and often constrained by the audience and goals. In the iterative nature suggested for the series of phases presented here, this means that there will often need to be a return to the audience and goals consideration, for further dialogue and elaboration of the assessment and evaluation purposes. Likewise, the context inventory will need to be consulted and perhaps modified in light of new information, as the assessment or evaluation team begins to weigh design options.

Questions such as the following will begin to surface and focus the selection process:

- Is there a need for large-scale assessment or evaluation beyond an individual classroom?
- Will the evidence required be experimental or quasi-experimental in nature?
- Is the primary focus on individual or group assessment?

2.5.1 Positivist evaluation designs

In evaluation contexts, when evidence is required for whether or how well the programme is working, the gathering of quantitative data (that is, a measurement of some kind) and a control or comparison group is often requested by one or more stakeholder groups. The basic design to be preferred in this case is true experimental or quasi-experimental. In these designs, the programme group students receive a treatment; the control group either receives nothing or it receives a different type of treatment. Both groups, when there are two groups, are measured in some way, generally with a type of test. This measurement can occur at different time periods: before and after the treatment (pre-test and post-test); after the treatment only (post-test); or at several times before, during and after the treatment (time series). In the case of programme evaluation, the treatment is the programme being evaluated, and the experimental group is the students in that programme. The control, or comparison, group is the students to which the programme students are being compared. The measurements that are taken generally involve tests of achievement in the language abilities or skills being taught by the programme. These can be language proficiency tests whose content is related to the programme curriculum in a general way, or they can be language achievement tests whose content is taken specifically from the programme curriculum.

The designs within the experimental and quasi-experimental family are distinguished by three main factors:

- whether or not there is a control, or comparison, group;
- how participants are assigned to a group (random or non-random);
- how many measurements are taken (pre-, post-, time-series testing).

2.5.1.1 Comparison-group designs

When there is a control group, and the participants are randomly assigned, we have the possibility for a 'true experimental' design. Classrooms can sometimes be more readily assigned in a random fashion than can students, and it may be that the evaluation team is primarily interested in results at the classroom level rather than the individual student level. Large-scale evaluations sometimes randomly assign schools or even school districts to the experimental programme or control group. However, the opportunity for random assignment is so rare in most language-programme evaluations that I will concentrate on the quasi-experimental designs.

The classic 'quasi-experimental' design involves a comparison between a programme group and some other group of learners, where the groups are 'intact', or the result of some non-random form of assignment to group. If measurements have been taken before and after the period of the treatment, or intervention (programme instruction), being evaluated, a statistical adjustment may be used in order to control for pre-existing differences between the programme and comparison group. This can be accomplished with the 'non-equivalent control group' (NECG) design, depicted in Figure 2.1. Here, the differences between the programme group and the comparison group after the intervention (post-test) are adjusted for pre-existing differences between the two groups, as estimated by the pre-test. This allows the evaluation team to feel reasonably confident that the differences at post-test time are due to the programme and not other systematic differences between the two groups.

Another quasi-experimental design is the 'interrupted time series with comparison group', or 'control series' design (Caporaso and Roos 1973: 22–4), depicted in Figure 2.2. Periodic measurements are taken at several intervals before the programme to be evaluated has been introduced (Time 1 through Time n), and

	Pre-instruction	**Intervention**	**Post-instruction**
Programme Group	pre-test	Programme instruction	post-test
Comparison Group	pre-test	Comparison instruction	post-test

Figure 2.1   Non-equivalent control-group design

(Note: The pre-test and post-test can be various types of measures, including surveys, which will be discussed in Chapter 3.)

	Time 1	Time 2	Time n	Intervention	Time n+1	Time n+2	Time n+ ...
Programme Group	M1	M2	M ...n	Programme instruction	M n+1	M n+2	M n+ ...n
Comparison Group	M1	M2	M ...n	Comparison instruction	M n+1	M n+2	M n+ ...n

M = measurements (tests or other measures of the language ability we are interested in affecting with the programme intervention)

Figure 2.2   Interrupted time series with comparison group

periodic measurements are then taken after the period of programme and comparison group instruction (the Intervention). Basically, the data gathered before the intervention period (Time 1 through Time n) is used to predict what the data would look like if the same pattern continued after the intervention (Time n+1 through Time n+ ...). The pattern of scores predicted from the measurements prior to the intervention period should look different from the pattern of scores actually observed in the post-intervention measurements, if the programme has had an effect.

2.5.1.2 *Programme group-only designs*

Just as it is rare to be able to randomly assign groups to programme and comparison treatments, it is often difficult or impossible to find a suitable comparison group. If only the programme group is available for measurement, then we have a set of quasi-experimental (some would characterise them as pre-experimental, or non-experimental) designs that are weaker than experimental or NECG designs, in terms of making causal claims about the programme and its effect on learning and achievement.

One example is the 'programme group with pre-test and post-test' design, the same design as depicted in Figure 2.1, without the comparison group. Because we have no measure of what would happen to a group of learners who did not receive the programme during the same period of time, the conclusions we can reach about the effect of the programme are clearly limited. However, when comparison groups are not available, this design at least allows the evaluation team to have something to say about change in student learning and achievement over the course of the programme. If the pre-test and post-test periods make use of multiple measures – proficiency tests, achievement tests linked to the programme's instructional goals, classroom observations, questionnaires concerning perceptions of the programme by teachers and students – the qualified conclusions that can be drawn from this design will be strengthened.

'Longitudinal designs' can also be useful when only the programme group is available for measurement, but data are available for the programme over longer periods of time than the period defined by the actual evaluation. One example of this is the use of 'panels', or 'cohorts', which represent the programme students over successive instructional periods of the programme. This might be a semester, several semesters or several years. If the programme has records of test scores and other measures for its students, these can be used to track student achievement. Data for these student cohorts can represent particular levels of the programme – for example, a beginning course, intermediate course and advanced course – and use successive cohorts in the particular levels to examine changes in proficiency and achievement over time. Similarly, cohorts representing particular years within the programme, or cohorts representing particular skill modules – for example, listening and note-taking, conversation, grammar – can be analysed separately or as an integrated programme (see, for example, Ross forthcoming). If the programme being evaluated represents an innovation that occurs during one of these successive cohorts, data from previous student cohorts can be used as a type of comparison group. To the degree that there are no systematic differences in the students in these cohorts over time, other than the changes in the instructional programme being evaluated, reasonably strong claims about programme effect can be made with this type of design.

Another programme group-only design that makes use of longitudinal data is the 'interrupted time series' design, discussed above. The design is the same as that depicted in Figure 2.2, without the row representing the comparison group. In this case, like the quasi-experimental, programme group only design, any change in the pattern of measurement from the pre-intervention period to the post-intervention period cannot be unambiguously claimed as being the result of the programme. We do not know what other factors may have been present in the instructional (and wider community) context that could explain the change.

2.5.2 Interpretivist evaluation designs

When evaluation audiences, goals, context and themes align around the basic idea that what we are trying to understand is a socially constructed entity that does not exist independently of our attempts to understand it – that it is, in essence, the result of our attempts, co-constructed with others, to understand it – then interpretivist-evaluation designs are appropriate choices. Various designs, or models, have been suggested in the literature, including the 'responsive model' (Stake 1975), the 'illumination model' (Parlett and Hamilton 1976) and the 'connoisseurship model'

(Eisner 1991). The details of these individual designs have been discussed elsewhere (Lynch 1996; Patton 1990). What they have in common, and what links them to the interpretivist paradigm, is an emergent, evolving nature to the design; a lack of manipulation of the programme setting; an engagement with the programme as it naturally occurs over the course of time; and a recognition of the multiple perspectives that exist within and inform any evaluation context.

The emergent nature of interpretivist designs is in stark contrast to the fixed, *a priori* nature of the positivist approach to evaluation. The interpretivist evaluation team will respond to programme participants and programme processes that they observe over the course of the evaluation, changing who they collect information from, when and how they collect it, as their understanding of the programme develops. The interpretivist designs remain open to issues and themes that suggest different conceptualisations of the programme (the independent variable, in positivist design terms), and to pursuing them with different data-gathering techniques and instruments than may have been originally planned. For example, the evaluation team may begin with a list of programme officials and participants from its initial interaction with the primary audiences. In the course of meeting with these preliminary contacts, the team may discover an aspect of the programme (a special learning centre, for example) that they were not previously aware of and which needs to be included in the overall evaluation design.

Interpretivist designs approach the programme as something to be observed and interacted with, rather than manipulated and measured. This means that the design must be very thorough in terms of the amount of information that it gathers about programme process and the experiences of the programme participants. Interpretivist designs are thus more descriptive, at times, than positivist approaches; however, they can also be explanatory. The lack of an experimental or quasi-experimental structure to the evaluation does not preclude these designs from drawing conclusions and forming interpretations that explain what sort of effect the programme is having and, more importantly perhaps, why and how it is having that effect. In this sense, interpretivist designs can do more than just form hypotheses; they can also provide a space for inquiry that tests these hypotheses as well. The hypothesis testing is done through further in-depth data-gathering (for example, through observation and interviewing) as the programme continues to operate as it normally would (rather than setting up a special experimental condition that manipulates the programme setting in some way). There is a 'progressive focusing' (Parlett and Hamilton 1976) from a holistic view of the programme to selecting particular aspects to look at in more depth, then back to the holistic view, and so on. This draws upon the notion of the hermeneutic circle and the methodology of philosophical hermeneutics (Gadamer 1989). For example, the evaluation-team members may begin their inquiry by each conducting independent, open-ended observations at the programme site (observing classes, meeting with teachers in the coffee lounge, talking with students in the common areas, attending programme functions). Each member's holistic impression could then be discussed to suggest more specific aspects of the programme that need to be examined. The team could examine these together, in turn, and then resume its independent observations to see how the findings from the more detailed and focused data-gathering fit the overall programme picture.

Interpretivist designs are inherently concerned with understanding the multiple perspectives that exist in relation to a programme and its meaning. This involves, most importantly, an investigation and understanding of the programme participant experience, what is known as the 'emic' view in anthropology. In order to capture the multiple perspectives and emic view, the evaluation team needs to schedule sufficient time in the programme setting and to structure the data-gathering so that all types of programme participants are included. Ultimately, the design needs a process whereby the multiple perspectives can negotiate with the evaluation team to arrive at some sort of consensus as to what judgements and decisions can be made about the programme. This process might be accomplished through a special meeting of the programme participants and stakeholders, through periodic small-group reviews of evaluation findings as the evaluation team begins to formulate them, or through something more formal, such as a mock trial of the programme (for example, the 'judicial model', Wolf 1975).

2.5.3 Mixed evaluation designs

As I mentioned earlier in this chapter, the interaction of audience, goals, context and themes may suggest the need for a design that draws upon elements of both the positivist and interpretivist paradigms. There are convincing arguments that the perspectives represented by these paradigms may be incompatible (for a summary, see Lynch 1996: 155–6). It is possible to have 'mixed strategies', where the design is primarily from one paradigm or the other, but to use data-gathering and analysis techniques from both (Patton 1990: 188–95). For example, a positivist NECG design could include in-depth interviewing of participants using qualitative data-analysis techniques (to be discussed in Chapter 6), along with pre-test and post-test measurements. In this scenario, the in-depth interview data would be interpreted within the positivist assumptions that the programme and its effect on learners was something independent of the evaluation team's attempt to understand it, that the programme and its effect could be objectively measured and understood as a causal relationship. The interview data and analysis would serve as additional confirmation of the effect measured by the test data. It would also provide additional evidence for external validity (to be discussed in Chapter 7).

A 'mixed design', on the other hand, attempts to combine the perspectives represented by the positivist and interpretivist paradigms. There are a variety of ways in which this could be carried out, but all of them run the risk of compromising one paradigm or the other. For example, to the degree that the positivist influence in the design calls for experimental manipulation of the programme setting, the interpretivist goal of understanding how the programme naturally occurs is made problematic. This, to a certain extent, assumes that the positivist and interpretivist inquiries are being conducted at the same point in time. Since most evaluation projects have a finite period within which to complete their work, most attempts at mixed designs will necessarily be conducting experimental-type inquiry and in-depth ethnographic-type inquiry at the same time. Assuming that the evaluation team can actually approach the context from both paradigmatic perspectives – with equal belief, understanding, and allegiance to both – it is possible to arrive at information that describes both measured effects from an objective view of the programme and a multiple perspective view of the programme that represents a co-construction and negotiation of its meaning (what the programme is, how it accomplishes this in relation to programme participants).

Mixing paradigms is a daunting task and requires the ability to play 'the doubting game and the believing game' (Elbow 1973) with one or more paradigms that may be initially incompatible with your research philosophy. It also can result in contradictory findings – there is no guarantee that the positivist evidence and interpretivist evidence will 'triangulate' around a single 'truth' – and will require reconciling different approaches to validity. Even though the evaluation team will normally be committed to, or guided by, a particular paradigm, an attempt at a mixed design can offer a richer set of information from which to make evaluation judgements and decisions. In other words, the importance in a mixed design may be the opportunity for the evaluators to step outside, for however briefly, their normal research worldview, and take in a different perspective on the programme and its setting.

Even if one paradigm or the other holds sway, even if one paradigm or the other is compromised, the resulting information and understanding may be more revealing than if only one paradigm had dictated the entirety of the design. An attempt at mixing designs can strengthen confidence in conclusions by providing evidence from one perspective that addresses contradictory or ambiguous evidence from the other perspective. For example, in my evaluation of the Reading English for Science and Technology (REST) programme (Lynch 1992, 1996), the positivist evidence from pre-test and post-test data were somewhat contradictory: some of the analyses for certain subtests suggested a significant effect for the programme, some did not. The interpretivist evidence from observations, journals and in-depth interviews, along with a content analysis of the test instruments, provided an explanation: the learners were being tested with an instrument that primarily measured aspects of language proficiency that they felt uncomfortable about and that, to a certain extent, represented language goals that they felt the curriculum was not preparing them for (specifically, general reading comprehension and listening comprehension as the language-proficiency goals represented by the tests, versus a curriculum focused on a reading-skills and strategies approach).

Likewise, evidence from the positivist side of the mixed design can help clarify findings from the interpretivist side. In the REST evaluation, I found that learners held contradictory views about the nature and purpose of grammar instruction within the curriculum. An analysis of the grammar subtest scores by classroom and level group allowed me to verify whether the reported differences in grammar instruction were related to differences in measurable language skills and knowledge (in this case, they were not).

Finally, when it comes time for the evaluation team to commit to a set of findings, conclusions and recommendations, the richness of evidence that accrues to a mixed design can be a useful validity check. In the REST example, if I had relied on the positivist evidence only, I would have concluded that the programme was generally a success (since most of the quantitative results suggested a significant effect for the programme, despite the subtest contradictions mentioned above). Had I relied solely on the interpretivist evidence, I would have reached a much less positive (no pun intended) conclusion. In the end, having access to evidence from both paradigm perspectives allowed me to endorse the first year of the programme in a qualified way, while being able to make specific suggestions for how the programme needed to be changed in the second year.

Another approach to mixed designs requires a longer period of time for the evaluation. It can be thought of as successive evaluation studies employing different designs. For example, the initial six months of the evaluation could be set up as a quasi-experimental design. This could be followed by another six months (or longer) in which an interpretivist design was followed. Of course, the order of design implementation could be reversed – there is no reason to assign automatically the positivist approach as the first – and with sufficient resources there could be another positivist study following the interpretivist one or, perhaps, a second implementation of both. Since it is unusual for evaluations to have the necessary funds and time commitments to carry on for this long, another option is for evaluation teams to coordinate across similar evaluation contexts; for example, it may be possible to find an evaluation done with an interpretivist design for a context that matches well with another where a positivist design could be carried out and the results compared and interpreted jointly (see McGrath et al. 1982).

2.5.4 Positivist assessment designs

McNamara (2000) discusses the development of language tests as a cycle and raises the question of 'who starts the cycle turning?' (p. 23). This is parallel to the concept of 'mandate', which Davidson and Lynch (2002) use to indicate the motivation for a test. This motivation includes such things as social, political and educational changes that lead to requests for new assessment instruments for the variety of purposes discussed in the previous chapter. For example, McNamara (2000: 23) presents the history of the Oral Proficiency Interview (OPI) and its motivation by the political needs of the Cold War climate in the United States. Given the need to gather intelligence information in a range of countries allied with the then United Soviet Socialist Republic, a test that focused on oral proficiency for a range of government workers (including 'spies') working in these countries, or with native speakers from these countries, was mandated.

Most often, the cycle of test development will be initiated by administrative officials from the upper levels of the bureaucratic chain of power and command, who then commission professional test developers. In educational settings, this means that testing mandates most often come from individuals other than those who will actually use the tests and who will be affected by their use (those who work in the specific teaching and learning contexts). Certainly, the test developers are most often external to the context of use – they are the professional testing experts who deliver the tests to the users (school administrators and teachers). Davidson and Lynch (2002) also discuss more internal mandates, and present a test-development procedure that includes teachers, and others normally seen in the 'user' role only.

2.5.4.1 Understanding the mandate

The first step in developing a language test is to understand what has motivated the test in the first place. Why is it being developed? Who is asking for it? Who will use it? This overlaps with the questions of purpose (for assessment) and audiences and goals (for evaluation) discussed in Chapter 1. In order to begin the test-development process, those who will design the test need to be able to answer these questions and to understand the various constraints that will be operating in the testing context. This includes issues such as whether the test will need to be kept 'secure'; that is, does the nature of the decisions being made from the test results require that test takers only see the test materials while they are actually taking the test, to guard against preparing answers in advance, coaching or cheating? It also includes consideration of whether there are particular schemes and notions of standards that need to be used for reporting the results, whether there are specific language-learning objectives that need to be measured, and what sorts of funding and timing (for test development and test administration) constraints exist.

2.5.4.2 Designing the test

The next step is to design the test. Depending on the purpose for assessment and the audience and goals for the use of the assessment information (including programme evaluation), this may take somewhat different forms. One distinction that has been made in the educational measurement literature that relates to these different purposes, audiences and goals is 'criterion-referenced measurement' (CRM) versus 'norm-referenced measurement' (NRM). CRM is an approach to testing that measures the individual in relation to a well-defined skill, ability or area of knowledge (which is the 'criterion'). NRM is an approach to testing that measures the individual in relation to how other individuals perform on the same test. (For more on the CRM–NRM distinction, see Brown and Hudson 2002; Davidson and Lynch 2002; Popham 1978.)

The CRM versus NRM approach to test design and development is further distinguished by the types of decisions we intend to make based on the test results. CRM is concerned with 'absolute decisions', as defined in Chapter 1. These decisions are about 'mastery', and need to be defined in terms of a level of the criterion ability, skill or knowledge. This definition of mastery is also discussed as 'standard setting'. NRM is concerned with 'relative decisions'; that is, how the individual is rank-ordered in relation to other test takers. In order for the rank-ordering to be meaningful, it needs to be in relation to some general notion of an ability, skill or knowledge as well. However, with NRM, the principal concern is with making certain that the test scores can be used to distinguish each individual test taker from the others.

For example, suppose a language school wanted to identify their top students in order to trial a new set of advanced materials. They want to do the trial with their normal class size (thirty) and, due to time constraints, they need to do it with students who are currently enrolled at their school. There are 120 students studying in their top level, but given the nature of the advanced materials, they want to identify the very best thirty students from that group. Hence, their decision needs to be a relative one, and they need a test that has been designed and developed within the NRM approach.

On the other hand, suppose that same language school needs to develop a new test to determine which of their students can be recommended for further study at the local community college. In addition to their normal selection criteria, the college has asked the language school for an empirically based recommendation as to the students' language-skill readiness for academic study in the first-year curriculum. Here, the decision context shifts from the relative to the absolute. The language school would probably not want to simply recommend their best thirty (or fifteen, or ten) students at any particular time (although there may be social and political factors that warrant other interpretations of how best to frame the decision). They would, in most cases, want to make an absolute decision for each student in relation to the criterion of language skills required for the first-year community-college curriculum. Are they ready for that level or not? This obviously involves a test that measures the particular skills identified as necessary for study in that curriculum, and for an identification of how much of those skills can be considered as sufficient. The first identification has to do with test content and target language-use analysis, to be discussed in the next section. The second identification has to do with defining mastery, or standard setting, which will be discussed in Chapter 4.

Because of the importance of the criterion in CRM, there has been an emphasis on defining test content in great detail. This relates to evidence for test validity. There has also been a closer association of CRM with classroom assessment and, in particular, achievement testing. However, some language-testing experts feel that definitions for tests and teaching activities need to be kept distinct (for example, Davies 1990). This fits better with the positivist perspective than with an interpretivist view, where teaching and testing are much more closely aligned. At the very least, teaching and learning objectives provide the basis for the clear definition of the criterion and content specification required by CRM.

Another way of considering purpose in the design and development of language tests is the notion of language for specific purposes (LSP) testing, which Douglas defines as:

> that branch of language testing in which the test content and test methods are
> derived from an analysis of a specific language use situation, such as Spanish for

Business, Japanese for Tour Guides, Italian for Language Teachers, or English for Air Traffic Control.

(Douglas 2000: 1)

This makes the argument that all tests lie on a continuum of purpose, from general to specific. CRM would probably be most relevant for the specific-purpose end; Douglas, while asserting that LSP tests could be norm-referenced (NR) or criterion-referenced (CR), acknowledges that 'CR testing offers an important perspective to LSP testing: the necessity of specifying precisely the level of ability or the domain of content that is to be the criterion for performance' (Douglas 2000: 16). Since the ability or domain of content derives from what Bachman and Palmer (1996) refer to as the 'target language use domain', LSP tests clearly need a precise definition of the characteristics of language that occur in the domain or situation of interest. This specification depends on an 'analysis of the target language use situation, authentic task, and interaction between language and content knowledge' (Douglas 2000: 4). Because of the need for detailed specification of situation, task, language and content knowledge, LSP testing is aligned with CRM, and in particular recognises the importance of detailed test specifications in the design and development of these tests. The details for test-specification formats will be presented in the next chapter.

2.5.4.3 Writing the test items

Once the test specifications are complete, the test items or tasks need to be produced. In the process, the test specifications (including the understanding and description of what is being measured) may need to be revisited and revised. Various considerations and formats for test items will be presented in the next chapter.

2.5.4.4 Conducting test trials

The final step in the test-development cycle (which, of course, can lead back to previous steps in the cycle) is the trialling of the test items or tasks. The term 'piloting' is also used, sometimes to signal a more informal 'trying out' of the test, or a portion of the test item/tasks. Whether there is an informal check on the item/tasks or not, it is important to have a formal pilot or trial, with operational conditions and a representative sample of test takers. That is, this step attempts to gather response data from the types of test takers who will be taking the test as it is intended to be used, under the same or similar conditions to the ones in which it will be administered. This results in a systematic collection of data that can then be analysed, as well as the possibility of feedback on the process from the test takers (through questionnaires or post-test interviews). This information is crucial to making certain that the test item/tasks are working the way they were intended to work, and therefore providing the information that the test users need. The use of response data from test trials for test development traditionally involves various forms of statistical analysis, to be presented in Chapter 4.

2.5.5 Interpretivist assessment designs

All of the steps I have presented for the design of positivist assessment will apply to the design of interpretivist assessment as well, although with some modifications. Instead of tests that measure the construct or criterion of interest, interpretivist assessment designs will produce procedures that will systematically gather information about language ability without measurement serving as the end goal. The way in which that language ability is conceptualised will be different in the interpretivist orientation, leading to choices for assessment format that are different from those that would be chosen for positivist assessment. So, for example, the step called 'conducting test trials' above would be labelled 'conducting assessment procedure trials' and this information will be analysed through qualitative techniques based in the interpretivist paradigm, rather than through statistical analysis. These differences will become clear when the development of positivist measures (Chapter 3) and the development of interpretivist procedures (Chapter 5) are presented.

These steps have been presented in a different form for interpretivist assessment design in the classroom context, especially with younger learners (primary, elementary, K-12 school levels), by Rea-Dickins (2001). The first stage of design is called 'planning' and includes an identification of the purpose for the assessment, choosing the assessment activity and preparing the learners for the assessment. The second stage involves implementing the assessment, but continues to need elements of design such as providing language and content 'scaffolding' (Hawkins 1988; Peregoy and Boyle 1997), an introduction of the assessment for the learners and initial feedback. The third stage that must be designed is the monitoring of the assessment activity. In addition to feedback to learners, interpretations from the evidence collected during the assessment can be shared with other teachers, and adjustments to the assessment activities can be made (such as changing the teaching and learning pairs or groups). The final stage involves the recording and reporting of assessment evidence outside the classroom context (for example, to school boards or other administrative bodies). All of these stages are iterative, allowing for the planning stage to be revisited following discoveries in the implementation and monitoring stages, for example.

2.6 VIGNETTES

The variety of audience–goals–context–themes–paradigm–design interactions for assessment and evaluation is extensive, but I want to illustrate the range of possibilities with a few vignettes. These examples come from actual assessment and evaluation contexts that I have worked in, although I have modified them to make for a clearer discussion of potential audience–goal interactions.

2.6.1 Vignette 1: short-term evaluation design for a university ESL programme

This first vignette involves a short-term evaluation of an ESL programme located in a university department (in this case, a department of education, offering a graduate degree in TESOL). The head of the department had requested a review of the ESL programme, which offered classes in general English as well as English for specific purposes. The students came from other countries to study ESL and were not enrolled in degree programmes at the university, although many were intending on eventually applying for tertiary study.

The primary audience for this evaluation was the department, including the ESL programme staff. The review had not been requested by the university but was, rather, internally motivated, in particular by the head of department. The evaluation was short term, with a four-day visit by a single evaluator (the Jet In-Jet Out variety mentioned in Chapter 1), and the goals were stated very generally, at least at first. The evaluator began the process with an understanding that the department wanted a primarily formative evaluation, information about the ESL programme that could be used to help improve it. As the evaluation proceeded, other goals began to emerge. Some were general: for example, the department wanted information that would help it decide about the balance between providing an essentially commercial programme (the fees from international students were significant for the university and department) and developing research and curriculum innovation. Other goals that emerged were more specific: the department, in particular the head of department, wanted to build a case for requiring all ESL programme teachers to have a relevant MA degree.

The evaluator was constrained in this context by the short-term time period for the evaluation, which was determined by the primary audience (a four-day visit, followed by a formal written report). Further contextual constraints included the lack of access to any sort of test or measurement data. These constraints, along with the initially general goals as communicated by the primary audience, led the evaluator to pursue an exploratory approach which made use of an interpretivist design similar to Stake's (1975) responsive model. The short-term nature of the evaluation meant that the design was actually formed as initial data were collected. The evaluator spent most of the four days attempting to clarify the audiences (primary and secondary), goals, context and themes beyond the initial information that had been conveyed via email prior to the visit. Although the evaluator came to understand that the primary audience, in particular the department head, might prefer a positivist conceptualisation of the programme and design for the evaluation, there did not seem to be sufficient time nor appropriate data-gathering possibilities to choose this direction.

What resulted was a series of interviews conducted with the department head, department-faculty members, ESL centre head, ESL centre coordinators and ESL centre teachers. The design also included a meeting with a group of the teachers to share with them the preliminary themes that had been raised in the interviews, in order to get their reactions and feedback before the final report was written. The evaluator also met with the department head and the ESL centre head after the preliminary themes had been constructed, and exchanged emails with both during the writing of the final report. This resulted in a co-construction of the programme and its effectiveness, the evaluator's attempts to synthesise the various voices encountered during the interviews and meetings carried out over the four-day visit.

2.6.2 Vignette 2: long-term evaluation design for a university ESL programme

The second vignette involves an evaluation of another university programme – an ESL programme that offered courses primarily to students already enrolled as undergraduates and graduates in a university-degree programme – that was carried out over a nine-month period. This evaluation was requested by the university, so the primary audience included representatives of the university administration as well as the department and ESL centre responsible for the programme. The latter included representation of the ESL teachers, who actively participated in the design of the evaluation as well as its implementation. Rather than a single expert, this evaluation employed a team of ESL experts, some from the city and country where the programme was located, and others from outside the country.

A formal set of evaluation goals was developed through dialogue between the evaluation team and the primary evaluation audience. In this process, the primary-audience concerns were communicated mainly by the administrators and teachers from the ESL centre. The head evaluator, who had been responsible for selecting the rest of the evaluation team, had established the general goals for the evaluation through dialogue with the head of the ESL centre at the beginning of the nine-month period. At that point, it was understood that the purpose of the evaluation was to provide feedback to the primary audience about the effectiveness of the centre in meeting its objectives and to provide information and recommendations to the centre for improving the programme. This was a classic combination of summative and formative goals, with the primary audience leaning towards a preference for quantitative evidence of student learning.

Once the evaluation team was selected, and the general goals established, the team met with the ESL centre staff to elaborate the goals and establish the evaluation design. During these discussions, three areas were established for the evaluation: an examination of the content of the centre's curriculum; the development of tests for the centre's curriculum; and a proposed study to measure change in learner proficiency over time (with a general ESL proficiency test). There were also visits to various components of the centre, such as the student self-access learning centre, to develop the evaluation team's understanding of the context and themes. An initial design was formulated, based on the primary audience's goals (to be able to measure student learning in relation to programme objectives), the context and preliminary themes (there were standardised proficiency tests in place as part of the selection and exit process; there was a desire for quantitative evidence of student learning and an expression of the theme of 'accountability' of the programme to its stakeholders) which was primarily positivist and quasi-experimental.

The evaluation team visited the programme again several months after the initial visit to continue the work on elaborating specific goals within the three areas identified. At this point the design began to change to a more mixed design, one that incorporated aspects of the interpretivist perspective and attempted to be responsive to the programme stakeholders in the development of the evaluation. In part, this was due to the difficulty with which the evaluation team had in finding the curriculum objectives that the measurement of student learning could be judged against. Since the documented course objectives were not always consistent with the understanding that came from the ESL centre coordinators and teachers, the evaluation team elected to pursue a multiple perspective view in order to arrive at a set of objectives that reflected the experience of programme participants. This construction of the course objectives evolved over several months of face-to-face meetings (the first two visits referred to above) and email correspondence between the evaluation team, the ESL centre head and the ESL teachers who were assigned to work with the team on the three areas (testing, curriculum and the learner proficiency study).

There was a third round of visits by the evaluation team to the programme setting, along with follow-up telephone interviews towards the end of the nine-month period. The evaluation team came to express the view that its overarching goal was to provide formative feedback and create processes (and tests) for ongoing programme self-study and development, not a summative judgement. The final evaluation report gave a series of review questions which demonstrated how the goals and design for the evaluation had evolved since the initial meetings. The design was ultimately structured around a quasi-experimental component (pre-test and post-test measures of student learning) combined with a more interpretivist component that focused on working collaboratively with the centre staff to develop a portrait of the programme. This portrait was designed to highlight areas for improvement, and to be integrated with the centre's ongoing curriculum development. The quasi-experimental component relied primarily upon the programme group only, pre-test and post-test design, since there was no appropriate comparison group available. A comparison group study was fashioned *ex post facto*, using test scores for learners who had exempted from the ESL programme in comparison to those who had just completed the programme. The interpretivist component examined participant perceptions of the programme, analysed curriculum content in terms of relevance to learner needs, and the match between curriculum goals and course materials and tests, and investigated teaching effectiveness. This inquiry was carried out collaboratively with programme participants through questionnaires, interviews, and document analysis, and made use of Eisner's (1991) connoisseurship model (evaluation-team members and primary-audience members using their expertise to arrive at critical guideposts for judging the curriculum). The final report itself was the result of preliminary drafts being circulated among the evaluation team and the primary audiences for feedback and clarification, which is further evidence of an interpretivist side to the evaluation design.

2.6.3 Vignette 3: a design for foreign language assessment in secondary schools

This vignette outlines a design for implementing assessment of foreign language achievement at the secondary school level. The assessment team had as its primary audiences the state board of education and local school administrators. These audiences were interested in quantitative evidence of individual student learning in relation to recent reforms in the teaching of foreign languages. The reforms focused on moving the curriculum away from strictly grammar- and translation-based teaching and learning to an approach that focused on oral communication skills.

These primary audiences and goals, thus, were very similar to a programme evaluation context. In this scenario, however, I want to focus on the design of an assessment instrument rather than the evaluation of a curriculum or programme. Another part of the primary audience for designing this assessment was the foreign-language teacher, as well as the foreign-language learner. The context and themes obviously included the atmosphere of curriculum change surrounding the shift to a communicative approach. The theory of language learning embodied in this curriculum change interacted with the primary audience's (state board and local school administrators) goals for quantitative accountability evidence, suggesting the need for a positivist approach to designing a language test.

The assessment team, in this case, consisted of two language testing experts who were hired as consultants on a larger, state-funded project designed to promote and develop the communicative approach to language teaching in the state's foreign-language curriculum (focusing on Spanish, French and German). They examined the curriculum objectives, spoke with project coordinators, and a focus group of foreign-language teachers from districts across the state. After a consideration of the primary audiences, goals, context and themes, the assessment team decided that a positivist approach was required. That is, they decided that the end goal for the assessment project was a test that would measure communicative language ability as defined in the objectives formulated for the larger curriculum-development project. This test would need to produce statistically reliable results and be correlated with the existing standardised tests that the state used to measure student achievement in foreign language.

Following the steps for test development outlined earlier in this chapter, the assessment team (now expanded to include a small group of test-specification and item writers) produced a set of test specifications for a listening subtest and a speaking subtest that would cover the range of language-proficiency levels assumed by the new state curriculum. Items for the subtests were then written by the team and piloted in a representative sample of foreign language classrooms. After statistical analysis of the piloted items, the tests were revised and operational forms were prepared for use in the next school year, to be given at the beginning and end of the year to all levels of foreign-language classes in a representative sample of high school districts across the state.

2.6.4 Vignette 4: one-teacher, one-classroom assessment design

This final vignette focuses the assessment context on an individual teacher and an individual classroom. It illustrates a frequent and consistent need in the language teaching classroom for ways of gathering information about the language ability of individual learners. In this scenario, then, the primary audience was composed of a teacher of sixth-grade (year 6 in the United States' K-through-12 system) Spanish in a heritage language programme (see UCLA 2001), the learners, and their families and community. The goal, in this case, was to understand the ways in which each individual student had learned in relation to a unit on the subjunctive (embedded in tasks involving making decisions between various plans for a traditional Mexican festival). The focus of the overall curriculum was on the communicative use of the language in situations that were meaningful and relevant to the student. The community for which this classroom existed was concerned about their children being able to use Spanish, an additional language to English for the children and the primary language of their parents or grandparents, as an educated Spanish speaker from the home country (Mexico and other Central American countries) would do. The teacher viewed language ability as something that could be measured and described on a continuum from informal conversational fluency to educated native-speaker proficiency.

Given this combination of audience, goals, context and themes, the teacher followed a primarily positivist design. The teacher used the steps for test development outlined earlier in this chapter and constructed a test of the subjunctive that made use of the types of decisions required by the instructional unit on planning a traditional Mexican festival. The format was selected so that questions that could be scored right or wrong. The test questions and correct answers were modelled after the language used in a videotape donated by one of the parents showing a group of Mexican officials planning a festival.

2.7 CONCLUSION

This chapter has laid out the basic steps that lead to the design of assessments and evaluations. I have attempted to demonstrate that a good deal of thought and planning happens before the actual assessment or evaluation project can begin. This thought and planning represent a complex interaction between audiences, goals, contexts and themes. In general, the resulting design needs to establish the feasibility of the goals, the priorities that exist among multiple goals, which audiences will be reported to, what form of evidence the audiences will be expecting, how the information reported will be used, and when the information will need to be reported.

To illustrate the complex interactions present in designing assessment and evaluation, I have presented several vignettes drawn from my experience with projects in different contexts. I consciously selected and modified these vignettes for a variety of purposes. Primarily, I wanted to show how audience, goals, context and themes can interact to lead to a particular paradigm and design. However, in choosing particular interactions, it should not be concluded that there is a strict determinism between this combination of factors and a paradigm design. A slight change in any of the combinations could easily lead to a different paradigm choice; for example, in Vignette 4, if the view of language on the part of the teacher had been slightly different and less amenable to a measurement view, the resulting design could have been characterised with a more interpretivist orientation. In part, I chose to give the one-teacher, one-classroom vignette a positivist solution to avoid oversimplifying interpretivist assessment as being what happens when individual teachers attempt to construct their own procedures for gathering information about individual learners. I want to avoid giving the impression that positivist designs are what we always use when the stakes are high, the scale is large, and we need to report to a variety of external stakeholders. I also want to avoid giving the impression that interpretivist designs are what we always use when we don't have the expertise to develop sophisticated tests or when the decisions to be made are limited to local concerns.

All of these vignettes, and the last one perhaps particularly so, hint at what the actual evaluations or assessments would look like as they were implemented. The focus here, though, is meant to be on the design of evaluation and assessment, not on their implementation, analysis and interpretation. The next four chapters will demonstrate how to move from designs to the actual gathering of information and the analysis of that information from the two basic paradigmatic perspectives.

EXERCISES

1. Think of one or two language programmes that you have been involved with, either as a teacher, or as a learner. Make a list of the primary and secondary audiences for an evaluation of that programme. Then try to identify what the goals for an evaluation of the programme might have been, from the different audience perspectives.
2. Revisit your list of audiences and goals from Exercise 1. Which paradigm is suggested as most relevant for the particular programme context?
3. Drawing on your experience as a language learner and/or teacher, make a list of your favourite teaching and learning activities. Now compare it with your list from Exercise 2, Chapter 1. What are the major differences between the items on the two lists? What would it take to make the teaching/learning activities into an assessment procedure?

SUGGESTIONS FOR FURTHER READING

(There are a set of narratives that focus on the mandate aspect of language assessment design presented in Chapter 5 of Davidson and Lynch, 2002, that may be useful complements to the assessment vignettes presented here.)

1. Weir, C. and J. Roberts (1994), *Evaluation in ELT*, Oxford: Blackwell Publishers. This book presents an introduction to positivist evaluation designs for second

language programmes. At this stage in your reading, focus on the first two chapters and perhaps one of the illustrative case studies provided in the second part of the book.

2. Rea-Dickins, P. and K. Germaine (1992), *Evaluation*, Oxford: Oxford University Press.

This book gives an introduction to a broad view of evaluation, including examples of the interpretivist perspective. For now, compare the first four chapters with the presentation of evaluation in Weir and Roberts.

3. McNamara, T. F. (2000), *Language Testing*, Oxford: Oxford University Press.

This book provides an introduction to the basic terminology and issues in language assessment. The relevant chapters for now are the first three, which offer definitions of testing terms and purposes, and examples of test formats.

Chapter 3

Developing measures of language ability and programme effectiveness

3.1 INTRODUCTION

Within the traditional, positivist approaches to assessment and evaluation, measurement procedures in the form of language tests are the primary sources of data for the decisions about individual language ability and language programme effectiveness. This chapter will describe the testing of separate language skills and integrative language ability. I will also discuss other measures, such as questionnaires, for both for assessment and evaluation.

3.2 TEST SPECIFICATIONS

As discussed in the previous chapter, an important starting point for test design and subsequent development is the test specification. There have been a variety of formats portrayed in the literature (Alderson et al. 1995; Douglas 2000; Norris et al. 1998). One influential format comes from the work of W. James Popham (1978) and his colleagues at Instructional Objectives Exchange. As presented in Davidson and Lynch (2002), the main components are: the General Description, the Prompt Attributes, the Response Attributes, Sample Item, and Specification Supplement. These components are discussed in more detail below.

3.2.1 General Description

This component provides a brief summary statement of the criterion and the theoretical perspective, purpose, motivation and context (mandate) that informs the testing of the criterion. McNamara (2000) uses the term criterion to designate the ability, skill or knowledge as it exists in some future context or situation, which corresponds to Douglas's (2000) target language use situation or Bachman and Palmer's (1996) target language use domain (for Douglas, the domain is something that the individual language learner constructs, more or less as a cognitive 'script' for understanding and relating to the criterion situation). Like Bachman and Palmer, McNamara uses domain to refer to 'the set of tasks or the kinds of behaviours in the criterion setting' (McNamara 2000: 25). The theoretical perspective for the criterion is provided by McNamara's use of the term 'construct' (2000: 13). The test construct defines the ability being measured, provides the theoretical understanding for the domain and guides the sampling of tasks and behaviours for the test.

Whichever of the definitions for domain, criterion and construct we adopt, the General Description (GD) component of a test specification needs to provide a clear summary of the language skill, ability or knowledge being tested, the theoretical perspective that informs what is being tested (how language and language use are understood), and the target setting or situation within which that skill, ability or knowledge will be used or performed. For the purposes of this discussion, criterion will be taken to include the construct (language skill, ability or knowledge being tested) as well as the target language use domain or situation.

3.2.2 Prompt Attributes

This component indicates what will be presented to the test takers, or how they will be prompted to respond on the test. Basically, this involves the selection of format for the test, at the item or task level, such as multiple-choice (MC), dictation, oral interview, cloze test or essay. The most important feature of the PA is sufficient detail in the description of what the test item or task will look like; that is, what will the test taker be asked to do? This includes specifying how the directions or instructions will be worded and presented, which Bachman (1990) and Douglas (2000) refer to as the 'rubric'. Information concerning characteristics for the entire test or subtest – how many tasks, how much time for each task, and so on – can be included here, or this information can be listed separately, in an appendix (see 3.2.5, 'Specification Supplement', discussed below).

The core of the Prompt Attributes (PA) concerns the characteristics of the actual item or task. Our specification of these characteristics needs to be clearly linked to the criterion, as informed by the test construct. In other words, if the test taker responds to our prompt, we need to know that this will give us information about the criterion we are trying to measure.

3.2.3 Response Attributes

There is unavoidable overlap between the PA and the next component of this test specification format, the Response Attributes (RA). This component specifies what the test takers will be expected to do in response to the prompt, or how they will interact with the PA. Generally, response formats are characterised by two types: 'selected response' and 'constructed response'. Selected response (also referred to as 'fixed response') involves item formats that ask the test taker to choose from a set of given responses; this includes, for example, multiple-choice, true-false and matching formats. In this sense, the set of given, or fixed, responses can also be seen as part of the PA, since they form part of what is prompting the test takers. The constructed response format requires the test taker to produce something other than what they are prompted with; that is, they may be required to fill in a blank with a word or phrase; they may be asked to respond to a question with a short written or spoken answer; they may be asked to speak or write an extended response to a given topic. Examples of constructed response formats include short answer, gap-filling, essay and oral interview. These formats will be discussed in more detail later in the chapter. Generally, for constructed response formats using extended written and spoken responses, the prompt will take the form of a text (the characteristics for that text will need to be detailed in the PA). The RA for such formats will need to describe how the test takers' responses will be judged, or what Douglas (2000: 67–71) refers to as 'characteristics of assessment'. The detail required for specifying the 'criteria for correctness' (see McNamara 1996 and Douglas 2000 for a complete discussion of this issue) as well as the scoring procedures, or how the test takers' responses will be judged against the criteria for correctness, may argue for putting it in the Specification Supplement, discussed below.

3.2.3.1 Authenticity of response

McNamara (2000) discusses authenticity as a characteristic of the test method, combining Prompt and Response Attributes. The degree of authenticity is determined in relation to the criterion language ability. Basically, an authentic test simulates, to the highest degree possible, the characteristics of the criterion and its setting. The 'highest degree possible' is mediated and constrained by issues of practicality; that is, it may not be feasible to include all characteristics of the criterion setting without the test being too long, too time-consuming, or too difficult to standardise and score. Of course, not all assessment contexts will be constrained to the same degree by these practical concerns, but for the development of measurement instruments and tests, especially large-scale testing, these particular practical issues will always be major factors in the design process.

The ultimate purpose for seeking authenticity in our language tests is to prompt a response from the test taker that will resemble language use in the criterion (or 'target') setting. As Bachman and Palmer (1996) remind us, this allows generalisation from test scores to language use in the criterion setting; that is, it strengthens our ability to make interpretations about the test takers' communicative ability beyond the test setting. However, as Douglas points out, 'Mere emulation of a target situation in the test is not sufficient to guarantee communicative language use' (Douglas 2000: 18). This relates to Widdowson's (1978) distinction between authentic and genuine, and Bachman's (1990) interactional versus 'real-life'. The authentic, interactional test will tend to engage the test taker's communicative language ability in relation to the criterion-setting characteristics. 'Merely emulating' results in a test that is genuine and 'real-life', in that it has the characteristics of the criterion setting, but may not be designed with the original, authentic purpose and audience assumed in the criterion setting. For example, a test may employ an article from an engineering journal as the reading text to which the test takers are expected to respond by answering questions concerning its main ideas and specific information. However, unless the test takers are the type of engineers (in terms of experience, background and motivation for reading the journal) assumed by the author of the article, then the test and task will not be fully authentic and inter-actional.

Finally, as mentioned above, not all assessment and testing contexts will have the same practical constraints. Depending on test purpose, the type and number of test takers, and the range of material support available for the development and administration of the test, authenticity will be in a trade-off situation with practicality. Being able to specify fully all of the criterion-setting characteristics in the test setting will usually be practically impossible.

3.2.3.2 *Relationship of the Prompt and Response Attributes*

Underscoring the potential for overlap between the PA and RA, the relationship between these two components has also been described with the features of 'reactivity', 'scope', and 'directness' (Bachman and Palmer 1996). 'Reactivity' exists when test items or tasks require interaction between the test taker and the test giver, such as in the oral interview test format. With this type of interaction, what is provided to the test taker (the prompt) changes depending on what the test taker does (the response). For example, test takers will receive questions, or prompts, that are tailored to their previous responses, with the test givers, or interlocutors, offering easier or more difficult language in order to encourage test takers to provide their best performance. Test takers may also receive some sort of feedback from the interlocutors which they can use to make their own judgement of how the test performance is going. In other test formats, there will be no reactivity; that is, the test taker will receive no feedback and there will be no direct interaction with the test giver. Computer adaptive tests, where the item or task presented to test takers is chosen by the computer based on how they did in relation to the previous items or tasks, is an example of indirect reactivity; there is no explicit interaction with the test giver, and no explicit feedback, but the prompt is tailored to the response using computer algorithms and test-item banks with pre-established item difficulty levels.

Bachman and Palmer's concept of 'scope' has to do with the amount of material in the prompt that must be taken in by test takers in order to generate their response. Some test items or tasks require an entire text (written or spoken) to be processed in order to provide an answer, such as skimming for the main idea. Other test items or tasks will have only a small amount of prompt input (such as a single-sentence multiple-choice format) or require a very small amount of the prompt input to be processed in order to generate the response (such as a locating-specific-information task). Douglas (2000) also discusses variety as a dimension of scope. Certain test items or tasks may require the test taker to synthesise information and ideas from a variety of prompt material, and this material may come from several previous subtest tasks. An example of this variety would be requiring the test taker to write a composition based on information presented in a lecture (perhaps from a previous listening subtest) and reading passage (perhaps from a previous reading subtest).

Bachman and Palmer's 'directness' has to do with how much the response is expected to go beyond what is provided in the prompt. A direct PA–RA relationship is where the PA provides most, or all, of what test takers need in order to produce their response. Examples of this would be selected response formats, or constructed response formats where the task is retrieving or paraphrasing information provided in the prompt materials. Indirect PA–RA relationships require the test takers to provide information that is not present in the prompt material, such as a constructed response format that asks test takers to relate a story from their past experience.

3.2.4 Sample Item

This component is used to illustrate the typical item or task that the specification is designed to produce. It answers the question: if test writers followed the specification the way it is intended to be used, what would the item/task look like? Although it can be positioned after the GD, it is generally more helpful to let specification users read and understand the specification components before seeing an example. This allows them to understand the details of what needs to be included in the prompt and what is expected in the response. Looking at a Sample Item (SI) first can lead the specification user to miss certain details, focusing on the more obvious characteristics represented there.

One of the classic problems for the test specification, however, has been the specificity of the criterion. How specific should we be in describing the skill, ability or knowledge to be tested? In the historical development of criterion-referenced measurement (CRM), the desire for clarity in the definition of the criterion led to more and more specific definitions and test specifications. As Popham (1994) has pointed out, this resulted in 'single-definition' criterion-referenced tests (CRTs), which defined the criterion with one specific item or task type. This led to a narrowing of instruction related to the criteria, since teachers took the particular item or task types as the object to be mastered. In the same way, giving too much prominence to the SI can lead to an overly narrow interpretation of the skill, ability or knowledge to be assessed. Interestingly, Popham has recommended a revised approach to specification writing that provides an elaborated GD and several 'illustrative items', or SIs that will represent the complexity of the criterion and encourage instruction that aims at 'generalizable mastery of the skill or knowledge domain being measured' (Popham 1994: 16–17).

3.2.5 Specification Supplement

As a final, optional component, the Specification Supplement (SS) is designed to store details that would be cumbersome or distracting from the reading and understanding of the spec for the first time. For example, the SS can include a listing of the types of magazines, journals or textbooks which would be appropriate as sources for reading texts. It might also include the actual rating scale (an example of 'criteria for correctness') to be used in assessing constructed responses, along with further detail on the process for using the scale. In this case, the RA could provide a description of the categories of language that will be assessed, with a reference to the rating scale in the SS.

3.2.6 Example Specification

To get a feel for what a specification looks like, Figure 3.1 presents one developed for the English as a Second Language Placement Exam (ESLPE) at UCLA.

3.3 TESTING SKILLS, SEPARATELY AND TOGETHER

There is a long tradition of discussing and categorising language tests based on the four skill areas of reading, listening, writing and speaking. This section will present issues that relate to the individual skill areas as separate test types, followed by examples of integrated skills testing. However, it should be noted that most tests will involve a combination of language skills. For example, it is rare, if not impossible, to have a test that measures listening and nothing else; usually some reading of text or speaking is involved as well. Perhaps it is best to think of the four skills not as part of the language ability being tested, but as 'the means by which that ability is realized in the performance of tasks in actual language use situations' (Douglas 2000: 38). For the purposes of this chapter, I will retain the notion of reading, listening, writing and speaking tests as both the means for testing and ability being tested, along with some examples of tests that integrate these modalities at the end of the section.

3.3.1 Tests of reading

3.3.1.1 Skills

The testing of reading is most often discussed in terms of skills and subskills that define the reading process (see, for example, Hughes 1989: 116–17; Lumley 1993: 233–4; Weir 1997: 43). Reading theory, and its models of the reading process, shapes the way these skills are conceptualised. The psycholinguistic (Goodman 1967; Smith 1971) and 'top-down' (Coady 1979; Steffenson et al. 1979) models of reading identify particular reading skills as being essential to successful reading. Hughes refers to these skills as 'macro' and Weir labels them as reading for 'global comprehension'. This range of skills includes:

- identifying the main purpose and audience for the text;
- skimming for main ideas;
- making propositional inferences;
- scanning for specific information;
- identifying the overall structure of the text and its arguments.

The 'bottom-up' model of reading (Gough 1972) focuses on skills that are commonly referred to as 'decoding', 'micro' (Hughes 1989), or 'reading for local comprehension' (Weir 1997: 43). These skills include:

Title: UCLA ESLPE TEST SPECIFICATION: Reading

(GD) General Description of the Criterion Being Tested: Examinees will demonstrate their ability to read genuine academic texts from general, non-technical university level materials or from genuine non-academic texts with content and language similar in difficulty and sophistication to the academic texts. The specific reading skills on which examinees will demonstrate their ability are:
  a) recognition of main ideas (and distinguishing them from supporting ideas)
  b) synthesis of information across more than one paragraph in the text
  c) recognition of opinions (and distinguishing them from information presented as fact)

(PA) Prompt Attributes:
Requirements for the Text: The reading texts for the test should have the following characteristics:
  a) academic content from an authentic university level text that is not overly specific to a particular field and does not contain extremely technical vocabulary, or general interest content from an authentic text that is aimed at a college-educated audience
  b) a self-contained section (with minimal or no editing to the original text) of 800 to 1200 words in length
  c) several rhetorical modes such as description, narration, argumentation, with a clear overall organizational structure (i.e., transparent markers such as section headings and logical connectors)
  d) examples, illustrations, anecdotes, graphs, charts, figures, and/or tables

Description of the Test Items: The examinees will be presented with multiple-choice (MC) format items. Each MC item will consist of a wh-question followed by four options, which may be either complete sentences or single phrases. One of the four options will represent the best answer to the question, according to the information in the text. The other three options (distracters) will depend on the type of question being asked. If the question is asking for a recognition of a main idea, distracters will be 1) statements which are clearly over-generalised or 2) ones which express ideas mentioned in the text, but are supporting ideas or otherwise not the main idea in question. If the question is asking for a synthesis of information, the distracters will be 1) statements which put information together that does not cohere for the text in question or 2) ones that represent a synthesis of information that goes beyond that presented in the text. If the question is asking for a recognition of definition or opinion, the distracters will be 1) statements that confuse statements of fact in the text with statements of opinion (or vice versa) or 2) ones that present definitions, facts, or opinions that do not occur in the text.

(RA) Description of the Answer Format: The examinees will have a separate answer sheet/card on which they will darken in their selection (A or B; A,B,C, or D) with a No. 2 lead pencil (for machine-scoring). They will be instructed to indicate their answer by marking the one best alternative for each test item.

(SI) Sample Item:
Which paragraph best expresses the main purpose of this essay?
A. Paragraph 10   B. Paragraph 11   C. Paragraph 13   D. Paragraph 16

(SS) Specification Supplement: *Texts:* Each Reading subtest should have two reading passages: one reading should have content from the natural sciences and the other should have content from the social sciences. *Items:* Specific information is supplementary information, supporting ideas, examples, illustrations, numerical information, and information retrievable from tables and figures. Main ideas may be characterised as main propositions or controlling ideas in the text and supporting ideas as particularisations, like illustrations, examples, anecdotes, and numerical or graphical information that work as detail. Suggestion: identify potential main ideas by the following procedures: read the material fast, skim or scan the text(s), read the first sentence of each paragraph, look for section headings, look for explicit organisational markers. Synthesis of information is a linking of one main idea with another idea, one main idea with supporting ideas or one supporting idea with one or more supporting ideas. For the purposes of the test, this should not include difficult or complex conceptual synthesis or tedious mathematical computations.

[This is a modified version of a specification revised in March 1992 by Brian Lynch. Previous versions of the specification were developed by Sara Cushing, Antony Kunnan, Charlene Polio and Brian Lynch.]

Figure 3.1   Example test specification

- recognising the meaning of grammatical structures (for example, present continuous tense for future time reference);
- recovering the referent from a pronoun;
- recognising the meaning of lexical items from morphology and context.

As Weir (1997: 43) points out, all 'reading for global comprehension' skills might include knowledge of the bottom-up skills mentioned above. This fits well with the 'interactive' model (Rumelhart 1977), which is currently a dominant influence in second language reading. This model emphasises the interaction between top-down and bottom-up skills, as well as the interaction between reader and author.

3.3.1.2 Texts

Reading tests usually involve having test takers actually read a text, and then indicate their understanding of the various aspects of the text (and their use of the various skills mentioned above) in one format or another. The selection of text type, then, becomes a major issue for developing tests of reading ability. These text types can range from magazine articles to newspaper columns, textbook chapters or excerpts, business letters, or advertisements. When deciding on the type of text to use, the following considerations may be useful.

1. Include a representative sample of texts, drawing upon the range of text types within the reading skill or skills being tested.
2. Choose a text with appropriate length, a length that requires the skills or construct to be tested and that will provide enough opportunity to test the skill across several items (for example, testing the ability to skim for the main idea will require a text with several paragraphs, or several main ideas; alternatively, there can be several shorter texts, each with its own main idea).
3. Have a number of texts presented within each test, in order to provide variety and to avoid having a single content that favours certain test takers over others.
4. Select text content that matches the skills being tested (for example, an encyclopedia-type text for testing the skill of scanning for specific information).
5. Select content that is interesting and engaging without being distracting or disturbing for the intended test takers.
6. Choose content that tests reading skills, not previous content knowledge.
7. Avoid content that is overly unfamiliar (from a cultural point of view) to the intended test takers.

3.3.1.3 Example reading tests

A variety of item or task formats have been used in the testing of reading ability, including both selected response and constructed response formats mentioned in the section on test specifications (RA). Note that the more 'constructed' the response format, the more the test will include writing skills as well as reading. Some illustrative examples are provided below.

Reading texts, or passages: newspaper articles; interview transcripts; advertisements; academic textbook chapters (whole or excerpts); short stories (whole or excerpts); recipes; instructions.

Item and task formats: multiple-choice; true-false; short answer; and from Valencia and Pearson (1987), cited in Cohen (1994: 233): summary writing; identifying questions most likely to help peers understand the text (selecting from a list); predicting content based on topic; determining the relatedness of vocabulary to text.

Example items:

1. Students read a newspaper article describing a story that contains several pieces of reported factual information (who, what, where, when). They are then presented with several statements for which they are instructed to identify as 'true' or 'false', according to the news story (true-false).

2. Students read an eight-paragraph excerpt from a high school textbook on biology. They are presented with several items that ask them to identify the main idea, definitions of key concepts and specific details from the passage. Each question is presented as an incomplete statement followed by a set of four alternatives from which they are to choose the best answer (multiple-choice).

3. Students read an advertisement for a new computer product. They are then instructed to answer a series of questions concerning the intended audience, the purpose of the product and specific information such as product features (short answer).

4. Students read a short text (one paragraph) describing a scene with multiple participants (e.g., several groups of people playing in a park). They are then presented with three or four picture illustrations of such a scene and are asked to choose the illustration that best represents the scene as described in the short text (picture multiple-choice).

5. Students read short (2–3 page) chapter from an introductory biology text that describes a natural process in scientific terms (e.g. photosynthesis). They are then presented with an incomplete diagram of the process and are asked to complete it using the information presented in the reading passage (diagram gap-filling).

6. Students are presented with the title and a first-page illustration (diagram or picture) for an article selected from their major field of study. They are asked to write a brief summary of what they think the article will be about, drawing on their background knowledge of the field (short answer).

3.3.2 Tests of listening

One of the central concerns for tests of listening ability is to clearly define the nature of 'listening'. Buck (1997) reminds us that when attempting to test listening, we need to remember several things:

1. Listening tests use *spoken* language as 'input'.
2. (Natural) spoken language is an 'acoustic signal', with the potential for lack of clarity, modification and speed (especially 'informal' speech).
3. (Natural) spoken language has 'non-standard' features, fillers and hesitations.
4. Spoken language occurs in 'real-time'; it must be captured 'on the run', and there is no 'text' (except with audiotapes) to refer back to.

3.3.2.1 Problems

This leads us to several problems. First of all, listening, like reading, is an internal process of comprehension; there is no observable product that directly represents listening. This means we need to devise response formats that allow test takers to communicate what they have understood, which inevitably means that we are also testing other language skills (speaking, reading and/or writing). The task of testing 'just listening', in isolation from other language skills, is perhaps the most vexing problem that has faced listening test developers. The answer to this problem, perhaps, is to see listening as an inherently interactive, integrated language skill.

Another problem, also articulated by Buck (1997), is that the process of listening differs depending on the purpose, interests and background knowledge which individual listeners bring to the task. Except for simple information transmission tasks, any spoken text may have a number of possible interpretations, and these will certainly not be limited to the interpretations the test writer imagines and creates. This means that there are complex aspects of listening, and complex listening tasks that we need to be able to test. For example, we need to test the ability to relate 'decoded' linguistic information to context and communicative purpose.

A final problem is the type of listening 'text' that should be used in our tests. Should 'natural' language be used, or should there be modifications (repetition of the text/passage; slow, deliberate delivery of speech; and so on)?

Each of these problems needs to be considered when designing tests for the particular language test situation. This, in turn, involves a consideration of the test criterion (construct and target situation). For particular test takers, with particular language use goals, or target language use situations, it may not be necessary to worry about testing 'just listening', there may be clear interpretations for the listening text, we may be interested in a relatively simple listening task, and the use of repetitive, slowly delivered speech may be appropriate.

3.3.2.2 Example listening tests

As with reading tests, most of the selected and constructed response formats discussed earlier can be used to test listening. As with reading tests, it is difficult if not impossible to test solely listening; other language modalities will inevitably form a part of the testing process. The following examples indicate a range of formats, from those that focus on listening to those that intentionally combine it with other skills. More examples of integrated skills testing will be presented at the end of this section, following 3.3.4, 'Tests of speaking'. The types of listening 'texts', or passages, and item or task formats presented below can be mixed and matched (for example, a news-broadcast recording with a matching format or with a re-ordering task), as the example items will demonstrate.

Listening 'texts', or passages: radio or television broadcasts of news; interviews; advertisements (recorded from original broadcasts or simulated with actors); recorded dialogues; recorded academic lectures (recorded from original or simulated); recorded directions or instructions (for example, how to drive to a particular location; how to bake a cake).

Item and task formats: multiple-choice; matching; re-ordering; short answer; gap-filling.

Example items:
1. Students listen to an audiotape recording of a news broadcast that presents a single news story. They are then instructed to select the picture that identifies the person described in the news story from four alternatives (multiple-choice).
2. Students view a videotape demonstrating the assembly of a bookcase from a kit. They then complete a task which asks them to put the sequence of events described in the videotape into the proper order from a scrambled list (re-ordering).
3. Students listen to an audiotape recording of an advertisement for a local restaurant. They are then instructed to complete a flyer for the restaurant that has certain missing information; for example: the business hours, days open/closed, name of the restaurant, type of food served (gap-filling).
4. Students view a videotape recording of an academic lecture from a university introductory-level psychology class. They are given an incomplete outline of the lecture which they are asked to complete (gap-filling), followed by several questions concerning the main concepts defined in the lecture (short answer).
5. Students listen to an audiotape recording of a dialogue between a father and son concerning their plans for the weekend. They are then asked to indicate which items from a list were associated with the father's expressed wishes for the weekend and which were the son's (matching).

3.3 Tests of writing

For tests of writing, several aspects of the test situation need to be considered. Hamp-Lyons (1990) identifies the task, the writer, the reader and the scoring procedure as being of primary concern.

3.3.3.1 The task

When formulating tasks for writing, 'conditions' such as length of time, medium of response (computer versus pencil and paper) and Prompt Attributes need to be specified. Prompt Attributes for writing include topic, content for the prompt, purpose, audience, cultural expectations, linguistic difficulty and rhetorical functions. It should also be noted that the choice of topic can limit or constrain the types of language that will be produced by the test takers. For example, a topic of 'how to use a pay phone' will be associated with the use of imperatives and process rhetorical organisation; 'a typical day in my home' will be associated with present tense and narrative, chronological structure and organisation.

It is also important to consider how many topics will be necessary to cover the 'domain' of interest. Do you need more than one question prompt to get at different types of writing within one domain (for example, different types of writing within the domain of 'academic writing')? And do you need different topics in order to have a variety so that no student is penalised or favoured because of special background knowledge?

The task needs to match the criterion. The Test writers need to be clear on whether they are trying to measure 'creativity', 'logic', 'ability to organise and express thoughts', or some other aspect of writing ability.

3.3.3.2 The writer

This aspect of the writing test situation concerns the characteristics of the person responding to the writing task. These characteristics include cultural background, gender, ethnicity, native language and personality, and they need to be taken into account when judging the meaning and interpretability of writing task performances. The test developer and the test task 'reader' will have their own expectations for the response that may be at odds with these characteristics; that is, test takers may not be able to respond (or may choose not to respond) according to expectations for reasons other than their writing ability. One way of thinking about this is that test takers need to engage with a topic provided by someone else and make it their own. Writers also convey affective and moral aspects of themselves in their writing, and readers of their texts will include reactions to these aspects of the writing in their judgements/ratings.

3.3.3.3 The reader

The research on how readers interact with texts (for example, Lumley 2002) has led to recommendations for reader/rater 'training', but there still needs to be more research on the 'effects' of rater training on the rating process (for example, Weigle 1994, 2002). What we do know is that the reader is crucial to the testing process. The reader provides the interpretation of the match between the response produced by the test taker and the criteria for correctness. This interpretation involves understandings of those criteria and the test taker's writing that may or may not be explicitly articulated by the reader and may or may not be consistent across ratings and other rater judgements.

3.3.3.4 The scoring procedure

Hamp-Lyons (1991) has identified several types of scoring procedures or methods for tests of writing. 'Analytic' scoring gives separate ratings for different aspects of the performance (for example, mechanics and punctuation, control of grammar). The term is not used much anymore, since its earlier versions (in the 1960s–1970s) tended to focus on superficial aspects of writing that could be quantified (for example, the number of spelling and grammar errors), but there are elements of it in some of the more recent 'holistic methods' (as opposed to 'holistic scoring' – see Hamp-Lyons 1991: 243).

Oller (1979: 386–7) gives an example of this type of the analytic approach. The test scorer/reader first rewrites the student's written text, rewording anything that does not conform to acceptable usage, and then compares the student text against the rewritten text, counting the number of error-free words (that is, words that appear in both the student and rewritten versions) and the number of errors (words in the student text that have been corrected or replaced in the rewritten text). The score is calculated as the number of error-free words minus the number of errors, divided by the total number of words in the rewritten text.

'Holistic' scoring was developed in response to the superficiality and overly mechanical aspects of the analytic approach to writing assessment. It represents the view that written texts have qualities that are greater than the (analytic) sum of their measurable parts. In this procedure a single score is given to the writing sample; this may be assisted by a scoring guide ('focused holistic scoring'). A significant disadvantage is that it is difficult for this procedure to provide detailed information about the test taker's writing ability, for diagnostic or feedback purposes. The reporting of a single score may not be meaningful to people outside the scoring context. A set of guidelines for scoring and example papers at different score levels can help, though.

However, holistic scoring is generally found to be unreliable, primarily because it requires the reader, or 'rater', of the writing sample to fit all of the various evidence of writing ability into a single score. Different raters may be attending to different aspects of the writing to different degrees in their effort to arrive at the single score. Also, reaching high levels of reliability assumes there is a 'true score' for each individual writer, but how to determine which individual rating is closest to that true score is a problem. If two raters disagree, which one is 'wrong'? If a third rater is brought in, does the fact that a third rating agrees more closely with one or the other of the first two ratings signify proximity to the true score? According to Hamp-Lyons (1990), however, the scoring procedure is probably not the place to focus for improving the validity and reliability of our assessment efforts; we need better understandings of the construct(s) of writing ability, and of how readers interact with writing texts. Note that writing ability, under the holistic scoring procedure, is seen as a unitary trait; it does not allow for the fact that second-language learners, in particular, may be at different stages of development in relation to different aspects or subskills of writing ability.

An example of the 'holistic' scoring procedure is the application of the American Council on the Teaching of Foreign Languages (ACTFL) 'proficiency guidelines' to samples of student writing by trained assessors. The guidelines are a set of descriptors for different levels of proficiency, ranging from 'Novice-Low' to 'Superior'. The descriptor for the Novice-Low level is:

> Able to form some letters in an alphabetic system. In languages whose writing systems are syllabaries or characters, writer is able to both copy and produce the basic strokes. Can produce romanisation of isolated characters, where applicable.

At the 'Superior' level, the descriptor is:

> Able to express self effectively in most formal and informal writing on practical, social and professional topics. Can write most types of correspondence, such as memos as well as social and business letters, and short research papers and statements of position in areas of special interest or in special fields. Good control of a full range of structures, spelling or nonalphabetic symbol production, and a side general vocabulary allow the writer to hypothesize and present arguments of points of view accurately and effectively. An underlying organization, such as chronological ordering, logical ordering, cause and effect, comparison, and thematic development is strongly evident, although not thoroughly executed and/or not totally reflecting target language patterns. Although sensitive to differences in formal and informal style, still may not tailor writing precisely to a variety of purposes and/or readers. Errors in writing rarely disturb natives or cause miscommunication.

> (ACTFL 1985)

'Primary trait' makes use of a separate scoring guide for each writing task or prompt, with a particular writing or rhetorical trait to be elicited (these 'traits' can be thought of as the 'aspects' of writing such as organisation, style, control of grammar). The trait is specified in detail as is the task and expected response, and sample papers and explanation of scores typically provided. At times this may be similar to focused holistic scoring, but with an emphasis on single aspects (traits) of writing and a clear connection to a particular writing task, in a specific local context. Although the ability to focus on just one aspect of writing seems like it would make the assessment task easier, and perhaps more reliable, Hamp-Lyons (1991: 247) reports that her research experience with writing assessment suggests that raters rarely attend to just one component of writing, and that judgements of one component influence judgements of others. A major practical drawback to this procedure is that a new scoring guide must be developed for each new writing prompt, task and context. In terms of washback effect for instructional settings, the emphasis on developing detailed scoring guides in the local context, for particular tasks or writing purposes, may be a positive influence on teaching and learning. On the other hand, this procedure may encourage a 'narrowing of the curriculum' around traits that are easy to describe and assess.

Weigle uses an example from Lloyd-Jones (1977) and his work for the National

Assessment of Educational Progress (NAEP) in the United States. The test takers are given a picture prompt and the following instructions:

> Look carefully at the picture. These kids are having fun jumping on the over-turned boat. Imagine you are one of the children in the picture. Or if you wish, imagine that you are someone standing nearby watching the children. Tell what is going on as he or she would tell it. Write as if you were telling this to a good friend, in a way that expresses strong feelings. Help your friend FEEL the experience too.
>
> (Lloyd-Jones 1977, as cited in Weigle 2002: 111)

The 'primary trait' for this test is 'imaginative expression of feeling through inventive elaboration of a point of view'. The scoring procedure uses a guide with different categories (for example, use of dialogue, point of view, tense) with a separate scoring scale for each. For example, the 'use of dialogue' category has the following scale:

0 – does not quote dialogue in the story
1 – direct quote from one person in the story. The one person may talk more than once. When in doubt whether two statements are made by the same person or different people, code 1. A direct quote of a thought also counts. Can be hypothetical in tense.
2 – Direct quote from two or more persons in the story.

(Lloyd-Jones 1977, as cited in Weigle 2002: 111)

The separate category scores are used to arrive at a single score for the essay.

'Multiple trait' is similar to analytic scoring, but does not focus on superficial aspects of writing that are easy to quantify, or traits that are impossible to quantify (for example, 'voice'). Multiple trait scoring is similar to primary trait procedures because it is grounded in particular writing assessment contexts, focusing on particular traits in the writing, established by careful description of those traits. Rather than focusing on a single trait, however, several are selected based on those which readers have been found to pay attention to in particular writing contexts. They are developed in relation to particular specified topic types or genres of writing, but do not (like primary trait) need to be rewritten/redesigned for each prompt. This development process involves obtaining data from raters as well as test takers in order to have an empirical basis for constructing the scoring guide descriptors. The scoring guide, once constructed, allows for flexibility in terms of how the rater uses it to assess individual samples of writing:

> A multiple trait instrument is an attempt to build up a scoring guide that permits readers to respond to the strands they have noticed whether these are all at the same quality level or are at several different quality levels.
>
> (Hamp-Lyons 1991: 249)

There are separate 'scores', then, for each trait, and these may or may not be combined for a single writing score. Weighting of scores is a tricky business, and equal weighting is advised unless a clear rationale for the weighting can be articulated and the results of combined weighted scores analysed statistically to make certain the desired effects of weighting are being realised. This procedure seems to combine the best of holistic and primary trait procedures, and can perhaps be seen as a blend of holistic and analytic (without the emphasis on mechanical, superficial, quantifiable aspects of writing).

An example of the 'multiple trait' scoring procedure can be found in the Michigan Writing Assessment Scoring Guide (Hamp-Lyons 1990; Weigle 2002). Student writing texts are rated against a guide that has three 'traits': 'ideas and arguments', 'rhetorical features' and 'language control'. The highest level, a '6', has the following descriptors for the Ideas and Arguments trait:

> The essay deals with the issues centrally and fully. The position is clear, and strongly and substantially argued. The complexity of the issues is treated seriously and the viewpoints of other people are taken into account.

The lowest level, a '1', has this descriptor for Ideas and Arguments:

> The essay does not develop or support an argument about the topic, although it may 'talk about' the topic.

The level 6 descriptor for the 'Language Control' trait is:

> The essay has excellent language control with elegance of diction and style. Grammatical structures and vocabulary are well-chosen to express the ideas and to carry out the intentions.

Level '1' for 'Language Control':

> The essay demonstrates little language control. Language errors and restricted choice of language forms are so noticeable that readers are seriously distracted by them.
>
> (all level descriptors as cited in Weigle 2002: 118–19)

These separate scores for the three traits may or may not be combined into a single, summary score.

Note that these traits are general enough to be used for a variety of writing prompts, and that they are somewhat similar to the 'categories' used in the primary trait scoring procedure. It may be that, as Weigle observes, 'the characteristics ascribed to multiple-trait scales have more to do with procedures for developing and using the scales, rather than the description of the scales themselves' (Weigle 2002: 109). That is, we will need to distinguish between scoring procedures and rating scales, and in doing so we will find that primary trait and multiple trait procedures may use similar scales which could be termed 'analytic'. They would be analytic in the sense that there are separate aspects of the writing – 'use of dialogue', 'tense', 'arguments and ideas', 'rhetorical features' – being assessed with separate sets of descriptors for the different levels of the scoring scale. All of the scoring procedures are formalised into some sort of rating 'scale', which is discussed in the next section.

3.3.3.5 Rating scales

Any scoring of a writing task makes use of a 'rating scale'. A test of writing that assigns a score of 1 to 100, for example, is a numerical rating scale. Each 'point', from 1 to 100, is a 'step' on the scale. Generally, rating scales have fewer 'steps', with descriptions of the ability or achievement level associated with each step. These descriptions are often called 'level descriptors': verbal descriptions of what performance or achievement at a particular level on a scale entails or requires, such as the examples given for holistic, primary trait and multiple trait scoring in the preceding section. These descriptors can make the scales more interpretable by test users; that is, it will be easier to understand the meaning of the verbal description of the scale point than it will to understand a number on a scale without any accompanying description. As North points out: 'A purely numerical scale like the TOEFL scale can mean quite a lot to insiders, but does not say much to someone unfamiliar with the TOEFL' (North 2000: 9). However, as discussed in McNamara (2000: 40–3), there are several problems associated with rating scales:

1. How can we provide clear, detailed level descriptors (CRM emphasises the importance of this) – as opposed to overgeneralised and relative statements like 'has a wide range of grammatical structures under control …'?
2. How should the 'end points' of the scale be determined, especially the higher end – without resorting to concepts like the 'native speaker' or 'expert user' (without defining what characterises those concepts and acknowledging the variation in performance and ability that such idealised categories might include)?
3. How many levels should the scale include? (Note the need to consider the 'point' on the scale where the important decisions are being made.)
4. How can the scale be made sensitive to progress or growth by individuals over time? (Along with determining the point on the scale where the important decisions will be made, the number of levels or distinctions between degrees of achievement or ability needs to be matched to the purpose of the assessment; for example, 'big picture' assessment versus classroom achievement assessment.)

In addition, the very act of constructing such scales may result in an over-simplification of the ability or achievement that we are attempting to measure (Brindley 1998; Clark 1985). North (2000: 11–12) acknowledges these problems, but offers a thorough and convincing list of the potential advantages in using rating scales, in this case scales of language proficiency. In addition to providing the language learner with a means of self-assessment, rating scales have the potential to provide a common framework to be used by different stakeholders in the assessment context (learners, teachers, administrators and so on), to provide a consistent reporting format for results from various levels of testing and assessment, to enable comparisons between educational programmes, and to provide links within various components of an educational and assessment system (placement testing, curriculum development, materials evaluation, exit and certification testing, and so on). A good example of this type of scale is the Common European Framework (Council of Europe 2002). These advantages also suggest an important role for rating scales as instruments for both assessment and programme evaluation.

Another issue with rating scales is the number of points, or 'steps', on the rating scale (for each evaluative criteria) that needs to be determined. North (2000) recommends five steps (scale points), citing research that shows maximum reliability being achieved with five, remaining constant up to nine, and falling off when there are three or less and eleven or more steps. Together with Popham's (1997) advice concerning the number of evaluative 'traits' to include in the rating scale, this means having scoring guides that have four–five 'traits', with each trait being scored on a five–nine point scale.

3.3.3.6 The rating process

Whatever the scoring procedure used, the assessment of writing usually involves the rating of writing samples produced by the test taker. As discussed by McNamara (2000: 35–6), this process includes:

- setting out the conditions under which the performance takes place (for example, length of time, type of task);
- agreeing upon the features of performance that are critical and the criteria for judging them;
- training the raters;
- judging the performances and allocating the ratings.

Rating is unavoidably subjective, even with CRM scales and instruments, the match between candidate performance and ability and the rating-scale criteria is mediated by rater judgement. As McNamara (2000: 37) reminds us, the 'referencing' of an individual to a criterion, the interpretation of scores in relation to a criterion, is influenced by chance factors which make rating a 'probabilistic' event: probabilities based on which raters were involved, which tasks attempted, what time of day the test was given and so on.

The chance variation in relation to raters can be seen as both between and within raters: certain raters may consistently rate candidates higher or lower than other raters do; certain raters may inconsistently vary their ratings across candidates and rating occasions.

3.3.3.7 Rater training

This is normally done through a procedure sometimes referred to as the 'moderation meeting'. The basic steps for this meeting are:

1. Raters-in-training are provided with sample performances to rate independently against a scale.

2. The ratings are compared and discussed. Usually there is a range of sample performances that have been rated in advance by experienced raters, and these experienced ratings are introduced into the discussion after the raters-in-training have had a chance to present their ratings. Where differences between the raters-in-training and experienced raters exist, these can be negotiated (the scale descriptors may need further specification), or the raters-in-training can be instructed to try and bring their ratings more into line with the experienced raters.

3. Raters-in-training rate another sample of performances; agreement between raters-in-training and with experienced rater judgements checked again. Raters-in-training who seem to be 'off' are counselled for how to bring their ratings into line with the experienced/expected ratings.

4. Raters move to operational, 'real' ratings of performances; the raters-in-training are monitored by experienced raters and counselled as necessary. For example, if particular raters are consistently rating lower than the other raters (when performances are double marked, this can be quickly identified), they can be given this information and reasons for their relative harshness can be discussed.

Fairness in the rating process is based on the notion that it shouldn't matter which rater individual candidates draw; they should receive the same rating regardless of individual rater. This can be seen as underpinning the process of rater training outlined above, too. There are 'expected' or 'true' ratings to which raters-in-training are judged against and their performance as raters is judged by how well they agree with these ratings and with each other. In Chapters 6 and 7, I will consider approaches to assessment that question this as the only way to conceptualise fairness (and validity); that is, these approaches to assessment attempt to see disagreement between raters as the source of valid information about candidate performance rather than as an indication of unreliability and a source of unfairness.

3.3.3.8 *Example writing tests*

Some of the selected and most of the constructed response formats discussed earlier can be used to test writing skills. Even the multiple-choice format has been used, although admittedly in a mostly indirect fashion. The following examples indicate possible formats, including selected response focusing on particular aspects of writing (for example, proof reading). The more direct tests of writing, of course, generally consist of a prompt that directs the test taker to perform some sort of writing task and may include some sort of reading passage to aid in the provision of a context for the writing task. More elaborate prompts, and linking of reading, listening and reading, will be considered in section 3.3.5, 'Testing the skills together'.

Prompts: text with errors to be revised or identified; incomplete form with instructions; topics with brief instructions; visual display (graph, picture) with associated writing task; reading passage with associated writing task.

Item and task formats: multiple choice; revision/editing; gap-filling; short answer; extended response.

Example items:

1. The test takers are presented with a paragraph for which each sentence contains an error (for example, grammatical, word choice, punctuation, cohesive markers). Each sentence is segmented into four parts, labelled in the multiple-choice fashion of A–B–C–D. The test taker's task is to identify the section of each sentence that contains the error (multiple-choice).

2. The test takers are given a multiple-paragraph text, which contains numerous errors (for example, grammatical, word choice, punctuation, cohesive markers). The task is to correct the errors, as if the test taker were revising/editing their own draft (revision/editing).

   (Note: for example items 1 and 2, samples of second-language writers' work, especially initial drafts, can be used to generate the types of errors to be included and/or the actual texts for the items.)

3. The test takers are given an incomplete application form, with instructions to fill in the form (gap-filling).

4. The test takers are given a graph which depicts a contrast (for example, amount of energy consumed per capita in three different countries) and are asked to write a short description of this information (short answer).

5. The test takers are given a job advertisement, with instructions to write a letter of application for the job, based on the requirements in the advertisement (short answer, extended response).

6. The test takers are presented with a brief topic (for example, 'Should cigarette advertising be banned?') and asked to write a 500-word essay (extended response).

3.3.4 Tests of speaking

3.3.4.1 The oral interview

The test method of preference for the testing of speaking ability has, over the years, become the oral interview. By engaging the examinee in an actual speaking interaction involving communication – responding to questions and prompts from the interviewer – the oral interview makes claims for being an authentic test of the ability to be measured.

Research has begun over the past decade to look at the nature of the interaction and communication that occurs in the oral interview. Some of it has found that the types of language that examinees are called upon to use is limited to phonology, lexico-grammatical features, but not to a wide range of discourse features. Further, the range of discourse features does not result or reflect the language proficiency of the examinees, but seems to be a function of the oral interview method. As Cohen (1994: 263) writes, 'it is still not possible through an interview format to assess the subject's ability to control conversation, produce topic initiations, or to assume responsibility for the continuance of the discourse'. Researchers like Perrett (1990) and Lazaraton (1991, 1996) see the range of discourse in the oral interview as specific to this method; that is, the oral interview test seems to be a genre of its own.

Of course, the interview as test depends on the set of criteria and scoring procedures that are used to assess the interview performance. If the assessment is holistic, different raters may use different criteria to arrive at their judgements, or may interpret analytic criteria in different ways. Raters who come from a second-language-teaching background may use very different criteria (or interpret existing criteria differently) from those from another professional background. For example, Lumley et al. (1994) found that ESL teachers rated more leniently than doctors when assessing the oral interview performance of medical students performing in a second language. In addition to differential effects of raters, research has shown that different interlocutors (the persons conducting the assessment interview) can have different characteristics and tend to have different behaviours that influence the nature of the oral interview (as well as other types of oral interaction) as a test, making the task harder or easier (Lumley and Brown 1996), and having an effect on the rating of interview performance (McNamara and Lumley 1997).

3.3.4.2 Other speaking test formats

When the basic structure of the oral interview is used without the 'direct' feature of live interlocutor, we have what is known as the 'semi-direct interview'. Examples are the Semi-direct Oral Proficiency Interview (SOPI) (Stansfield et al. 1988) and the Speaking Proficency English Assessment Kit (SPEAK) (ETS 1985). The live interlocutor is usually replaced by a tape-recorded voice that, along with a written instructional booklet of some sort, prompts the test taker with various questions and tasks. This means that the semi-direct format requires audiotape recording and playback equipment, such as in the typical language-laboratory setting. The semi-direct tests also tend to deviate from the traditional interview format, using a variety of tasks instead. The typical tasks that are used for the semi-direct interview are:

- Personal conversation: the test taker is asked a series of personal question (for example, 'What is your name?', 'What country do you come from?').
- Reading aloud: the test taker is presented with a printed text which he or she is instructed to read aloud.
- Completion: the test taker is given a series of incomplete sentences, in writing, and is asked to read and complete the sentences (for example, 'When the weather is hot, I …').
- Giving directions: the test taker is asked to give directions, from a given point A to a given point B, using a printed map that has these points, various locations and street names indicated.
- Detailed description: the test taker is prompted with a picture, drawing or photograph, and asked to describe it in as much detail as possible.
- Picture sequence: the test taker is given a series of pictures that depict a narrative, and is asked to 'tell the story' presented in the picture sequence.

- Giving opinions: the test taker is given a topic, such as 'the threat of global warming', and is asked to offer his or her ideas or opinions.
- Responding to situations: the test taker is given a situation, such as 'a friend invites you to a movie that you've already seen', and is asked to give a response.
- Explaining graphical information: the test taker is given information in the form of a table or graph and is asked to explain it (for example, 'Explain what this schedule tells you about the availability of trains from City A to City B').

Cohen (1994: 271–3) reports on taking an SOPI in Portuguese and identifies the following as potential problem areas for this assessment procedure:

- The conversational questions need to be similar to the kinds of questions that arise in typical conversations, rather than the types of questions that occur in oral interviews.
- There needs to be sufficient time given to the test taker for preparing a response.
- When using visual stimuli such as maps, special cognitive abilities required for interpreting the map need to be minimised.
- Instructions for completing the speaking tasks may need to be given in the target language, in order to 'set up' the response, and to further simulate typical conversational and other speaking contexts.
- Whether the topics and situations chosen will be interesting and engaging for the test taker needs to be carefully considered.

There are a variety of other task types that can be used to test speaking ability. Some involve setting specific rhetorical functions for an individual test taker, such as asking for a definition of a technical or semi-technical term that the test taker is presumed to know, or asking the test taker to offer an apology or a compliment. These latter functions usually involve the general task type of the role play, where a situation is simulated by giving the test taker a certain amount of information concerning the setting and imaginary participants, and asking him or her to complete the scenario.

Another type of task involves a prepared demonstration or presentation. This may be a formal or informal lecture or speech on a designated topic, or a summary of a newspaper article or other text. In the latter case, the focus on speaking ability can be maintained by allowing test takers to use a text that they have read in their first language, giving the summary in the second language being tested. Rather than testing the individual in isolation, many of the speaking test formats can be used with pairs or groups of test takers.

3.3.4.3 Scoring procedures and scales

The discussion of scoring procedures and rating scales in the preceding section on writing tests is relevant to tests of speaking ability as well. The types of scoring procedures – analytic, holistic, primary trait, multiple trait – and considerations for rating scales are essentially the same, as are the observations on the rating process and rater training. However, the specific traits and evaluative criteria used for assessing speaking do, of course, differ from those used for writing. The following are examples of rating scales used in speaking tests that will give a sense of these differences.

ACTFL Proficiency Guidelines for Speaking: this is a holistic scale, and as with the ACTFL Proficiency Guidelines for Writing discussed earlier in this chapter, there are nine levels with descriptors indicating the abilities that characterise each level. For example, the lowest level, 'Novice-Low', is described as:

Oral production consists of isolated words and perhaps a few high-frequency phrases. Essentially no functional communicative ability.

The most advanced level, 'Superior', is characterised by:

Able to speak the language with sufficient accuracy to participate effectively in most formal and informal conversations on practical, social, professional, and abstract topics. Can discuss special fields of competence and interest with ease. Can support opinions and hypothesize, but may not be able to tailor language to audience or discuss in depth highly abstract or unfamiliar topics. Usually the Superior level speaker is only partially familiar with regional or other dialectical variants. The Superior level speaker commands a wide variety of interactive strategies and shows good awareness of discourse strategies. The latter involves the ability to distinguish main ideas from supporting information through syntactic, lexical and suprasegmental features (pitch, stress, intonation). Sporadic errors may occur, particularly in low-frequency structures and some complex high-frequency structures more common to formal writing, but no patterns of error are evident. Errors do not disturb the native speaker or interfere with communication.

(ACTFL 1985)

Cambridge First Certificate in English (FCE), Paper 5 (Interview): this is a multiple trait scoring procedure and, in Weigle's (2002) terms, an analytic rating scale. There are six evaluative criteria: fluency, grammatical accuracy, pronunciation/sentences, pronunciation/individual sounds, interactive communication, and vocabulary resource. Each of these categories is rated against a six-point scale (0 to 5), with descriptors for each level. For example, the descriptors for fluency are:

5: Comfortable at natural-speaker speed and rhythm in everyday contexts, though there may be some hesitation when speaking on more abstract topics.

4: In everday contexts speaks with minimal hesitation. Hesitation when discussing abstract topics does but does not demand unreasonable patience of the listener.

3: Does not hesitate unreasonably in everyday contexts though may experience some difficulty with more abstract topics.

2: Unacceptable hesitation even in everyday contexts.

1: Speech very disconnected.

0: Not capable of connected speech.

(UCLES 1987: 148)

Speaking Perfomance Scale for UCLA Oral Proficiency Test for Non-Native Teaching Assistants: this is another multiple trait procedure, analytic rating scale adapted from the Interagency Roundtable oral proficiency 'interview' by Janet Goodwin for use with a task-based oral proficiency test designed for international teaching assistants at UCLA. There are seven evaluative criteria: pronunciation, speech flow, grammar, vocabulary, organisation, listening comprehension and question-handling. Each category is scored on a five-point scale (0 to 4) with descriptors for each level For example, the descriptors for pronunciation are:

4: rarely mispronounces
3: accent may be foreign; never interferes; rarely disturbs native speaker
2: often faulty but intelligible with effort
1: errors frequent, only intelligible to native speaker used to dealing with non-native speakers
0: unintelligible.

(Goodwin 1990)

3.3.4.4 Example items

1. The test taker is given a set of four photographs depicting a particular theme (for example, working in an office environment). A test interlocutor guides the test taker in a conversation about the photographs, using a set of questions prepared in advance for this topic that are designed to engage the test taker's speaking ability without relying too heavily on factual knowledge concerning the particular theme. The interview/conversation is tape-recorded and the test taker's performance is rated using an analytic scale similar to the Cambridge FCE scale discussed above.

2. The test taker (in this case, a health professional who has immigrated to an English-speaking country and is being tested as part of a professional certification process) is asked to respond to an interlocutor who is role playing the part of a patient at a health clinic. The interlocutor/patient is given instructions for the role play, which establish the setting, why the interlocutor/ patient is visiting the clinic, and what should be attempted in the interaction with the test taker/health professional. A third-party test administrator observes the interaction and rates the test taker using a holistic scale similar to the ACTFL example described above, but tailored to the communicative abilities expected in a health professional–patient interaction. (Also see McNamara and Lumley 1997.)

3. The test taker is given ten sentences, taken from an introductory level university course in engineering, to read out loud into a tape-recorder. The test taker's recorded responses are rated against a scale similar to the UCLA Non-Native Teaching Assistant Speaking Performance scale described above.

4. Several days before the test, the test taker, an international teaching assistant in biology at a university in the United States, is given instructions to prepare a presentation on a typical biology-lab experiment for an audience of under-

graduate students studying biology. Instructions include the time limit for the presentation, and guidelines to make certain the test taker does not prepare a memorised speech. The test taker presents the experiment to an audience of two undergraduate students and two test administrators, and fields questions from the undergraduate students. The two test administrators view a videotape of the presentation and rate the test taker against a scale similar to the UCLA Non-Native Teaching Assistant Speaking Performance scale described above. The undergraduate students submit their impressions of the presentation via a brief questionnaire, filled out immediately after the test. A third test administrator assigns a final score using the two test administrator ratings and the undergraduate student questionnaires. (Also, see Douglas and Selinker 1991.)

3.3.5 Testing the skills together

As mentioned at the beginning of the previous section, although there is a tradition in language testing of addressing the four skills separately, there is also a tradition that argues for testing the skills together. In the early days of language testing, there was a move away from 'discrete-point' test, which were designed to measure separate elements of language, such as particular grammar points, to what were termed 'integrative' tests, which were designed to measure many elements of language at the same time (see Carroll 1961/1972).

Of course, the discrete-point versus integrative distinction does not quite capture the testing-skills-separately versus testing-skills-together distinction. Many of the examples discussed previously for testing each of the language skills separately can be considered integrative tests, in that they require the test taker to use several elements of language at the same time in order to complete the test task. For example, the typical writing test that asks the test taker to respond to a prompt by writing a multi-paragraph essay combines elements of grammar, vocabulary knowledge, rhetorical organisation, punctuation and spelling. In the discrete-point tradition, each of these elements would have been tested separately, with separate items for separate subelements (for example, separate grammatical points). As language-teaching methodology moved away from a focus on isolated linguistic elements to a focus on communication, so testing moved to forms that would capture the integrated nature of language skills being used for communicative purposes.

Another way of describing this move is one from test formats that were more 'indirect' to ones that were more 'direct' measures of the language ability being tested. These labels, indirect or direct, are not always useful since it can be argued that all tests are more or less indirect measures of the ability being tested. However, they capture the important notion of asking test takers to demonstrate their ability through a task that requires them to actually perform that ability. If we want to test someone's ability to engage in conversation, for example, a direct test will ask that person to actually converse with another. The fact that it is a test, and not a 'real' conversation, means that it is less direct than if we were able to capture such a real conversation on videotape, but it is more direct than if we asked the test taker to read a paragraph out loud. This also means that, to a certain extent, the notion of direct versus indirect overlaps with the notion of authenticity: direct tests will tend to be more authentic than indirect tests, in the sense of more closely approximating the language behaviour that would occur in the non-testing context that calls for the ability being tested.

Examples of integrative tests that are of varying degrees of directness are the dictation, the cloze and the C-test. These are discussed extensively elsewhere (for example, Alderson 1979, 2000; Bachman 1985, 1990; Brown 1980, 1983; Klein-Braley 1985).

3.3.5.1 Communicative tasks

The influence of communicative language teaching and languages for specific purposes methodology has resulted in language tests that use communicative tasks as the focus of their procedures. Rather than have separate tasks to test reading, writing, listening and speaking, language testers began to use tasks that consciously combined the skills. For example, the 'interview topic recovery task' (Cohen 1994: 260) has test takers interview an interlocutor for the purposes of obtaining information concerning a particular topic (for example, interviewing recent immigrants concerning their adjustment to the new country) and then reporting back, orally on their findings. This task, however it is recorded and evaluated, obviously involves the test takers' speaking and listening skills. It could be fashioned to include reading and writing skills as well, by having the test takers read relevant background material before the interview and then report back after the interview in writing.

Another example of this approach to language testing is the 'storyline test' (Cohen 1994: 227–9), where there are separate tasks that focus on particular skills, but a common theme, or storyline, running across the tasks. One example cited in Cohen (1994: 227–8) is from Swain (1984), who used 'finding summer employment' as the storyline, and constructed writing tasks (a letter, a note, a composition and a technical report) and speaking tasks (a job interview and a group discussion).

In a similar vein to the storyline test, Bachman et al. (1995b) describe the development of a test for the Education Abroad Program of the University of California, for students who are being placed in an immersion language experience in Spain or Germany. The tasks included viewing a videotaped lecture in the target language, reading an article either referred to in the lecture or related to its main theme, and participating in a role play where the students ask the lecturer for clarification about some aspect of the lecture and reading.

A final example of task-based tests that combine the language skills was developed by a group of students in my Language Testing class (LING 439/539) at Portland State University (Outeiriño et al. 2002). Their test was designed for adult ESL learners in a community-college setting, and attempted to measure the ability of the test takers to respond to employment ads via voicemail. The tasks involved reading a set of job advertisements (taken from Portland Community College ESL course materials, which were patterned after authentic local newspaper classified ads), choosing one to respond to, reviewing a set of possible job-ad voicemail questions, calling the phone number listed in the job ads and leaving a message in response to the voicemail prompt (there was one phone number representing a hotel with a variety of jobs; the phone number belonged to one of the test constructors, connected to an answering machine with a voicemail prompt asking a series of questions from the 'set of possible job-ad voicemail questions'). The test takers' recorded responses were rated with a scoring guide that assessed the degree to which their responses indicated understanding of the voicemail questions and the degree to which their responses were understandable to 'a native speaker of English accustomed to non-native speakers'.

3.4 OTHER MEASURES FOR ASSESSMENT AND EVALUATION

In addition to tests, there are a variety of other measures that can be used to gather data for assessment and evaluation purposes. Most of these fall under the method-ology generally referred to as 'survey'. Brown (2001) provides a thorough description for surveys, focusing on interviews and questionnaires as the primary instruments. Henerson et al. (1987), in addition to discussing survey instruments, describe the use of structured observation for the measurement of attitudes in programme evaluation. The following sections will summarise the key issues for constructing these measure-ment tools. Interviews and observation, as interpretivist approaches to assessment and evaluation, will be discussed further in Chapter 5.

3.4.1 Surveys

Surveys are probably used most often for programme evaluation rather than individual language assessment. Generally, we use survey interviews and question-naires to find out about attitudes, perceptions and opinions in order to answer questions about groups of language learners or language programmes. However, it is possible to use these instruments for individual assessment purposes as well; for example, surveys can provide us with measures of individual language ability (as self-assessed by the individual). As with language test data, these individual measures used for language assessment purposes can then be aggregated into group measures for language programme purposes. As such, surveys serve the larger purposes for assessment and evaluation discussed in Chapter 1: both formative assessment and evaluation for diagnosing and improving individual language learning and programme effectiveness, and summative decisions about the individual and the programme.

3.4.1.1 Question types and content

There are a range of question types that surveys can answer, including experience, opinions, judgements and attitudes. When deciding on questions for assessment and evaluation purposes, the most important rule is to have a clear use for the answers to the question. You should be able to tell in advance exactly what you will do with the information that each survey question gives you. It is a bad idea to construct a survey with questions that seem interesting, but have no specific use for your assessment or evaluation goals. For example, if you are going to ask questions about student attitudes towards aspects of the language programme curriculum, what is the point of asking these questions? Are student attitudes towards the curriculum something the evaluation audiences want to know about; that is, do the goals for the evaluation include measuring student attitudes? Are these evaluation goals and questions framed specifically enough to be measured with survey questions (or are they too general and open to a variety of interpretations)? If you are going to ask students to self-assess on aspects of their language ability or achievement, how will these data be used to make decisions? Will the data be combined with other assessment information to arrive at a final grade, or will they be used for diagnostic purposes only?

These question types can address different sorts of content, in terms of assessment or programme evaluation information to be gained. One area of content, making use of the opinion and judgement question types, is the importance of particular language skills or programme objectives. Allied with this content is the emphasis placed on these skills and objectives in the programme. The two areas of content can be combined in a survey known as a 'need–press' interaction analysis (Henning 1987: 149). Individual learners (and other programme participants, such as teachers) are asked to judge the importance (need) of particular language skills or abilities, and then to judge their emphasis (press) in the teaching programme. By comparing judgements of how important something is perceived to be with how much attention it receives in the instructional setting, areas of individual learner development and programme objectives that may need improvement are identified.

A version of the press (curriculum emphasis) type of content can be found in the concept of 'opportunity to learn' (see, for example, McDonnell 1995), which looks at whether learners have been given the chance to study and learn skills or knowledge being measured. Typically, opportunity to learn (OTL) is measured with survey questions that ask the teacher to judge the degree to which the skill or content necessary for answering particular test items has been part of the teaching programme. The types of survey questions being used to measure OTL can also include judgements of teacher background and experience, the availability of instructional materials, specific course offerings and teaching methods as indicators for interpreting learner achievement.

Another area of content, particularly important for programme evaluation, is 'instructional programme coherence' (Newmann et al. 2001). Coherence is judged, in part, by the match between need and press discussed above. However, it also includes an examination of the match between assessment procedures and instructional objectives, the coherence of these assessments over time, staff working conditions and expectations, and allocations of school resources. The assumption is that programme coherence will be related to student achievement. This assumption has recently been examined in the language-teaching field by Ross (forthcoming).

3.4.1.2 Formats

Once there is a clear use defined for the survey data, and the question types chosen, the question format needs to be chosen. One format distinction will be the use of self-report versus other-report. In self-report survey questions, we will be asking individuals – students, teachers, administrators and so on – to give us information about their own experience, attitudes, abilities and so on. In other-report, we will be asking individuals – students, teachers, administrators and so on – to give us their perceptions concerning the experience, attitudes, abilities of others. For example, we might survey teachers concerning their perceptions of student abilities in relation to particular components of the language programme; or we might survey students about their perceptions of their teachers' abilities. Again, we would want to have clear uses for this information, rather than constructing survey questions because the answers might be interesting.

With both self- and other-reports, there are further choices for measurement format. The 'alternative-answer' format provides the survey participant with a single choice from among two or more alternatives. For example, questions can be posed requiring a 'Yes' or 'No' answer:

> Are you able to read newspapers in English and understand the main ideas in most articles?
> Yes ____ No ____

There may also be several alternatives from which to choose:

> What part of the programme helped your language learning the most? (Choose *ONE*.)
> Listening to academic lectures _____
> Reading and writing for academic assignments _____
> Seminar discussion skills _____

This format can be used with both structured interview and questionnaire surveys. For interview surveys, it is important to keep the questions reasonably short, and the alternatives reasonably few in number, in order for the participant to be able to process and respond. For example, I once completed a survey interview over the telephone. The person conducting the survey asked me questions like: 'Would you agree or disagree with the following statement: "We currently have enough scientific evidence concerning the relative impact of commercial and recreational fishing on the ocean wildlife habitats in Oregon so that we can make appropriate decisions about whether or not there should be areas designated as protected wildlife zones."' This is probably too much relatively complex information to be processed and responded to in an oral-interview format. Especially when the survey participants are responding in a second language, care should be taken to make the task manageable.

Another format is the 'checklist', where there may be more than one possible response from the survey participant, and where the presence or absence of an ability or behaviour is what we are trying to measure. Here are two examples, one for an individual learner self-assessment and one for a teacher as part of programme evaluation:

1. Which of the following are you able to accomplish successfully using [your second language]? Check *all* that you are able to do.
   Write a letter to a friend _____
   Request medical information over the phone _____
   Ask for directions from a stranger _____
   Fill out a job application form _____
   Read the newspaper for current world events _____
2. Which of the following teaching materials did you use regularly (each week) in your class? Check *all* that apply.
   Videotaped lectures _____   Authentic reading materials file _____
   Information gap activity file _____   Role play file _____
   Reading rate builders _____   Extended reading file _____
   Radio programmes _____

The success of the checklist depends on providing all the relevant options. An 'Other' category can be added, but this tends to introduce a range of options being indicated under that category. Usually when using the 'Other' option, it is helpful to ask the participant to give an example or examples. The checklist format can work well in questionnaires, but becomes difficult to manage in an interview survey. With an interview, this type of information would probably be better handled as a 'Yes' or 'No' alternative-response format.

Another alternative is the 'ranking' format, where survey participants are presented with a list that they are asked to rank-order in some way: from least to most important, from least to most frequent and so on. For example, language learners might be asked to self-assess their language skills with the following ranking format:

How would you assess your ability in the following language skill areas? Please indicate your strongest skill with a '5', your next strongest skill with a '4', and so on (your *weakest skill* will be given a '1').
Understanding lectures   _____
Understanding the textbook   _____
Speaking in seminar discussions   _____
Writing argumentative essays   _____
Writing summaries   _____

The advantage of this format is that it forces the participants to indicate the relative strength, importance, interest and so on, that the language abilities or aspects of the language programme hold for them. The problem is that it may lead to a false sense of distinction between the abilities or programme aspects. The participants may feel equally capable in some or all skills; they may actually judge certain or all aspects of the programme equally. One solution to this problem is to allow participants to assign the same rank number to items that are judged as equal (for example, three of the items receive a '5' and the other two receive '2' and '1'), although this makes the quantification and analysis of the responses a bit more complex and some researchers advise against it (Henerson et al. 1987: 69). It is also a good idea to limit the number of items being ranked; Henerson et al. (1987: 69) suggest no more than five items.

The 'Likert scale' format provides alternative answers on a scale. This is somewhat different than the issue of rating scales discussed previously for language tests. There may be some similarities when the survey is a self-assessment of language abilities, but it will normally not include the level of descriptive detail for each evaluative criterion that was found in language test rating scales. This format is useful for measuring the degree to which participants find aspects of their language learning or the language programme important, enjoyable or successful. The Likert scale most often used is an 'agreement scale'. Statements concerning the object of survey interest are constructed, and for each statement the survey participant is asked to respond by indicating his or her level of agreement; for example, by choosing one of five responses:

Strongly Agree – Agree – Undecided – Disagree – Strongly Disagree.

As an example, we might provide programme participants with a series of statements concerning curriculum objectives:

For each of the following statements, indicate your agreement or disagreement by selecting one of the following:
Strongly Agree – Agree – Undecided – Disagree – Strongly Disagree.
1. There is sufficient time spent on reading skills instruction.
2. There is sufficient time spent on listening skills instruction.
3. There is sufficient time spent on writing skills instruction.
4. There is sufficient time spent on grammar instruction.
5. There is sufficient time spent on vocabulary instruction.
6. There is sufficient time spent on speaking skills instruction.

These responses can be quantified by assigning a numerical value to each category (for example, 5 for 'strongly agree', 4 for 'agree', and so on).

Like the checklist format, the Likert scale is easier to use with the questionnaire than with the interview survey. If there are a small number of points on the Likert scale (with simple, one-word descriptors, as in the agreement–disagreement version), and the statements are kept reasonably short, it may be possible in an interview survey. However, it is probably not a good idea to attempt an interview survey using Likert scale items with second-language learners in the second language.

A major issue with Likert scales is the number of points to select from, and the tendency of some participants to choose the middle point, rather than declaring a clear position (agree or disagree; important or unimportant). In order to avoid this tendency for some to 'sit on the fence', researchers recommend using an even number of scale points (Brown 2001: 41).

3.4.2 Structured observation

In addition to tests and surveys, observation can be used to measure individual language abilities and provide data for language programme evaluation. I am making a distinction here between structured and unstructured observation. This is probably best conceived as a continuum rather than a dichotomy, and at the highly structured end of the continuum there are 'observation schedules' and 'checklists'. The advantages of highly structured observation approaches are that they provide a helpful focus and systematicity to a potentially overwhelming experience. They are also designed to quantify the observations, which provides a basis for comparability across observations and the ability to judge the reliability of measurement. The disadvantages are that the observation is constrained, and may miss things that are not identified prior to the observation. The verification of characteristics or ideas about the programme to be evaluated is emphasised over the discovery of characteristics and generation of new ideas about the programme. Observation techniques from the more unstructured end of the continuum will be discussed in Chapter 5.

The first step in using a structured observation is to decide what will be observed. In the case of individual language assessment, this will be similar to the criterion 'traits' being measured by a test. In fact, any language test involving a performance that can be observed could be measured with an observation schedule or checklist. The difference will be in the level of detail that the schedule or checklist provides as compared with the rating scale or scoring rubric used in a test. This is because the structured observation will most usually be carried out in real time, and the observer will need relatively economical (short, concise) descriptors to refer to when making the judgements required by the schedule or checklist. Of course, if the performance being observed can also be videotaped, a more complex schedule or checklist can be applied with the advantage of multiple viewings.

Checklists provide an inventory of the aspects of language or programme activity that have been determined as the object of measurement. For example, we may decide that it is important to measure interactions between students engaged in pair work in the language classroom. The checklist would be constructed with characteristics of pair interactions that we expect (based on theory) to observe. Each time the characteristic is observed, the corresponding item on the checklist is marked. The measurement would be the frequency of occurrence for those characteristics, based on the tallies on the checklist. Note that the checklist can be designed to keep track of individual learners (for individual language assessment) as well as for tallying interaction characteristics for the class as a whole (for programme evaluation).

For example, Figure 3.2 shows two checklists (partial): one for individual language learner assessment of pair interaction (where the √ marks indicate single occurrences of the characteristic), and one for observation of an entire class.

The more complex the category schemes are for representing the characteristics to be observed and measured, the more they tend to be referred to as observation schedules or coding schemes. As an example, we might design an observation scheme

Checklist for individual learner:

Student Name: _____

Characteristic	Occurrence	Total
1. asks for clarification	✓ ✓ ✓	3
2. repeats what partner said	✓ ✓ ✓ ✓	4
3. interrupts	✓ ✓	2
4. gives opinion	✓	1
...		

Checklist for entire class:

Class: _____   Date: _____   Time: _____

Characteristic	Occurrence	Total
1. Student asks for clarification	✓ ✓ ✓	3
2. Teacher asks for clarification	✓ ✓	2
3. Teacher paraphrases student	✓	1
4. Student answers teacher question	✓ ✓ ✓	3
...		

Figure 3.2   Example observation checklists

for observing a complete language-class period. The scheme would need to include the larger categories of classroom characteristics and activities; for example, participation patterns, language content, language form, materials. Within each of these major categories there could be subcategories such as teacher, student and further distinctions such as types of participation pattern, language content, language form and materials. Figure 3.3 gives an example of such an observation schedule (partial view).

By recording the characteristics as they occur in real time, this schedule becomes a record of the sequence of these language classroom behaviours, with each row in the sample schedule above representing an ordered and specific occurrence (with either the 'start time', or the amount of time taken, recorded in the leftmost column: 'Time') rather than a cumulative tally as in the checklist. This makes more complex measurement possible, since the frequency of occurrence offered by checklists can be extended to the frequency of particular sequences (for example, student-initiated abstract language followed by student response abstract language) as well as the total amount of class time characterised by particular behaviours or sequences of behaviour. For a good example of an observation schedule see Spada and Frohlich (1995), the Communicative Orientation to Language Teaching (COLT).

	Participation				Language Content			
Time	Teacher		Student		Teacher		...	
	initiates	responds	initiates	responds	concrete	abstract	...	...

Figure 3.3   Example observation schedule

3.5 CONCLUSION

In this chapter I have presented a variety of instruments for gathering language assessment and programme evaluation data. In the positivistic approaches, language tests are the primary type of instrument used for these purposes. In order to guide the development of language tests, I have used the concept of the test specification as central to that process.

I have attempted to give examples of the wide range of language tests that exist or can be created. These tests can focus on particular language skills – listening, reading, writing and speaking – or measure a combination of language skills necessary for completing particular tasks.

In addition to language tests, I have presented examples of surveys (structured interviews and questionnaires) and structured observation for collecting language assessment and programme evaluation. The use of unstructured (or less structured) interviewing and observation in interpretivist approaches will be discussed in Chapter 5. This chapter has focused on instruments that allow for quantification of the language abilities and programme outcomes (and processes). In the next chapter, I will discuss the methods for analysing these quantitative data in order to make decisions and judgements about learners and programmes.

EXERCISES

1. Decide on some aspect of language ability that you think is important for second-language learners (for example, listening to academic lectures for main ideas and specific information; requesting information at the doctor's office; filling out job applications) and write a test specification for it.
2. Remove the sample item from your test specification in Exercise 1 and give the rest (GD, PA, RA and SS, if there is one) to another person. Ask them to write a sample item from your spec. Compare the sample item they write with your original.

3. Write five items for a questionnaire designed to have learners assess their reading ability, using at least two different formats (for example, ranking, checklist and Likert scale alternative response).
4. Write five items for a questionnaire designed to have learners evaluate a programme focused on reading skills, using at least two different formats. Compare these with your items in Exercise 3.

SUGGESTIONS FOR FURTHER READING

1. Alderson, J. C., C. Clapham and D. Wall (1995), *Language Test Construction and Evaluation*, Cambridge: Cambridge University Press.

Chapters 2 and 3 of this book provide a useful complement to the treatment of test specifications and test item formats presented in my own chapter. Certain item types that I do not cover, such as the C-test and dictation, are discussed by the authors.

2. Brown, J. D. (2001), *Using Surveys in Language Programmes*, Cambridge: Cambridge University Press.

This book provides a detailed account of constructing and using surveys – questionnaires and interviews – primarily for programme evaluation purposes. At this point in your reading, focus on the first three chapters, which cover purposes for surveys, the design of survey instruments and the gathering of data using surveys.

3. Clapham, C. and D. Corson (eds) (1997), *Encyclopedia of Language and Education, Vol. 7: Language Testing and Assessment*, Dordrecht: Kluwer Academic Publishers.

This volume contains chapters on all the major issues in language assessment. At this stage in your reading, I would suggest looking at the chapters on assessing the skills of listening, reading, writing and speaking.

Chapter 4

Analysing measurement data for assessment and evaluation

4.1 INTRODUCTION

In this chapter I will present the analysis of measurement data in three major sections: test-item analysis, the analysis of non-test measures and statistical analysis for making inferences about individual learner ability and language-programme effectiveness. Test-item analysis, and associated techniques for estimating reliability can be viewed as a part of the test-development procedures discussed in the previous chapter; that is, they are techniques that are used to improve tests during the piloting and revision stages prior to operational use. However, I present them here because of their methodological kinship with the other statistical analysis procedures involved in assessment and evaluation.

In order to keep the scope of this chapter, and this book, manageable, I will not be introducing basic statistical concepts concerning measures of central tendency and dispersion, correlation and analysis of variance. If these are not familiar concepts, the reader may wish to consult Hatch and Lazaraton (1991), Brown (1988, 2001), or consult the *Dictionary of Language Testing* (Davies et al. 1999).

4.2 ANALYSING TEST DATA

Procedures for the analysis of language test data have been developed through classical test theory (CTT), generalisability theory (G-theory) and item response theory (IRT). These three approaches will be discussed and compared in terms of their usefulness and thoroughness in providing information about individual language ability. Within the discussion of CTT, variations particular to criterion-referenced measurement (CRM) will be identified.

4.2.1 CTT item analysis

CTT approaches to item analysis include the computation of item difficulty, item discrimination and distracter analysis (for multiple-choice items). 'Item difficulty' is the proportion of examinees that answer the item correctly (also called the 'p value'). There are various ways to interpret this information – a p-value of .85 (85 per cent of test takers answered the item correctly) could be taken as evidence the item is 'easy'; a p-value of .25 (25 per cent answered incorrectly) could be seen as evidence of a 'difficult' item. The higher the p-value, the 'easier' the item is for the examinees, leading some to prefer the term 'facility index'. In CTT, the 'ideal item' (p = .50), is one in which 50 per cent of the examinees get the correct answer. Items with extremely high (or extremely low) item difficulty would be considered bad items. We would also need to look at its discrimination.

'Item discrimination' describes the relationship between the examinees' answers to the item and their answers on the total test. That is, it answers the question: if examinees are scoring high on the test overall, are they also answering this item correctly? In CTT, especially when using norm-referenced measurement (NRM), where the main goal is to rank-order examinees and make relative decisions, the ideal item is one that discriminates highly. The guidelines given by Popham (1990: 277) suggest that a discrimination of .40 and higher is a sign of a 'very good' item, and that anything less than .20 is a sign of a 'poor' item. Items with discrimination indices between .20 and .40 can probably be improved through revision.

In addition to using estimates of item difficulty and discrimination, when the test items are in multiple-choice format, another technique for analysing the quality of items is 'distracter analysis'. Basically, this technique involves counting the number of examinees who select each alternative in the multiple-choice answer format. The incorrect alternatives are called 'distracters' – distracting examinees from the correct answer. It is also important to know how the examinees did on the test overall; that is, we need to identify whether the individuals who selected each alternative performed well or poorly on the test overall. The reason for this is that we would expect those examinees who are doing well on the test overall – those who have a high total test score – to select the correct alternative and avoid the distracters. Likewise, we would expect those who are doing poorly on the test overall – those with low total test scores – to choose one of the distracters rather than the correct alternative.

4.2.1.1 Example calculations for item analysis

Item Difficulty (p): when the items can be scored as right or wrong, correct or incorrect, this is a very simple calculation:

1. For each item, assign a '1' for a correct answer and a '0' for an incorrect answer.
2. Count the number of examinees who get the item correct (the number of '1's).
3. Divide the total from the second step by the total number of examinees.

For example, using the data in Table 4.1:
The 'p-value' or item difficulty for Item 1 is:
2 (the number of examinees who got it correct; who have a '1');
divided by 6 (total number of examinees);
= .33
The 'p-value' or item difficulty for Item 4 is:
5 (examinees getting it correct);
divided by 6 (total number of examinees)
= .83

Table 4.1   Example data for item analysis

Item/Examinee	Item 1	Item 2	Item 3	Item 4	Item 5
Yuko	0	0	0	1	1
Jean-Luc	1	0	1	0	1
Mercedes	1	1	1	1	0
Hameed	0	0	1	1	1
Kolya	0	0	0	1	1
Sam	0	1	1	1	1

Item Discrimination (d): the statistic used for item discrimination represents how well getting the item right or wrong matches up with the test taker's total scores on the test. This information is calculated and averaged across all test takers, providing us with a single number that says how well the information this item gives us matches the information we get from the rest of the items on the test. The most accurate way to calculate item discrimination is with a computer programme, using an 'item-to-total', or point-biserial correlation. An easier, somewhat less accurate, method for calculating item discrimination can be done 'by hand', or with a calculator.

This method is presented for items scored right-or-wrong (1 or 0) in Popham (1990: 275–7):

1. Calculate a total score (number of items correct) for each examinee.
2. Order the examinees by total score.
3. Divide the examinees into a 'high' group and a 'low' group, with equal numbers in each. (This can either be done by dividing the rank-ordered scores into two equal halves, or – for a more accurate analysis – by using the top and bottom 25 per cent (or, with smaller numbers of examinees, the top and bottom 33 per cent).)
4. Calculate the item difficulty (p-value) for each group separately.
5. Subtract the item-difficulty value for the 'low' group from the item difficulty for the 'high' group.

For the example data in Table 4.1, with the top and bottom 33 per cent approach, we would order the examinees as follows, from highest score to lowest:

Mercedes (4)
Sam (4)
Jean-Luc (3)
Hameed (3)
Yuko (2)
Kolya (2)

The 'high' group (top 33 per cent) would be Mercedes and Sam; the 'low' group (bottom 33 per cent) would be Yuko and Kolya.

The 'p-value' for Item 1 for the 'high' group is $1+0 = 1$;
divided by 2 (remember to divide by the number of examinees in the high or low

group this time, not the total number of examinees);
= .50.
The p-value for the 'low' group is $0+0 = 0$;
divided by 2;
= 0.

The 'discrimination index' (d) for Item 1 is:

the 'high' group p-value (.5) minus the 'low' group p-value (0)
= .50.

Distracter Analysis: this form of item analysis involves counting the number of examinees who select each alternative in the multiple-choice answer format, along with determining how they did on the test overall. For example, suppose that for the following multiple-choice item ($p = .50; D = -.33$) with four alternative responses (the correct response is marked with a *), we have the following distribution of examinee responses (from Popham 1990: 279):

	A	B*	C	D	Omit
Upper 16 students	2	5	0	8	1
Lower 15 students	4	10	0	0	1

The information in this distracter analysis gives us a reason for the negative discrimination ($D = -.33$): there is something about alternative 'D' that is attracting half of the test takers in the 'upper' group (and none of the students in the lower group are selecting D); that is, too many of the better students are selecting the wrong answer. Also, alternative C is not attracting any students, which is generally seen as an undesirable characteristic for any item. Normally, each incorrect alternative should be 'distracting' at least some of the test takers.

Here are some further examples of distracter analysis for multiple-choice items.

Item 1.	*a.	b.	c.	d. (= alternatives)
	50	12	13	25 (= no. of responses)

From a difficulty point of view, this looks like a promising item: 50 per cent get it right, 50 per cent get it wrong, with all distracters drawing some responses. However, if we calculate the distracter distribution separately for the top one-third students (overall test score) and the bottom one-third students (overall test score), we combine item difficulty with item discrimination information, and we get the following picture for Item 1:

	*a.	b.	c.	d.
upper ⅓	8	5	4	16
lower ⅓	28	2	3	0

More people in the lower one-third (low scorers, overall, on test) are giving the correct response than people in the upper one-third (high scorers on test). Also, distracter 'd' is attracting too many of the upper group.

Item 2.	a.	*b.	c.	d.
upper ⅓	0	20	6	7
lower ⅓	0	20	7	6

We see that Item 2 is not discriminating between high and low scorers – equal numbers are getting the item correct, and the distracters are attracting the same number of responses from both high and low scorers as well. Also note that distracter 'a' is not drawing any response.

Item 3.	a.	b.	*c.	d.
upper ⅓	3	25	3	2
lower ⅓	11	5	5	12

For Item 3, 'b' is attracting too many high scorers; it may be a 'possible' answer.

Item 4.	a.	b.	c.	*d.
upper ⅓	2	2	1	28
lower ⅓	20	2	4	7

Item 4 is discriminating well. Note that 'a' may be a 'developmental error'; that is, it may be a mistake that learners make at early stages of their language acquisition.

4.2.2 CRM item analysis

With CRM tests we can use the same item-analysis techniques as in CTT, but we would interpret the results differently and, with respect to discrimination, we would apply somewhat different approaches. In CRM, we would not automatically consider an item to be giving us bad information if the item-difficulty estimate was high (indicating an 'easy' item) or low (indicating a 'difficult' item). It would depend on what the item was measuring and who the examinees were. If we give a set of items that are designed to measure some specific language skill or ability to a group of students before they receive instruction on that skill or ability (the criterion), then we would expect a low item-difficulty index. On the other hand, if we give those same items to the students after instruction, then we would expect a high item-difficulty index – that is, we would expect a 'p-value' of .75 or greater, indicating that most of the students had mastered the learning objective.

Similarly, we would not consider an item to be 'bad' simply because it had a low item-discrimination index. That would indicate that it wasn't able to distinguish between examinees very well. In a CRM context, where we are expecting students to learn the criteria that we are attempting to test, we do not necessarily require this discrimination between individuals. We do require discrimination between those that have learned the criterion and those who have not. So, discrimination from a CRM point of view amounts to distinguishing between those who have received instruction and those who have not, or between those who have mastered the criterion and those who have not.

To estimate this CRM type of discrimination, we need two groups of examinees:

a group before instruction begins and a group who have received instruction; or a group judged to be 'masters' of the criterion and a group judged to be 'non-masters'. We then give our test items to both groups, and calculate p-values (item difficulty) for each group on each item. Subtracting the p-value for the uninstructed group from the p-value for the instructed group (or the non-masters from the masters) gives us an estimate of how well each item 'discriminates', in this case between those who are thought to have achieved the criterion being measured from those who have not. This is called the 'difference index'.

For example, look at the following item statistics:

Item 1	p-value
Instructed Ss	.85
Uninstructed Ss	.25

The 'difference index' for this item would be .60, indicating that the item is discriminating well between students who have received instruction on the criterion being measured and those who have not.

Item 2	p-value
Instructed Ss	.40
Uninstructed Ss	.35

The 'difference index' for Item 2 would be .05, indicating that the item is not discriminating well. It appears to be difficult or confusing for even the instructed students; it may not be measuring what was taught.

4.2.3 Item analysis with subjective scoring

For some of the testing formats presented in Chapter 3, the notion of individual test items does not capture the nature of the assessment. The oral interview, for example, is usually not taken to be a series of independent items, but is an integrated performance, or procedure. Furthermore, this type of performance is not scored 'objectively' (that is, it is not scored as either right or wrong); it is generally scored 'subjectively', on some sort of rating scale, as described in Chapter 3. However, even with a performance-based test, there may be different tasks, or questions asked, and if these can be judged, rated, or scored separately, then we are still able to use the item-analysis techniques used for objective scoring.

The main difference will be the fact that there is no 'right' or 'wrong' answer, but a judgement (hence, the term 'subjective' scoring) about the performance on a particular task, or in relation to a particular trait, or evaluative criterion (such as 'pronunciation', 'fluency', 'organisation', 'grammar' and so on). If there is more than one person doing the judging, then we have different sets of scores for our test takers on the same test or procedure. We can still aggregate those different scores, and compute an 'average' score across the judges, or raters, and we can total the average scores for the different parts (tasks, criteria) that have been scored. So, in principle, we can compute 'item difficulty' (the average score on any task or criterion, across

Table 4.2 Example data – speaking assessment

Eval. Criteria→ Students ↓	Pronun.	Fluency	Organisation	Vocabulary	Grammar	Total Score
José	5	4	4	3	4	20
Kim	3	3	5	5	5	21
María	4	4	4	4	4	20
YuYin	5	5	5	4	5	24
Sam	3	3	2	2	3	13

all test takers and all raters), and 'item discrimination' (using the 'total score' on the performance and seeing how well individual tasks/criteria correlate against it; or using the total score to form 'upper' and 'lower' groups, and comparing their difficulty values).

In order to interpret these results as we do with objectively scored items, we need to convert the scores into proportions. For example, if we have an item-difficulty estimate for a task, or for an evaluative criterion, on a speaking performance, and that item difficulty (the average item score) is 3, then we need to express it as a proportion out of the total possible score (note that with items scored 0 or 1, the total possible score is 1, and so the proportion is automatic). If the rating scale for that task or evaluative criterion is a 0 to 6 scale, then the total possible score is 6, and the item difficulty would be $3 \div 6$ or .50.

For item discrimination, we can either correlate the item score with the total score for each of the test takers (the resulting correlation coefficient will be on a scale of -1.0 to $+1.0$), or we can use the total scores to order the test takers, find the upper- and lower-score groups, and then calculate item-difficulty values for the two groups, using the transformation to proportions described above.

Table 4.2 gives some example data for a speaking assessment. The columns are the 'evaluative criteria' which define the subskills for the 'criterion' being assessed (for example, 'the ability to speak communicatively and accurately in academic discussion groups').

Each evaluative criterion is judged on a 1- to 5-point scale – the scale descriptors will generally be worded uniquely for each evaluative criterion. Note that these data show the students being rated by only one rater. With multiple raters, you would need to average the scores on each evaluative criteria for each student. Note also that a total score is calculated for each student (José = 20; Kim = 21; María = 20, etc.). However, a total score may not be as revealing as reporting the score profile, with individual evaluative criterion scores (for example, José and María have the same 'total score', but different profiles).

For the most part, with subjective scoring and multiple raters (always recommended), we are interested in the degree of agreement between the individual raters. This leads to the next aspect of test analysis: reliability, or the consistency of measurement. In the case of subjective scoring, we are interested in how consistent raters are among themselves, or how much they agree on their ratings of individual test takers: inter-rater reliability. But first, we will examine reliability for objective scoring.

4.2.4 Reliability

When we talk about reliability, we are referring to the consistency of our measurement. Since no measurent that we attempt will be perfectly consistent, we have the concept of 'measurement error'. Error is anything that is inconsistent with the measurement of the skill or ability we set out to measure. For example, if a particular examinee is unusually tired while taking the test, the results of that test will be influenced by this factor of tiredness, which is not a systematic part of the skill or ability we want to measure. This type of influence is difficult or impossible to predict and it is a temporary characteristic. The examinee would receive a different test score on the day she or he was tired than on another day when she or he was not tired. The measurement from one day to the other would be inconsistent, signalling error in our measurement, expressed as an inconsistency across testing occasions. Reliability, or consistency of measurement, is important in positivist testing theory since it is a necessary, but insufficient, requirement for validity. If our measurement is not consistent, if it contains too much error, then we cannot make claims for it being valid (or measuring what we say it is). Another way of thinking about reliability is as a concern with identifying the sources of error in our measurement, that is, the things we don't intend to measure.

4.2.4.1 Sources of error

There are many possible sources of measurement error. Examples include an examinee's motivation towards the test, distractions such as noise in the test environment, the general anxiety level of the examinee and aspects of the test administration, such as explanation of procedures. Many of these sources are, for the most part, random in nature; they cannot be systematically predicted in terms of their effect on the examinee's test score. There are sources of error that are more systematic in nature, however. For example, attributes of examinees such as their test-taking ability ('test-wiseness'), cognitive style and background knowledge can have an effect on their test performance. This effect can be systematic, but it is not the result of the ability or skill we are trying to measure (unless we are measuring test-taking ability, cognitive style and so on). Bachman (1990) has also identified systematic sources of error having to do with the test procedure itself, which he calls 'test method facets'. So, the answer format for the test – multiple choice, for example – is a test method facet that can have a systematic effect on an examinee's test performance. This systematic effect may be the same across all individuals taking the test, or it may be different for some individuals. The important point is that, to the extent the effect is unrelated to the skill or ability we are trying to measure, it is a source of measurement error.

4.2.4.2 Estimation techniques

The basic concept used by CTT for estimating reliability is the notion of the 'true score'. This is the ideal measurement for an individual that we would get if we were able to measure without error. Since there will always be some amount of measurement error, we can think of any score we actually obtain, or observe, as being composed of the true score plus error. This gives us the following relationship between true scores and observed scores:

Observed Score = True Score + Error.

Reliability, then, is the proportion of the observed score that is without error, or the ratio of the true score to the observed score. The more error our measurement has, the smaller that ratio will be, resulting in a smaller reliability estimate. The estimate for reliability, then, is a proportion – a number that will vary from 0 to 1. A reliability estimate of 1 would indicate that the true score (score without error) was equal to the observed score; therefore, the observed score would be seen to contain no error. A reliability estimate of .5 would indicate that the true score was half as large as the observed score; therefore, the observed score would contain as much error as it did true score. A reliability estimate of 0 would indicate the observed score was total error (no true score).

4.2.4.3 Internal consistency techniques

Since we cannot observe or know with certainty what someone's true score actually is, we need techniques for estimating reliability from observed scores. There are three basic approaches to this estimation, each associated with a different type of measurement error. The first approach is called 'internal consistency', and it attempts to identify sources of error internal to the test instrument or procedure. The basic idea is that all the items on the test should be giving similar information if they are measuring the same thing. To the extent that different items show different patterns of response from the examinees, this is taken as evidence of measurement error; the test is inconsistent within itself. Of course, it must be kept in mind that it is not actually the test instrument that is inconsistent or unreliable, but the measurements we obtain from it for a particular group of examinees. Reliability is always a property of a set of measurements, not the test itself.

Most of the techniques for estimating internal consistency reliability are variations on the same theme: divide the test into two halves and correlate the responses for one half with the other. If the test is perfectly reliable, that is, if the test is perfect in its internal consistency, then the correlation between the examinees' responses to one half of the test with the other should be 1.0. The question becomes: how do we divide the test into two halves? Do we take the first half of the items and correlate them with the second half? Do we take the even-numbered items and correlate them with the odd-numbered items? We need to make certain that the two halves are each representative of the test overall and are not influenced by their items having different content or being affected by the order in which they were responded to by the examinees.

The estimation most often used for internal consistency reliability is 'Cronbach's alpha'. It represents an average of all possible test-half correlations. It allows for the estimation of reliability when the items are scored other than right–wrong, for example if items are given partial credit, or scored on a judgement scale. The formula is:

$$\alpha = k/k-1 \; (1-\Sigma s_i^2/s_x^2)$$

where:

k = the number of items on the test

Σs_i^2 = the sum of the item variances

s_t^2 = the total test-score variance.

If the formula seems imposing, fear not: most computer applications, like the Statistical Package for the Social Sciences (SPSS), available for Windows-based operating systems (SPSS 2002), will perform the calculation for you, as will be discussed later in the chapter.

4.2.4.5 Test-retest

When the source of error is thought to be different behaviour over time, from one test occasion to another – that is, when reliability is conceptualised as consistency over time – the approach for estimating reliability is termed 'test-retest'. This involves giving the test items to a group of examinees on one occasion and then giving the same test items to the same examinees again on a later occasion. The scores on the first test are then correlated with the scores on the retest – a high correlation would suggest that the test measurements have been consistent over the two occasions. The decision about the time interval between occasions is crucial, since if the test is repeated too soon after the first administration, the examinees may still remember their original answers. A high correlation may be the result of examinees simply remembering the way they answered the first time and doing so again as an automatic response. A low correlation, on the other hand, may be the result of some examinees remembering and giving their original answers and others not doing so. If the time interval between the two tests is too long, the examinees may have changed; they may have improved at different rates on the skill or ability being tested. A low correlation may be the result of this differential improvement, rather than a lack of consistency in the test items themselves over time. On the other hand, a high correlation might indicate a consistency in the test measurement, if all the examinees had improved at the same rate.

4.2.4.6 Equivalent forms

When the source of error is thought to be changes in the characteristics of the test items from one form of the test to another, the approach for estimating reliability is equivalent forms. This is essentially the same as estimating internal consistency, only the two halves of the test being correlated are two different sets of test items, designed to measure the same criterion. The consistency being estimated is from one form (one set of items) to another – that is, it asks the question 'How equivalent are these two forms of the test?' Like test-retest, the scores on one test form are correlated with the scores on another. Unlike test-retest, this estimation procedure can be done on one test administration occasion. The two test forms (for example, Form A and Form B) would be randomly distributed to a single group of examinees, with each individual taking only one test form. The scores from those taking Form A (a random half of the total group of examinees) would be correlated with those taking Form B (the other half of the group). Test-retest can also be combined with equivalent forms as reliability-estimation procedures.

4.2.4.7 Inter-rater reliability

When the test procedure involves 'subjective' scoring – having 'raters' judge a language performance, using a rating scale or scoring guide – there is another source of measurement error to reckon with: the individual raters or judges. This source of error is identified with estimates of inter-rater reliability. The ratings or scores given to the test takers by a particular rater or judge are correlated with the ratings/scores given by all other judges.

Since obtaining estimates for inter-rater reliability is not as straightforward as with estimating internal consistency, I will provide the details for the calculation. To get the correlations between individual rater scores, you need to use a computer statistical package like the previously mentioned SPSS. Using SPSS, you would type in the data (individual ratings for each student in the rows of the data spreadsheet; the different raters' ratings forming the columns). In Table 4.3's example data, there are ten students being rated by three raters. Then, in SPSS, select (from the top menu bar) 'Analyze' → 'Correlation' → 'Bivariate'. Select the 'variables' (which are the columns, representing raters) and move them into the 'variables' box. The default is 'Pearson' (a type of correlation), which you can use; then click 'Okay', and the program will compute your correlation matrix, which will look like the section of Table 4.3 labelled 'SPSS Corelations' (VAR1 is Rater 1; VAR2 is Rater 2; VAR3 is Rater 3).

In addition to providing the correlations necessary for inter-rater reliability, these statistical packages can do basic item analysis and internal consistency reliability estimation. In SPSS, for example, under the 'Analyse' procedure, select 'Scale' and then 'Reliability'. The options for the reliability subprocedure allow you to select 'descriptives' for Item, Scale and Scale-if-item-deleted: this gives you item difficulty and item discrimination statistics.

In the SPSS correlation matrix, there are three correlation coefficients, one for each pair of raters (Rater 1 with Rater 2 = .711; Rater 1 with Rater 3 = .742; Rater 2 with Rater 3 = .894). These correlation coefficients then need to be corrected for the fact that the data are not taken from a truly 'interval' scale (rating scales are 'ordinal' in nature – 'steps' that are not truly equidistant from each other), using the Fisher Z transformation (see Hatch and Lazaraton 1991: 533, 606, for explanation and table of transformation values). Using the Fisher Z transformation values (in this case, .889, .955 and 1.442), the correlations are then averaged (that is, we add all

Table 4.3   Sample data: Inter-rater reliability

Rater → Students ↓	1	2	3
1	5.00	5.00	5.00
2	4.00	5.00	5.00
3	4.00	4.00	5.00
4	3.00	3.00	4.00
5	3.00	4.00	4.00
6	4.00	3.00	4.00
7	5.00	5.00	5.00
8	5.00	5.00	5.00
9	2.00	3.00	4.00
10	4.00	3.00	4.00

SPSS Correlations

		VAR1	VAR2	VAR3
VAR1	Pearson Correlation	1	.711[a]	.742[b]
	Sig. (2-tailed)		.021	.014
	N		10	10
VAR2	Pearson Correlation		1	.894[a]
	Sig. (2-tailed)			.000
	N			10
VAR3	Pearson Correlation			1

[a] Correlation is significant at the 0.05 level (2-tailed).
[b] Correlation is significant at the 0.01 level (2-tailed).

coefficients and then divide by the total number of coefficients), and this average correlation (in this case, 1.095) is used in the following formula:

$R_{tt} = n\, r_{AB} / 1 + (n-1)\, r_{AB}$

Where:

n = the number of raters

r_{AB} = the average of the corrected (Fisher Z transformation) correlations between the raters

R_{tt} = the inter-rater reliability estimate, *after it is transformed back to Pearson*, using the Fisher Z transformation table again, this time from Z to Pearson.

The calculation would be:

$[3\,(1.095)] / [1+2(1.095)] = 1.028$

This correlation, 1.028, is the Fisher Z coefficient, which now needs to be transformed back to the Pearson scale, resulting in:

$R_{tt} = .77.$

The inter-rater reliability for these data is estimated to be .77, which as with all estimates of reliability means that 77 per cent of the observed test-score variability can be attributed to true-score variability; or, conversely, we can interpret this to mean that 23 per cent of our measurement may be due to error.

4.2.4.8 Acceptable reliability

For any of our estimates of reliability, what is considered acceptable? This question has no definitive answer. In the research literature, you will see estimates ranging from .60 to .90 being described as 'acceptable'. However, a reliability of .60 is on the extreme low end of acceptability. Generally, for assessment and evaluation purposes we expect the reliability of our measurements to approach the .90 level. Of course, it depends on the stakes of the decisions being made. The higher the stakes, the more serious the decisions being made, the higher the reliability we will need to justify the decisions being made from the measurement data.

4.2.5 CRM 'dependability': G-theory

The discussion of reliability in CRM has adopted a different term: 'dependability'. This is because CRM is less concerned with the type of consistency based on a notion of 'relative error'. Relative error signals the fact that in classical test theory (and NRM), the consistency of measurement is conceptualised in terms of item variance in relation to persons (examinees) only. In other words, error is considered to be homogeneous or coming from the same source (or, at least, the estimation identifies only one source at a time: internal, test-retest, equivalent forms) and that this source is always random, unsystematic. CRM is interested in 'absolute decisions' in relation to the criterion being measured, and therefore needs to treat error as 'absolute' (meaning it sees error as composed of different sources of variability, sources that interact with each other and with the criterion being measured). Since it is interested in absolute decisions, the concern is for the 'dependability' of those decisions, and this can be estimated using a different approach to measurement theory known as 'generalisability theory' (G-theory).

In G-theory, the CTT concept of 'true score' is recast as 'universe score', taking all possible conditions, or sources of variance, into account. The CTT concept of error as random and homogeneous is replaced in G-theory by a concept of error as including multiple and systematic sources (sources of variance, or variability in test scores). Particular sets of conditions in the measurement procedure – a set of items, a set of raters, a set of occasions on which the measurement is conducted – are termed 'facets'. For example, if a group of four people are rating the written texts produced by students on a test of writing, those four people form the 'rater facet' (with four 'conditions') for that measurement procedure.

When using G-theory, the test developer or researcher defines which facets will be considered of interest and importance in a particular testing context. These facets are referred to as the 'universe of admissible observations'. For example, in a study done by Lynch and McNamara (1998), a test was investigated in terms of trained raters (native English speakers) and items defining characteristics of ESL speaking ability. In this case, the 'universe of admissible observations' consisted of the rater facet (four persons, or 'conditions') and the item facet (twenty-three items, or 'conditions'). Although only four conditions for the rater facet and twenty-three conditions for

Table 4.4   G-study (variance components for 'single observations' = one item)

Effect	Variance Component	% of total variance
Persons (p)	.011	5.37
Items (i)	.061	29.76
pi, e	.133	64.88

the item facet were sampled, it is assumed in G-theory that these are representative of the infinite set of possible conditions in each facet. Once the facets and their conditions have been identified, a 'generalisability study' (G-study) is carried out which estimates the amount of variability in the test scores that each facet accounts for, or their relative effects on the overall test-score variability. These effects are estimated using a procedure known as analysis of variance (or ANOVA), which allows for an estimation of how the facets interact with each other and with the 'object of measurement' (the persons taking the test). The G-study provides estimates for percentage of total variability in the test scores across all test takers that each facet (and interaction) accounts for. These estimates are called 'variance components' and can be used in turn to estimate the reliability, or dependability, of inferences drawn from these test scores. Table 4.4 gives an example set of G-study variance components where 'items' is the single facet being used.

The next phase of G-theory analysis is the 'decision-study' (D-study). The purpose of the D-study is to see how different numbers of conditions for the facets, in different combinations, will affect the reliability or the dependability estimate. That is, the test developer or researcher wants to know how many conditions of a facet – how many raters, for example – will be necessary to achieve a particular level of reliability/dependability. This introduces another 'universe': the 'universe of generalisation', or the particular number of conditions for each facet and their combination that we want to consider using, or 'generalising' to. An individual's 'universe score', the G-theory replacement for CTT's 'true score', can be thought of as the average for an individual across this universe of generalisation. Any number of D-studies can be designed to estimate the change in reliability/dependability when we change the number and combination of conditions in our facets of interest. One D-study might be designed to estimate the reliability/dependability of our decisions when we use three raters and twenty items. Another might be designed for two raters and thirty items. The changes in dependability across the D-studies allows us to choose the best 'design', given our resources and desired level of reliability/dependability. We might be willing to settle for a reliability/dependability estimate of .80, achieved with one rater, for example, even though increasing the number of raters to three would increase the reliability/dependability to .85. In a context where we had limited funds to pay raters and where a .80 reliability/dependability was traditionally acceptable, a one-rater design might be the best choice.

4.2.5.1 Relative versus absolute decisions

In CTT, the norm-referenced view is only interested in ranking test takers, or making reliable distinctions between individuals. This means that when considering test-score variability, the only variation of interest is that which is directly attributable to persons (the test takers). Items (or ratings given by raters) are assumed to be of equal difficulty (or harshness). Even if the items (or raters) do vary in difficulty (or harshness), the rank-ordering of the persons will stay the same, only the average scores for the individual test takers will change (becoming lower if the items are difficulty or raters harsh). Since the rank-ordering is not affected, the reliability of such 'relative decisions' will not be affected.

However, if we are interested in 'absolute decisions', as we are from a CRM view, the effect of variation in item difficulty or rater harshness is important. If our test is being used to determine who will qualify for a particular class or position, and a score is set to determine that level of ability, then it does matter whether the items are difficult or easy, and whether the raters are harsh or lenient. If the items vary in difficulty, or the raters vary in harshness, then these facets are independently contributing to the variability in the observed test scores. If some of the items are more difficult, or some of the raters are more harsh in their ratings, then this factor alone will bring the average scores for all individuals down. This means that using the observed test scores to decide who is qualified will result in selecting fewer people than if the items or raters had less variability. Another way of thinking about the problem is that when a facet has an effect, when there is a large amount of variability in the test scores due to this facet, then we need to add more conditions of this facet (more items, more raters) in order to lower the variability that it causes. When we increase the number of conditions for a particular facet, three related things happen:

1. the better we have sampled that facet;
2. the less variability it will have;
3. the more we minimise the effect that it has on our observed scores.

In order to determine the consistency of measurement with G-theory, there are two estimates of error we can use: one for relative decisions, one for absolute. The estimate for relative decisions is generally referred to as a 'generalisability coefficient'. In the case of absolute decisions, error is calculated differently, using more information from the facets that have been identified (such as items and raters). This estimate is generally referred to as a 'dependability coefficient'.

Because the amount of variability attributed to the object of measurement (persons) will change depending on the number of conditions for each facet, the reliability and dependability estimates will also change. Table 4.5 provides a comparison of these estimates across varying numbers of conditions for the facets (items and raters, in this case). As we add raters and items to the measurement process, our reliability and dependability increases. Note that the dependability estimates are always smaller than the generalisability estimates. This is due to the way the two estimates are calculated (with more information being included in the estimate of dependability).

It appears that for this measurement procedure, adding an additional rater improves the reliability and dependability more than adding an additional set of

Table 4.5   Reliability and dependability estimates from D-studies

Raters	Items	Generalisability/ reliability (NRM)	Dependability/ (CRM)
4	23	.955	.870
3	23	.943	.836
2	23	.919	.776
1	23	.853	.637
4	16	.952	.866
3	16	.938	.832
2	16	.913	.771
1	16	.846	.632
4	8	.939	.851
3	8	.925	.816
2	8	.897	.755
1	8	.823	.615

(Modified from Lynch and McNamara 1998: 166)

items. For example, beginning with the smallest number of conditions for each facet (one rater and eight items), there is an increase in dependability from .615 to .632 if eight items are added, without adding a rater; there is an increase from .615 to .755 if one rater is added, without adding items. With four raters and eight items we achieve slightly better dependability (.851) than with three raters and sixteen items (.832). If our goal is reliability or dependability in the high .80 to .90 range, then we will need at least four raters for dependability (four raters, sixteen items = .866), and at least two raters for reliability (two raters, eight items = .897). Ultimately, the test developer, in consultation with the test users, will need to make decisions about the value of increasing reliability or dependability versus the cost of adding conditions to the facets (for example, increasing the number of raters or items).

I hope that the brief description offered here will allow the reader to interpret published G-theory statistics, and to determine whether their use will be of benefit to particular assessment contexts the reader may encounter. G-theory analysis is accessible via a software package developed by Robert Brennan, called GENOVA, available for both Macintosh and PC platforms (Brennan 1992, 2001). A detailed explanation of the calculation of generalisability and dependability estimates can be found in Brown and Hudson (2002).

4.2.6 Item response theory (IRT)

Just as G-theory was a response to the problems and inadequacies of CTT, so item response theory (IRT) was developed to address the limitations of both CTT and G-theory. The main inadequacy that CTT and G-theory share is that they do not provide an estimate of individual ability; they can only establish an interval of measurement, or range of scores within which the 'true score', or the individual's actual level of ability, will fall.

IRT attempts to overcome these limitations in the accuracy of measurement by providing an estimate of individual, or person ability, that is independent of the group of test takers, and the set of items, from which the test data come. It does this through a mathematical model that hypothesises the existence of a latent trait: an unobservable, psychological variable that underlies the performance we are observing and trying to measure. IRT specifies parameters, or types of information about the characteristics of the item, that it will use to model mathematically the item responses. Example parameters are: discrimination, difficulty, and guessing (that is, the probability of low-ability person getting item correct). It is further hypothesised by the model that these characteristics accurately describe the relationship between the observed performance on any item and the underlying latent trait or ability. These hypotheses are then 'tested' against the data from a particular test. If the data pass the test, if they fit the IRT mathematical model, then the estimates of individual person ability are said to be 'sample free', meaning they do not depend on the particular group of test takers that the original data came from; and the item-difficulty estimates are said to be 'item free', meaning they do not depend on the particular set of items used on the test. These characteristics of sample-free and item-free measurement are also referred to as 'invariance'.

4.2.6.1 Assumptions

There is a fair amount of controversy over the question of the assumptions of the IRT models, in particular the assumption of 'unidimensionality'. I will not go into these arguments, but will merely point out that the assumptions underlying any statistical model are important to address (for further discussion, see Hambelton et al. 1991; Henning et al. 1985; Henning 1988; McNamara 1990).

4.2.6.2 The logit scale

IRT is a 'probabilistic' model of test performance. That is, it expresses the estimates of person ability and item difficulty in terms of probabilities: what is the probability that a person of ability X would get an item of difficulty Y correct? The units of this probability, which define the scale of measurement in IRT, are called 'logits'. This scale is centred on zero and can vary in both positive and negative directions. Positive values on the logit scale indicate greater person ability and greater item difficulty (or greater harshness on the part of raters). Negative logit values indicate lower ability, easier items (or more lenient raters). Logit values typically range between +2 and –2, as depicted in Figure 4.1.

4.2.6.3 Different IRT models

An infinite number of IRT models are possible, depending on how many charac-teristics of the measurement procedure can be related, or expressed, mathematically, in relation to performance on the test. Perhaps the most commonly used IRT model is the one-parameter, or Rasch model. The sole parameter used in this approach is item difficulty. In this case, then, it is assumed that only item difficulty is influencing

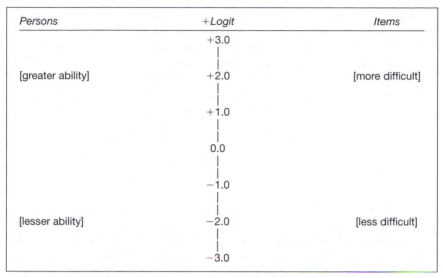

Persons	+Logit	Items
	+3.0	
[greater ability]	+2.0	[more difficult]
	+1.0	
	0.0	
	−1.0	
[lesser ability]	−2.0	[less difficult]
	−3.0	

Figure 4.1   The logit scale

test performance. For example, this means that all items are assumed to discriminate equally, and that there is no guessing that affects how individuals do on the test. The estimate of the item-difficulty factor is a logit value that corresponds to the ability logit value where the probability of getting the item correct is .50 (50 per cent). The larger the logit value for the item difficulty, the more difficult the item is, and the greater the ability required to have a 50 per cent chance of getting it correct.

The two-parameter model adds the characteristic of discrimination to the calculation. This parameter, like the others, will be estimated in terms of logits: a positive value approaching 2 is considered good discrimination; a negative value is not discriminating well. The three-parameter model includes the two previous parameters, item difficulty and item discrimination, and adds the characteristic of 'pseudo-chance', or 'guessing' (an estimate of the probability that a person of low ability will get an item correct). This means that the item-difficulty parameter will have a probability of one-half the difference of the guessing parameter probability and 1. For example, if the guessing-parameter probability for an item is .10, then the difficulty parameter will have a probability of .45 (halfway between .10 and 1.0), identifying the point on the ability scale at which a person will have a 45 per cent chance of getting the item correct.

4.2.6.4 Many-facet Rasch measurement

While maintaining the one-parameter IRT model, the 'many-facet' extension of the Rasch model allows the estimation of the effects for additional characteristics of the measurement process on the estimation of the latent trait, or underlying ability. Such characteristics are parallel to the facets discussed in the preceding section on

G-theory. An example of an additional facet would be rater severity. The 'many-facet Rasch measurement' model includes the effect of the relative harshness or leniency from individual raters in the estimation of the person ability and item difficulty. That is, just as the score that individual test takers receive – the measure of their ability – is adjusted for the differences in item difficulty, so the estimates of item difficulty and person ability are adjusted for differences in rater harshness. The model also analyses the interaction, or combination, of the rater facet (and any others we may choose to identify) with persons and items (and other facets). When particular combinations are showing a systematic difference – for example, if a particular rater is systematically rating a particular person differently, both in comparison to other raters and in comparison to the particular rater's judgements of other persons – this is identified in the many-facet Rasch 'bias analysis'. As with the other IRT models, this approach also identifies inconsistent patterns: particular raters who are inconsistent in their own rating; particular items that demonstrate no consistent pattern and that do not fit the overall model of the data. This inconsistent pattern will not provide reliable measurement information and is labelled as 'misfitting'. Misfitting raters, items, or persons (or other elements for any facet) can be excluded from the analysis (or modified/retrained in the case of items and raters) to improve reliability.

For example, in the Lynch and McNamara (1998) study, out of 83 persons in the sample, 4 were found to be misfitting. Since this represents almost 5 per cent of the total sample, it is a cause for concern. The misfitting persons could either be excluded from the analysis, or they could be examined more closely in terms of background characteristics to suggest mismatches with the measurement procedure (for example, it may be that the misfitting persons come from previous educational experiences that did not prepare them for the measurement format being used).

Examining the item statistics in the Lynch and McNamara study, two items out of twenty-three were found to be misfitting. This result would suggest that these items are measuring something different from the other items. In this case, the items were in fact ratings of task performance (for example, rating the fluency of a role play), using a rating scale, it may also suggest that there were disagreements between the raters on how to interpret the rating scale for particular task judgements.

The many-facet Rasch analysis detected no misfitting raters, which meant that the judgements, or ratings, from the raters in this measurement procedure were providing reliable information about person ability. When it occurs, the presence of misfitting raters signals an inconsistency in measurement for which the Rasch model cannot adjust. Had there been any misfitting raters in the Lynch and McNamara results, the problem would need to be pursued through changes in rater selection and training.

The advantages of using IRT models are significant. They allow us to correct for measurement error within the estimate of person ability and item difficulty; in a sense, the mathematical model recycles information from persons and items back into the calculation of ability and difficulty. When certain persons are of greater or lesser ability, and certain items are more or less difficult, the final scores assigned to individuals reflect these relative differences. Another important benefit is the ability to tailor tests to particular individuals or groups of individuals. In particular, we can design computer-adaptive tests, where the items that each individual receives are selected based on how they respond to previous items. This allows us to arrive at a reliable estimate of the individual's ability with a minimum amount of items (and test-taking time). Finally, IRT models, with their item and sample-free characteristics, have provided a more precise method of equating test forms. With a small set of 'linking items' (whose difficulty estimates are known and expressed on the logit scale), a new form (set of items) can be given and the resulting item and person estimates adjusted to the previous form (the set of items that the linking items came from).

There are some disadvantages to using IRT, however. In most cases, especially for two- and three-parameter models, large sample sizes are needed in order to achieve reliable estimates. Also, the assumptions of the IRT models, discussed above, are difficult to meet. And, as this brief introduction has probably made clear, IRT is complex and requires specialised computer software and expertise in order to generate and interpret the analysis.

As with G-theory, an explanation of how to calculate IRT statistics is beyond the scope of this book. The goal here was to present a description that will allow you to interpret generally IRT statistics, and to decide upon their usefulness in your particular assessment contexts. The one-parameter Rasch model is available in several software packages, with many-facet Rasch measurement, including Linacre (1988) and Wu et al. (1996). A thorough explanation of the IRT models and statistical calculations can be found in McNamara (1996) and Brown and Hudson (2002).

4.3 ANALYSIS OF NON-TEST MEASURES

The data from non-test measures discussed in Chapter 3 – survey questionnaires and interviews, structured observations – will, for the most part, be analysed in ways similar to tests. If the survey format is a Likert scale, statistics parallel to item difficulty and discrimination can be calculated. However, we will not necessarily be expecting particular levels of difficulty or the ability to discriminate between test takers. If the Likert scale or ordered scale is being used as a self-assessment (or other-assessment) of language ability, then discrimination becomes an issue, depending on the purposes for the assessment or its potential use for evaluation. If, on the other hand, the scale is being used to indicate opinion or level of satisfaction, we would not expect nor need the sort of discrimination required from tests where the objective is to make relative decisions concerning individuals. That is, we are using this survey information, in general, to obtain a measure of opinion or attitude, not of a pre-determined language-achievement goal or level of language proficiency. In this case, we would analyse the survey data by first calculating descriptive statistics: central tendency and dispersion (using a statistical package such as SPSS or a spreadsheet such as Excel 2000). For each item on the survey instrument, the mean, or average, score (or the median or the mode) and some measure of dispersion or variability such

Table 4.6   An example five-item Likert scale (1–5) survey response rata and descriptive statistics for ten participants

Participant	Item 1	Item 2	Item 3	Item 4	Item 5
1	3	4	4	5	3
2	4	4	4	4	3
3	3	3	4	4	3
4	5	5	4	5	5
5	4	4	4	4	3
6	3	3	3	3	4
7	4	4	4	4	4
8	3	3	3	4	5
9	4	4	4	4	4
10	5	4	4	5	5
Average	3.80	3.80	3.80	4.20	3.90
Standard Deviation	0.79	0.63	0.42	0.63	0.88
Range	3 to 5	3 to 5	3 to 4	3 to 5	3 to 5

Table 4.7   An example five-item alternative answer (with Yes = 1, No = 0) survey response data and percentages for 'Yes'

Participant	Item 1	Item 2	Item 3	Item 4	Item 5
1	0	0	0	0	1
2	1	1	1	1	0
3	1	1	1	0	0
4	0	0	0	0	0
5	1	1	1	1	1
6	1	1	1	1	1
7	1	1	1	1	0
8	0	0	0	1	1
9	1	1	1	1	0
10	1	1	1	0	0
Percentage 'Yes'	70%	70%	70%	60%	40%

as the standard deviation (or range, or minimum and maximum scores) can be calculated. An example of these statistics is given in Table 4.6.

For alternative answer and checklist survey formats, as well as most structured observation schemes, the data are usually analysed by calculating frequencies and percentages. In the case of a yes–no alternative-answer format, for example, we would count the number of 'yes' answers and the number of 'no' answers, and then express those totals as percentages of the whole. An example of this type of analysis is given in Table 4.7.

Percentages may also be useful for analysing Likert-scale or ordered-scale data. For example, it may be useful to determine the percentage of survey participants who answer with a particular score for each item. In the example Likert-scale data shown in Table 4.6, for Item 3, 80 per cent of the participants indicated '4' (disagree), which is the highest percentage answering in that category for any of the items.

For the ranking format, the method of analysis becomes somewhat more difficult. Rather than individual items, for which individual statistics can be calculated, the

Table 4.8   Example ranking format response data (five subitems)

Participant	Subitem 1	Subitem 2	Subitem 3	Subitem 4	Subitem 5
1	1	3	4	2	5
2	1	3	4	2	5
3	2	3	4	1	5
4	2	3	4	1	5
5	2	4	3	1	5
6	1	3	2	5	4
7	1	3	4	2	5
8	3	2	4	1	5
9	5	4	2	3	1
10	1	3	4	2	5

ranking format has subitems that depend on each other for their 'score'. In the example response data in Table 4.8, the numbers 1 through 5 for each of the 5 subitems correspond to a rank-order: for each participant, each subitem has its own unique number (rank), unlike the Likert scale or alternative response formats, where different items can receive the same number (scale rating or 0/1).

To summarise, or describe, these ranked subitems, it is possible to calculate average rank scores across survey participants, in a similar fashion to calculating the mean for Likert-scale scores. And a measure of dispersion, or variability, could be calculated as well. The problem is that the traditional measures of central tendency and dispersion (mean and standard deviation) are designed for interval or strongly continuous scale data, not rank-ordered data. It may still be useful to summarise rank-ordered data with a mean (or median) score. For example, in the response data in Table 4.8, on the average, survey participants ranked Subitem 5 as '3.1' on a scale of 1 to 5 (5 being most important). It may also be meaningful to describe the individual subitems being ranked in terms of their dispersion. In the example data, the range of rankings given to Subitem 5 was from 1 to 5 (note that the one participant who ranked it as '1' seems to have ranked all subitems in a fashion opposite to that of most other participants; this may be an indication that the participant 'reversed' the scale, interpreting '1' as 'most important' instead of the intended 'least important', for example).

In addition to providing summary information, these descriptive statistics for the survey and structured-observation data can be used to determine how well the instrument is functioning as a measure. For example, if a Likert-scale format has items that everyone answers with the same 'score', it is important to examine the item to determine whether this unanimity is warranted. It may be the case that everyone agrees perfectly on the particular item, but it may also be an indication that the item needs revision. Similarly, items that a large number of participants do not answer should be examined. Finally, there may be items where you are expecting agreement, or lack of agreement-based on prior experience and/or theory. If the item responses vary from those expectations, the items in question may need to be re-examined and revised.

The final check on how well these instruments are functioning as measures will come from a reliability analysis. For Likert-scale formats, reliability is estimated in the same way as for test instruments. Cronbach's alpha will be the technique to use, since it allows for non-dichotomous scoring; that is, it can handle the scale 'scores' as opposed to requiring a 0–1, wrong–right scoring. A note of caution is in order with survey instruments that have multiple sections that may be measuring different things; one section may be designed to measure attitudes towards teaching activities, another section may be designed to measure preferred learning strategies. Reliability, at least as estimated with internal consistency techniques such as Cronbach's alpha, is telling us about consistency across all items. With different sections of the survey measuring different things, we would not expect that consistency; that is, we would not expect our participants to be answering the same for items in one section as compared with items in another section. It would be more appropriate to calculate reliability separately for each section.

4.4 ANALYSING MEASUREMENT DATA FOR ASSESSMENT AND EVALUATION DECISIONS

The level of analysis described in the previous sections is primarily carried out to develop, or improve, the measurement instruments in question. Some of this information, such as the descriptive statistics, can also be used for the next level of analysis: making assessment and evaluation decisions. For assessment decisions, the focus on the individual means that we use the test-score data and non-test measurement as a summary of the individual's ability or skill in the area being measured. This summary – the score on the test, response pattern on the survey, or the frequencies in a structured observation – is used to decide something about individual learners. Have they mastered the course objectives? Are there particular aspects of classroom interaction that they are having trouble with? How do they compare with other learners (in a class, or some other group norm)?

For evaluation decisions, the focus tends to be more on the group. The test or non-test measurement data need to be aggregated and summarised in order to make decisions about a classroom or a programme. Is this class, on average, meeting the curriculum objectives? Are there particular aspects of the curriculum where learners are experiencing difficulties? How does achievement by the learners in this programme compare with learners in other programmes?

4.4.1 Assessment decisions

One of the first considerations in making assessment decisions is the decision type. As discussed in the previous chapter, these can be thought of as 'absolute' or 'relative' decisions. When making absolute decisions, we are attempting to establish whether individuals have mastered or achieved at a particular level for some language skill or ability. Mastery decisions basically involve comparing the individual score to a predetermined score level, or passing score, taken to represent the 'performance standard' that describes mastery (this standard is the assessment specification of the 'content standards' mentioned in Chapter 2). Such a performance standard is 'a conceptual boundary between acceptable and unacceptable levels of achievement' (Kane 1994: 433). In setting these standards, there is judgement involved. There is an entire literature on standard-setting techniques, which I will not be able to cover in this discussion. Suffice it to say that there are systematic procedures that have been proposed and used in the setting of standards for mastery decisions (see, for example, Berk 1986; Brown and Hudson 2002; Hudson 1989; Shepard 1984). In general, they all involve expert judgement on what constitutes acceptable and unacceptable levels of ability, and on the match between passing scores on particular tests and the conceptual performance standard that defines mastery. For example, in the Angoff (1971) method, a panel of experts rates each item on a test of the ability to be mastered, assigning a value that expresses the probability that someone who is a master (minimally) would be able to get the item correct. These values are then summed and averaged across the experts, and the resulting total score becomes the standard (basically, a percentage score on the test that defines the minimally competent person). This method, and others that rely on experts estimating the probability that test takers will answer items correctly, has been criticised and new alternatives are being proposed, such as the model proposed for the United States' National Assessment of Educational Progress (Pellegrino et al. 1999).

When making relative decisions, we are interested in comparing the individual learner's score to other individuals, or groups of individuals, called 'norm groups'. A representative sample is taken from the norm group – for example, from all students in a particular school district, or a representative sample across an entire nation – and group statistics are calculated. Individual scores can either be directly compared with the norm group, determining whether they are above or below the group average, for example, or they can be 'standardised' by using the norm-group mean and standard deviation to compute a new score on the same scale as the norm group. Another way of analysing individual test scores in relation to a norm group is to compute 'percentile scores'. The percentile score is based on a scale of 100, and tells you, with one number, where each individual student's performance is located in relation to all the other students in the norm group. According to Cohen (1994: 98), this can be done with a single classroom (or group of classrooms) of students, where the individual classroom (or group of classrooms) serves as the norm group. It is computed by first ordering the student scores on an assessment from lowest to highest. For any individual score, the number of students scoring higher than that individual is then added up. To that is added *half* the number of students who got the same score as that individual, and this sum is divided by the total number of student scores. The final product is multiplied by 100 to put it on the percentile scale. As a formula, this looks like:

Percentile Score (rank) =
$$\frac{[(\text{number of students above score}) + (1/2 \text{ number of students at score})]}{(\text{total number of students})} \times 100$$

Another decision which may be investigated in an absolute or in a relative sense, concerns individual improvement over time. Especially in a classroom-achievement context, we are often interested in how much individual learners have changed in relation to a particular skill or ability, or in terms of general proficiency. This change is traditionally measured with the 'gain score', which in its simplest form is the difference between two test scores taken at different points in time (for example, at the beginning of a period of instruction and again at the end of instruction). This may be more of an absolute decision – how much has the individual gained in relation to the language ability being measured – or a relative decision – how much has the individual gained in comparison with others in the same class (or other classes)?

Of course, any set of individual test or non-test measurement data can be aggregated in order to represent group standing or achievement, and therefore be used for evaluation decisions as well as assessment.

4.4.2 Evaluation decisions

The analysis of measurement data for evaluation decisions is generally associated with the quasi-experimental (QE) designs discussed in Chapter 2. The techniques for using measurement data for evaluation decisions presented in this chapter are for comparison between non-equivalent groups, comparisons between programme subgroups (for example, comparing survey-data responses between teachers and students), and within programme group comparisons (for example, pre-test compared with post-test for programme students).

4.4.2.1 Choosing measures of programme effect

When deciding on tests or non-test measures of programme effect, parallel to assessment concerns, the evaluator needs to be clear on whether the decisions to be made are absolute or relative. Generally, we need to know whether the programme effect, as represented by group scores, is meaningful in relation to mastery of programme objectives. Thus, as Hudson (1989) has pointed out, criterion-referenced tests (CRTs), and the absolute decisions in relation to the criterion objectives they are designed for, are inherently tied to most programme evaluation efforts. In order to make accurate judgements about programme effects, it would seem obvious that our measures need to be sensitive to the objectives and types of instruction being carried out in those programmes (what Beretta, 1986, has called 'programme fair' tests). This clearly calls for CRTs, with their focus on developing tests that measure a distinctly defined language skill or ability, and for evaluation purposes, the criterion being measured would be the instructional objectives of the language programme (Bachman 1989).

The data from CRTs can be used in both QE designs where there is a comparsion group, as well as in pre-experimental and *ex-post-facto* designs where there is only the programme group. In the QE case, problems arise when the comparison-group is receiving a programme that has significantly different instructional objectives. There may need to be two sets of CRTs: one for the programme group and one for the comparison group. When, as is usually the case, the comparison group outperforms the programme group on the tests designed for the comparison-group curriculum, and the programme group outperforms the comparison group on the tests designed for the programme group curriculum, it becomes difficult to make any clear judgements concerning the effectiveness of the programme being evaluated.

Another option is to use a 'programme neutral' measure, one that measures language ability more generally (for example, a norm-referenced test (NRT)). The problem with this option is the NRT's lack of sensitivity to the curriculum objectives, and therefore the programme's effectiveness in relation to those objectives. The most important comparison, perhaps, is the 'programme fair' one, or a comparison that uses the test designed for the programme being evaluated. If the programme group does not outperform the comparison group on that measure, it will be difficult to argue for the programme's effectiveness. If the programme group does outperform the comparison group on the 'programme fair' test, but shows no significant differences on the 'programme neutral' test, an argument may still be made for the programme's effectiveness, especially if the NRT's lack of relevance to important programme objectives can be demonstrated (via item-content analysis, for example).

4.4.2.2 Choosing statistical analyses: designs with a comparison group and post-test only

For evaluation contexts that have access to a non-equivalent comparison group, there are a variety of statistical analyses available. In the case where the evaluation team has only been able to gather test or survey data at the end of an instructional period, the analysis is limited to simple group-mean comparisons. This can be done using the 't-test' or ANOVA procedures available in most statistical software packages such as SPSS, where the test or survey data are interval or strongly continuous ordinal scale data (that is, the scores progress from low to high in such a manner that the intervals between each score are considered to be reasonably equal: a score of 23 is 1 greater than a score of 22, is 1 greater than a score of 21 and so on). Basically, this means that the data should have close to a normal distribution, with a mean score that describes the central tendency of the data, and a dispersion or spread of scores that allows for at least two standard deviations above and below the mean. For a more extensive discussion of the data requirements for t-tests and ANOVA, the reader is directed once again to Hatch and Lazaraton (1991) and Brown (1988, 2001).

The comparison being made with these statistical analyses is between the two group means (programme group and non-equivalent comparison group) on a post-instructional measure (test or survey). For example, the measure could be a test of language achievement, and a significant difference between the group means (with the larger group mean belonging to the programme group) would signal that the programme group had outperformed the comparison group. The lack of pre-test data, as well as the quasi-experimental nature of the design, means that our interpretation of this significant difference cannot unambiguously claim a causal connection between the programme and the superior performance of the pro-gramme group. The programme group may have been at a higher level of language ability than the comparison group before the instructional period began. There may be other, systematic differences between the two groups (for example, previous instructional experience) that could account for the difference in their performances at the end of the instructional period.

Where the test or survey data cannot be considered interval or strongly continuous, and where the distribution of the scores is clearly non-normal, the comparison of the two groups (programme and comparison) can be made using 'non-parametric' statistical tests. The non-parametric equivalents for comparing group means are the Wilcoxon Rank Sums and the Mann Whitney U tests (Hatch and Lazaraton 1991: 274–7). Like the t-test and ANOVA, non-parametric tests are available in most statistical software packages such as SPSS.

Another method of analysis that can be used where data are limited to post-test comparisons on non-interval scales is 'Chi-square analysis'. This is a statistical test that allows the evaluator to determine whether or not there is a relationship, or a dependency, between the programme and the outcome measure. This relationship is not a causal one, however. If the Chi-square statistic is significant, the most we can say is that there is a dependence between the programme (being in the programme versus being in the comparison group) and outcome or effect (scoring high or low on the test). In cases where the original measurement data from the post-test – test scores or survey data – do not meet the requirements of interval-like data, Chi-square is particularly useful since it works with frequencies derived from subgroups based on the original measurement data. The frequencies that programme evaluation looks at are how many persons scored high or low (or responded in particular ways to a survey) from each of the groups (programme and comparison) that have been tested. So the first step is to establish some way of categorising or grouping the participants. With a post-test of achievement, the categories could be various ranges of scores: for example 0 to 33 per cent, 33 to 66 per cent, 66 to 100 per cent. These categories would be crossed with whether the persons were in the programme group or the comparison group. Each person in the evaluation study would be counted in one of the resulting combinations, as depicted in Table 4.9.

If the programme were having a positive effect on achievement, then we would expect there to be greater frequencies in cell C than in cell F (and vice versa for cells A and D). Chi-square would allow us to say whether the observed frequencies were likely to be due to chance, or whether they represent a signficant dependence. Again, it does not allow us to say for certain that the programme caused the achievement, but it can be used to make a qualified claim about programme effect. In the case of the post-test-only design, above, the claim would be highly qualified, unless we had information to suggest that the programme and comparison groups were equivalent on the outcome measure before the instructional programmes began (that is, at pre-test time).

Group comparisons can also be made with survey frequency data. Responses to survey questions can be used to categorise members in the programme group and

Table 4.9   Frequency data group comparison

Post-test Score →	0–33%	33–66%	66–100%
Programme group	A	B	C
Comparison group	D	E	F

Table 4.10   Example survey Chi-square analysis

	Pre-test – 'Yes'	Pre-test – 'No'	Post-test – 'Yes'	Post-test – 'No'
Programme group	40	60	70	30
Comparison group	45	55	50	50

comparison group and then analyse the resulting frequencies using Chi-square analysis. For example, participants could be grouped based on how they answered a particular survey question or set of questions (yes or no, or Likert scale) at pre-test time compared with how they answered the question set at post-test time. For an alternative response survey item, answered 'yes' or 'no' – for example, a question such as 'Do you feel confident about your ability to hold a conversation in language X?' – this analysis would look like Table 4.10. A greater change from 'no' responses to 'yes' responses on the part of the programme group relative to the comparison group, with a significant Chi-square statistic, could be taken as evidence that the programme was having a salutary effect on this aspect (confidence in conversational ability) of the curriculum. Chi-square analysis can be done with spreadsheets such as Excel and statistical packages such as SPSS.

4.4.2.3 *Choosing statistical analyses: comparison group with pre-test and post-test*

With NECG designs we can choose between two basic analysis strategies: change-score analysis and regression adjustment (Judd and Kenny 1981:107). Change-score analysis refers to the comparison of gain, or the difference between pre-test and post-test scores, between the programme and comparison groups. One such analysis computes an 'effect-size'. Another technique that requires a comparison group, pre-test and post-test is the 'standardised change-score analysis'. Here, 'change score' means the same thing as 'gain score' in the effect-size analysis. One of the advantages of this technique is that it makes an adjustment for contexts where the groups may be learning at different rates (such as in language-programme evaluation settings where non-randomly assigned, intact classrooms are being compared). I have presented the details of these analyses elsewhere (Lynch 1996: 97–100).

The second major strategy for the analysis of NECG designs is 'regression adjustment'. Basically, this adjustment is a statistical alternative to randomised assignment to programme or comparison groups, which, as discussed in Chapter 2, theoretically ensures that the only systematic differences between the two groups at post-test time would be the result of what they experienced in their instructional setting (programme or comparison). We can approach this feature of randomised experiments by adjusting the scores for all students (programme and comparison group) at post-test time to account for pre-existing differences at pre-test time. One technique for doing this is 'analysis of covariance' (ANCOVA). Most statistical packages, such as SPSS (2002), can perform this analysis (see Lynch 1996: 100–3).

The estimate of programme effect that is produced by ANCOVA is affected by unreliability in the pre-test, or covariate. This can be compensated for with a reliability adjustment that estimates what the true score for the pre-test would be (Judd and Kenny 1981: 114). Another procedure that overcomes the reliability problem and increases the precision of the programme effect estimate is 'structural equation modeling' (Maruyama 1998). This is a complex statistical procedure for which specialised statistical software exists (Bentler 1995; Bentler and Wu 1995; Muthén and Muthén 1998).

Where appropriate data exist, the group comparison can be between the programme being evaluated and a 'norm-group' statistic, using the same techniques presented above. This comparison can also be made in a simpler fashion by calculating the percentage of programme group students at or above the norm-group mean. This norm group can represent various levels of comparison, from a representative sample of language students across a nation to a representative sample of students in a particular school district.

Rather than collecting data only at one or two points in time, certain evaluation designs call for 'longitudinal data' collection, as discussed in Chapter 2. Where the resources exist for this approach, the resulting statistical analyses can be revealing, adding the important dimension of trends and fluctuations over time into the evaluation picture. Although it may be more difficult to analyse and interpret these data statistically, they provide an important view for something as dynamic as second-language learning. One approach to longitudinal analysis makes use of the 'interrupted time series with comparison group', discussed in Chapter 2. With this design, the data gathered before the programme was introduced (the intervention period) is used to predict what the data would like if the same pattern continued after the intervention. In Figure 4.2, the data points designated by C (comparison group) and P (programme group) represent scores on a measure of language ability at the various time intervals before (Time 1 through Time 3) and after (Time 4 through Time 6) the programme intervention period. As discussed in Chapter 2, if the programme is having an effect, the observed data for the post-intervention measurements should demonstrate a different pattern from the pre-intervention measurements. In Figure 4.2, although the programme group shows an increase in its score after the intervention period, it is no greater than would be expected given the rate of increase in scores prior to the intervention (that is, if a line is drawn through the Time 1–3 points, and through the intervention period, it will match up with the scores at Time 4–6). In the example in Figure 4.3, the programme group demonstrates a larger increase than the comparison group following the intervention period, and this increase (at Time 4 to Time 6) is greater than would be expected from the Time 1 through to Time 3 scores, giving us evidence of a positive effect for the programme.

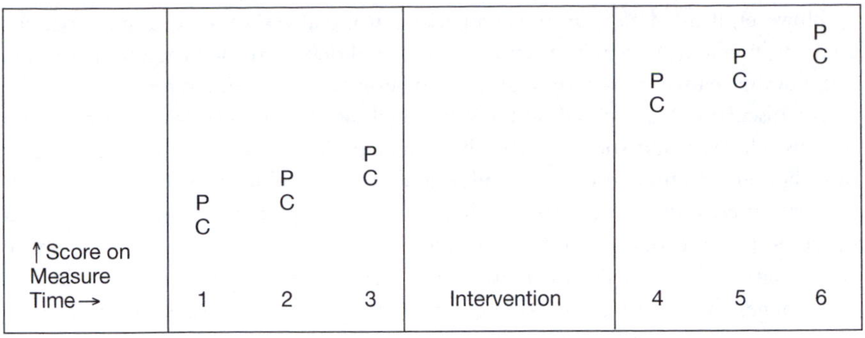

P = programme group; C = comparison group

Figure 4.2 Interrupted time series with comparison-group analysis: no programme effect

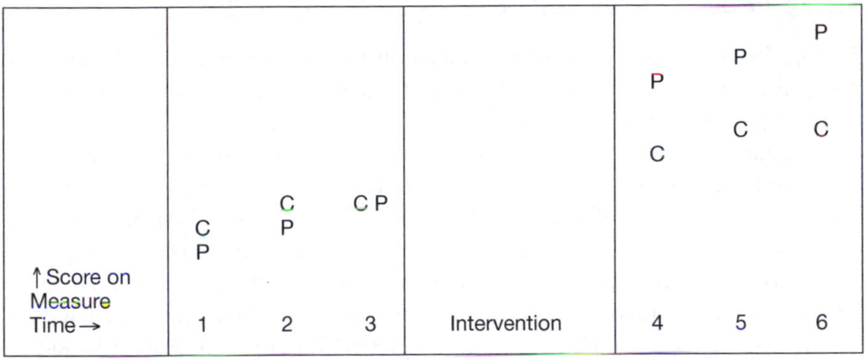

P = programme group; C = comparison group

Figure 4.3   Interrupted time series with comparison group analysis: programme effect

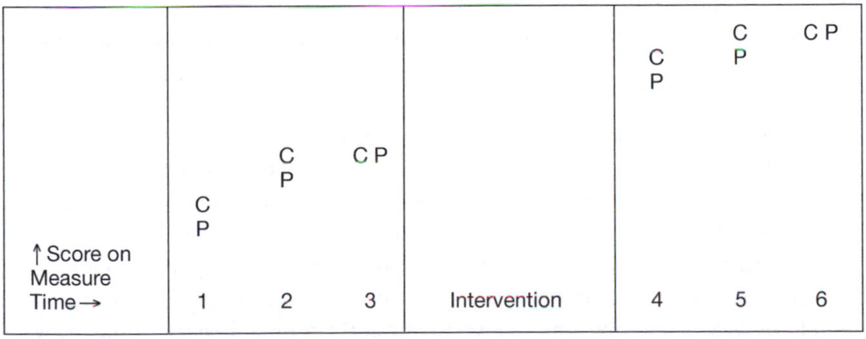

P = programme group; C = comparison group

Figure 4.4   Interrupted time series with comparison-group analysis: uncertain programme effect

However, if the data from the comparison group also shows a change in pattern after the intervention period, then we are less confident that the programme was the cause of the change in pattern. Figure 4.4 demonstrates this outcome.

My discussion has focused on the visual analysis of graphical data for time-series designs. There are statistical analyses that can be performed with time-series designs, but they are mathematically complex and were developed primarily for such activities as economic forecasting, rather than for group comparisons. The patterns of scores (pre-intervention and post-intervention) that were visually analysed above can be statistically modelled as 'trends', and 'intervention models' exist which look at the changes that occur in post-intervention trends (see Mellow et al. 1996, who report on the use of time-series designs with individual second-language learners; also see Caporaso and Roos 1973: 27–9 for statistical tests of pre- and post-intervention differences that take trend into account).

4.4.2.4 Choosing statistical analyses: no comparison group available

Perhaps in most cases, programme evaluation will not be able to make use of a comparison group against which to judge the measurements made with the programme group. Although it becomes impossible to make causal claims about the programme and its effects, measurement data can still be analysed in order to provide evidence for evaluation decisions. When pre-test and post-test data are available, paired t-tests or repeated-measures ANOVA (available as standard procedures in most statistical packages such as SPSS) can be used to determine whether any gains in test scores (or changes in survey response) are statistically significant. There are problems with interpreting simple gain, or change scores (differences between post-test and pre-test scores), however, and the preferred method of analysis would be to use 'residual change scores', which basically represent the difference between the post-test score and the score that is predicted on the post-test from the pre-test score using regression analysis (Judd and Kenny 1981: 108–9 fn.). The regression analysis required to compute the predicted values for the post-test scores is available in most statistical packages such as SPSS.

Where the measurement data do not meet the requirements of interval-like scale and normal distribution, the equivalent non-parametric procedures are the 'Sign' test and 'Wilcoxon Matched Pairs Signed Ranks' test (Hatch and Lazaraton 1991: 294–300), or gain groups can be established and Chi-square analysis used, as discussed for comparison-group analyses. While a significant difference between pre-test and post-test will not establish the programme as the cause of the change, it does provide a means of establishing whether the observed change is worth paying attention to or not. Establishing that there was a statistically significant increase in achievement test scores over the course of an instructional period is important and useful evidence when reporting to a variety of evaluation audiences. Similarly, with survey data, being able to report a significant change in attitude or self-assessment of ability over the course of an instructional period can be important evidence by which to judge the programme.

Another way of making comparisons when the data are restricted to programme participants is to examine survey responses from different 'programme subgroups', such as teachers and students. The same statistical tests mentioned above can be used to determine whether these subgroups differ from each other or have experienced change over time in terms of attitudes, opinions and perspectives on various aspects of the programme (such as the importance of particular curriculum activities). For example, it may be useful to know whether teachers and students differed in their response to a survey statement such as, 'Being able to use a variety of reading skills is important for academic success', answered on a Likert scale of 1 to 5, with 5 representing 'Strongly Agree', 4 representing 'Agree', 3 representing 'Neutral', 2 representing 'Disagree' and 1 representing 'Strongly Disagree'. Suppose that the teacher and student responses to this survey item resulted in group-mean scores of 4.5 for the teachers and 2.0 for the students. The group-mean scores could be compared for significant differences, using t-test, ANOVA, or the non-parametric test equivalents discussed earlier. A significant difference would be evidence that teachers and students disagree over the importance of reading skills in the programme, at least in terms of their relationship to academic success. If this were an important component (and belief) of the programme, it could help explain achievement-test results (for example, if achievement on reading was low, student attitude and lack of motivation may be an explanation), or suggest areas for further investigation and programme improvement (for example, surveying the students in more detail concerning their attitudes and opinions about reading skills; enhancing the introduction of reading skills in the curriculum with a clear rationale and evidence of its importance for academic success).

If survey questions have been designed to measure the 'need–press' comparison discussed in Chapter 3, these data can be compared across programme subgroups as well. For example, if the 'need' survey item discussed earlier ('Being able to use a variety of reading skills …'), had a 'press' version (one that asked about 'the emphasis given to reading skills in the programme instruction'), agreement between the two subgroups could be compared on this as well. It may be that teachers feel sufficient attention is being given, but that students perceive a relative neglect of these skills in the programme. The differences between the evaluation of need (importance) versus press (emphasis) could also be compared across the two subgroups. Similar comparative analyses can be made for programme features such as opportunity to learn (OTL) and programme coherence, also discussed in Chapter 3.

It may also be important to look at changes in attitude, opinion, or perspective over time. For example, it may be useful to know whether teachers and students changed their response pattern to a survey statement such as 'Correct pronunciation is essential for successful communication', answered on a Likert scale of 1 to 5, with 5 representing 'Strongly Agree', 4 representing 'Agree', 3 representing 'Neutral', 2 representing 'Disagree' and 1 representing 'Strongly Disagree'. Table 4.11 presents hypothetical group-mean scores on this item over the course of an instructional period (Time 1 and Time 2). The group-mean scores could be compared for each subgroup separately, using matched t-test, ANOVA, or non-parametric tests to

Table 4.11   Programme subgroup comparison: change over time

Programme Subgroups	Survey Q. Time 1	Survey Q. Time 2
Teachers	2.0	2.0
Students	4.5	2.5

determine change over time (for example, before and after instruction). Subgroups could also be compared with each other, using t-test, ANOVA, or non-parametric tests for differences at both Time 1 and Time 2. The teachers appear not to have changed their opinion about pronunciation – they tend to disagree that it is important for successful conversation – but the students appear to have changed from agreeing fairly strongly to disagreeing that pronunciation is important for conversation. Assuming the difference between the students' group mean at Time 1 and Time 2 is statistically significant, we can interpret this as evidence that the students have changed their opinion over the course of the programme. If the programme is emphasising speaking skills other than pronunciation, this could be interpreted as a successful outcome; that is, the students appear to have realised that their success in communication is not tied as closely to pronunciation as they thought before their participation in the programme. Comparing teacher and student group means at Time 1 and Time 2 would provide further evidence of this change: assuming that the difference in group means is significant at Time 1 and non-significant at Time 2, the students have changed their opinion to coincide with that of their teachers over the course of the programme.

When the survey includes 'ranking format' items, it is possible to make comparisons between programme subgroups using correlational analysis. Consider the fictitious data in Table 4.12, where the subitems refer to components of the curriculum that have been ranked in terms of their importance as perceived by the survey respondents (in this case, teachers and students). The question we are interested in answering is 'What is the relationship between the way teachers and students rank-order these curriculum components?' By computing a mean rank across all teachers for each subitem (curriculum component), and another set of mean ranks for the students, we have two sets of ranks that can be correlated to determine the degree of relationship.

Since the data are rank-ordered, the appropriate correlation to use is 'Spearman-rho', which can be computed by most statistical software packages, such as SPSS. If a spreadsheet software package, such as Excel, is used, the correlation will be performed using the Pearson Product Moment. Table 4.13 shows the correlation between the teachers' rankings and the students' rankings using the Pearson correlation coefficient, and Table 4.14 shows the Spearman-rho correlation coefficient for the same data. A negative correlation signals that the teachers and students are ranking these curriculum components in the opposite way: components (subitems) that are ranked high by the teachers tend to be ranked low by the students, and vice versa. The correlation is statistically significant at the level usually set for these studies ($p \leq .05$), which means that the observed correlation is not likely to be due to chance.

Table 4.12   Ranking-item data: teachers and students ranking curriculum components (subitems) in terms of importance

Teachers	Subitem 1	Subitem 2	Subitem 3	Subitem 4	Subitem 5
1	1	3	4	2	5
2	1	3	4	2	5
3	2	3	4	1	5
4	2	3	4	1	5
5	2	4	3	1	5
6	1	3	2	5	4
7	1	3	4	2	5
8	3	2	4	1	5
9	5	4	2	3	1
10	1	3	4	2	5
Mean rank	1.9	3.1	3.5	2	4.5

Students	Subitem 1	Subitem 2	Subitem 3	Subitem 4	Subitem 5
1	5	3	2	5	1
2	5	3	2	4	1
3	3	3	1	4	1
4	3	3	2	5	2
5	4	2	4	5	1
6	5	2	4	1	2
7	4	2	1	4	1
8	3	4	2	5	1
9	1	1	4	3	5
10	4	2	1	4	1
Mean rank	3.7	2.5	2.3	4	1.6

Table 4.13   Pearson correlation of teacher and student mean rank orders

	Teachers' mean rank	Students' mean rank
Subitem 1	1.9	3.7
Subitem 2	3.1	2.5
Subitem 3	3.5	2.3
Subitem 4	2	4
Subitem 5	4.5	1.6
	Correlation coefficient	−0.98
	Significance (2-tailed)	.004

Table 4.14   Spearman-rho correlation of teacher and student rank-orders

	Teachers' mean rank	Students' mean rank
Subitem 1	1.9	3.7
Subitem 2	3.1	2.5
Subitem 3	3.5	2.3
Subitem 4	2	4
Subitem 5	4.5	1.6
	Correlation coefficient	−0.90
	Significance (2-tailed)	.037

Table 4.15   Alternative answer item response data

Student	Yes	No
1	x	
2		x
3	x	
4	x	
5	x	
6	x	
7		x
8	x	
9		x
10	x	
11	x	
12		x
13	x	
14	x	
15	x	
Frequency of response	11	4
Mean score	.73	.23
Percentage	73%	23%

The magnitude of the correlation (.98 for Pearson and .90 for Spearman) tells us that the relationship is very strong: the high rankings for teachers are matched by very low rankings from the students, and vice versa. This would be strong evidence that the teachers and students disagree on the relative importance of the curriculum components, which could be useful information in making decisions about programme success and which aspects of the programme should receive future attention.

It is also possible to examine the programme subgroups independently using survey data. Individual survey questions can be analysed in a number of ways: calculating group means, frequencies, or percentages. For example, a survey question such as: 'Does your teacher correct your grammar mistakes in class?', with a possible alternative response format of 'Yes ___ or No ___', could produce the data set shown in Table 4.15. The analysis of survey data such as these allows us to decide whether or not a majority of the students perceive particular classroom practices in the same way. In the example above, 73 per cent of the students report that their teacher is correcting their grammar mistakes in class. This result would then be compared with programme objectives; if the programme is designed to focus on grammatical form and provide feedback to the students on their grammatical accuracy, then this would be evidence towards programme success. If, on the other hand, the programme is designed to avoid overt error correction in class, then the example data might signal a failure of this objective and suggest an area for programme improvement.

Single subgroups can also be investigated using 'ranking format' survey items. Using the example data for students presented earlier in Table 4.12, we can calculate a series of correlations, using the Spearman-rho statistic, to investigate how well the students agree or disagree about the ranking of curriculum components. The resulting correlation matrix is displayed in Table 4.16. Because none of the correlations are significant at the level usually presumed for statistical significance

Table 4.16   Spearman-rho correlations for students' ranking of survey
subitems 1–5

		Subitem 1	Subitem 2	Subitem 3	Subitem 4	Subitem 5
Subitem 1	Correlation	1.000	.040	.047	−.067	−.350
	Sig. (2-tailed)	.	.912	.898	.854	.321
	N	10	10	10	10	10
Subitem 2	Correlation		1.000	−.312	.610	−.432
	Sig. (2-tailed)		.	.381	.061	.213
	N		10	10	10	10
Subitem 3	Correlation			1.000	−.096	.583
	Sig. (2-tailed)			.	.792	.077
	N			10	10	10
Subitem 4	Correlation				1.000	−.444
	Sig. (2-tailed)				.	.199
Subitem 5	Correlation					1.000
	Sig. (2-tailed)					.
	N					10

($p \leq .05$), meaning that the correlations are likely to be due to chance, it is difficult
to interpret the results. Most of the correlations are small in magnitude (ranging
from −.35 to .61) anyway signalling weak relationships at best. When we compared
the teachers' mean rankings with the students' mean rankings earlier, the results
suggested that the teachers and the students disagreed on the importance of these
items. The separate analysis for students provides the important additional information that the students are not agreeing among themselves, either. It should be kept
in mind, however, that part of the failure to reach statistical significance and the low
magnitudes is the result of having such a small sample of data (only ten students).
Remember also that if the correlations are computed using a spreadsheet such as
Excel, the calculations will use Pearson correlation, which is not as appropriate for
rank-ordered data. Table 4.17 gives the Pearson correlations for the same data, for
comparison purposes.

Analyses of survey data on OTL and programme coherence can also be performed
on these single subgroups using these same statistical procedures. A more sophisticated statistical analysis of survey data, using 'structural equation modelling' for
simultaneously investigating both interrelationships between the survey-item
responses and relationships with other variables such as language proficiency has
been presented by Purpura (1999). With an 'interrupted time series' design, as
presented in Chapter 2, the same analysis discussed above for the time series with
comparison group can be conducted. Without the comparison group, we cannot be
as certain that the programme alone caused any observed change in pattern. It does
allow us to determine whether or not there was a change in the pattern of language-
ability development after the experience of the programme intervention. If there
is no change in pattern, the programme does not appear to be having an effect. If
there is a change in pattern, this evidence can then be weighed against other possible

Table 4.17　Pearson correlations for students' ranking of survey subitems 1–5

		Subitem 1	Subitem 2	Subitem 3	Subitem 4	Subitem 5
Subitem 1	Correlation	1	.261	−.149	−.071	−.716
	Sig. (2-tailed)	.	.466	.681	.845	.020
	N	10	10	10	10	10
Subitem 2	Correlation		1	−.470	.524	−.620
	Sig. (2-tailed)		.	.170	.120	.056
	N		10	10	10	10
Subitem 3	Correlation			1	−.427	.575
	Sig. (2-tailed)			.	.218	.082
	N			10	10	10
Subitem 4	Correlation				1	−.423
	Sig. (2-tailed)				.	.224
	N				10	10
Subitem 5	Correlation					1
	Sig. (2-tailed)					.
	N					10

explanations for the change, such as the presence of other factors outside the programme that might affect language learning (for example, the introduction of public television programming in the language being learned).

Another type of longitudinal analysis involves the use of 'panels', or 'cohorts' representing groups of students from the programme over successive instructional periods, or years. One technique compares the programme group against a norm-group statistic. This analysis is usually reported as percentages of students in the programme group who are at or above the norm-group standard (see, for example, Hess 1999). This standard can be determined as the norm-group average, or can be established using the standard-setting procedures mentioned earlier in this chapter. For example, Table 4.18 presents fictitious data showing percentages of programme group students who score at or above the group average for a norm-group representing ESL students across the state in which this programme exists. The longitudinal data represent the programme across five years, with each year representing the students' end of school year test scores. These data can be analysed to see if the programme results in achievement consistently over time, and if there have been modifications to the programme in particular years, how those changes affect student achievement. The example data depicted in this table indicate that the programme students are performing reasonably well against the state group norms, and that this performance was steadily improving with the exception of Year 3. The evaluation team would need to search for information about changes in the curriculum, or other events occurring that year, in order to explain the temporary decline.

In addition to longitudinal studies comparing programme panels against a norm-group statistic, panel studies can be analysed without a norm group using 'hierarchical linear modelling' (Bryk and Raudenbush 1992). Hierarchical linear modelling (HLM) allows us to compare the variance in measurement that is due

Table 4.18   Example longitudinal analysis: comparison against norm group standard

	Year 1	Year 2	Year 3	Year 4	Year 5
Programme Student Achievement (percentage of students at or above norm-group average)	70%	75%	65%	75%	80%

to individual learner differences within the panels (for example, particular years or instructional periods) against variation across the panels (in the case of successive instructional periods, this is across time), in addition to examining how measures of proficiency and/or achievement are affected by other variables such as changes in programme structure. The HLM approach was used by Ross (forthcoming) to examine how changes in programme coherence affected achievement across six years of a two-year programme (six panels, each with Year 1 and Year 2 students), controlling for pre-programme proficiency by using TOEFL entry scores as a covariate. This analysis used three hierarchical models: a baseline model that compares the six panels, in terms of their achievement in the different skill domains (Year 1 and Year 2 for: listening/oral presentation; reading/seminar; writing); a second model which added the pre-programme proficiency of all learners in each skill domain (the TOEFL as covariate); and a third model which added the measure of programme coherence for each panel. The HLM analysis produces an estimate of the effect of programme coherence, using the differences in coherence across the six panels, on learner achievement, while controlling for pre-programme proficiency. This allows the programme evaluation team to identify particular year and skill combinations (for example, Year 2 reading; Year 1 listening) where more or less coherence has the greatest effect on student learning. In turn, this can provide the basis for deciding where to focus time and resources on improving aspects of the programme such as coherence. The statistical analyses required for HLM are sophisticated and can be carried out through general statistical packages such as SPSS or with specialised computer software (for example, Raudenbush et al. 2000).

4.5 CONCLUSION

The link between language assessment and programme evaluation is perhaps most evident in this chapter. The test data for all of the quantitative techniques presented for programme evaluation come from instruments developed according to the principles outlined for language tests in the previous chapter. Instead of using the test or survey data for decisions about individuals, however, the scores are examined at the group level to make inferences about the effects of programmes.

Just as there are a variety of ways to analyse test results, there are a variety of ways to analyse programme evaluation data. Wherever possible, a multiple-strategies approach is advocated. When the context allows for the use of G-theory and IRT in addition to the more traditional approaches to test analysis, they should be pursued. Any programme evaluation that makes use of multiple quantitative analyses will provide stronger and more convincing evidence than an evaluation that relies on a single analysis.

However, knowing what the individual student or the programme has produced, in terms of a test score or a group-average score, will not always give us the information we need to make decisions. It will not always allow us to understand the process that led to those results. For a fuller understanding of both individual language ability and language programme effectiveness, we need to turn to methods motivated by the interpretivist paradigm. Approaches for developing assessment instruments from this perspective will be presented in the next chapter.

EXERCISES

1. The following data represent an item analysis (using the SPSS Reliability procedure) for an intermediate-level ESL class final examination. The test items are for the Reading Subtest, which has 15 items (ITEM 16–30). The column labelled 'MEANS', which is the item means, or average score for each item (= 'item difficulty'). The last column, 'C.I-TOTAL' gives you the discrimination index ('corrected item-to-total correlation').

ITEM	MEANS	C.I-TOTAL
16	0.500	0.267
17	0.819	0.332
18	0.750	0.041
19	0.900	0.135
20	0.955	0.172
21	0.750	0.041
22	0.932	−0.129
23	0.682	0.134
24	0.909	0.307
25	1.00	0.0
26	0.773	0.268
27	0.682	0.274
28	0.614	0.029
29	0.773	0.332
30	0.932	0.393

- What is the most difficult item?
- What is the easiest item?
- What item discriminates the best?
- What item discriminates the worst? (Do *not* consider Item 25.)

2. Examine the G-theory 'D-study' table below, and answer the following questions:

D-study (4 raters, 23 items)

Effect	Variance Component	% of total variance
Persons (p)	.580	87.0
Raters (R)	.057	8.5
Items (I)	.002	0.3
pR	.022	3.2
pI	.003	0.5
RI	.000	0.0
pRI, e	.003	0.5

- What can you say about the effect of raters and items upon persons' test performances based on this table?
- What do you think would improve the dependability of this test the most – increasing the number of raters or increasing the number of items?

3. Look at the following test scores, expressed in IRT 'logits'. Which is the person with the highest ability? Which person displays the lowest ability?

Person	Ability Score (logits)
1	−0.18
2	+1.58
3	+0.49
4	−1.98

4. Look at the following IRT item statistics, expressed in 'logits'. Which is the most difficult item? Which item is the easiest?

Item	Difficulty Score (logits)
1	+2.43
2	−1.58
3	+0.89
4	−1.06

5. Do the items in 4, above, 'match' the range of person ability in 3, above. Draw a 'map' which puts the persons on one side of a vertical scale of logit values, and the items on the other side of that scale:

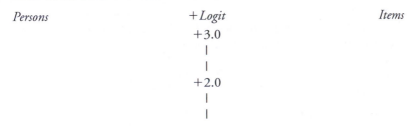

Persons	+ Logit	Items
	+3.0	
	|	
	|	
	+2.0	
	|	
	|	

Persons	+Logit	Items
	+1.0	
	|	
	|	
	0.0	
	|	
	|	
	−1.0	
	|	
	|	
	−2.0	
	|	
	|	
	−3.0	

SUGGESTIONS FOR FURTHER READING

1. Popham, W. J. (1990), *Modern Educational Measurement* (2nd edn), Englewood Cliffs, NJ: Prentice Hall.

Popham provides an introduction to basic testing concepts. See, in particular, the chapter on general item-writing guidelines, as well as additional information on standard setting, and criterion-referenced measurement versus norm-referenced measurement.

2. McNamara, T. F. (1996), *Measuring Second Language Performance*, London: Longman.

This book provides the best explanation of item response theory that I am aware of, as well as an excellent chapter on the models of language ability that are used by language test developers and other researchers.

3. Brown, J. D. and T. Hudson (2002), *Criterion-referenced Language Testing*, Cambridge: Cambridge University Press.

Once you have understood the basic idea behind criterion-referenced measurement versus norm-referenced measurement, this book will give you a detailed account of how to use the various statistical procedures associated with language testing. It provides the most thorough account of CRM to date.

4. Brown, J. D. (2001), *Using Surveys in Language Programmes*, Cambridge: Cambridge University Press.

Following on from the suggested reading for Chapter 3, I recommend Brown's Chapter 4, on the statistical analysis of survey data.

ANSWERS TO EXERCISES

Exercise 1:
- Most difficult item = Item 16
- Easiest item = Item 25
- Best discriminator = Item 30
- Worst discriminator = Item 22

Exercise 2:
- (D-study results) Raters account for more of the variability in test scores than Items; they are having a greater effect on the test scores than Items.
- Because the Raters are having a greater effect on test scores than Items, we would increase the reliability/dependability more by increasing the number of Raters.

Exercise 3:
- Highest ability (IRT logits) = Person 2; Lowest ability = Person 4.

Exercise 4:
- Most difficult item (IRT logits) = Item 1; Easiest item = Item 2.

Exercise 5 (locations indicated on the logit scale are roughly approximate):

Persons	+Logit	Items
	+3.0	
	|	1
	|	
	+2.0	
2	|	
	|	
	+1.0	3
3	|	
	|	
1	0.0	
	|	
	|	
	−1.0	4
	|	
	|	2
4	−2.0	
	|	
	|	
	−3.0	

Chapter 5

Developing interpretivist procedures for language assessment and programme evaluation

5.1 INTRODUCTION

Interpretivist procedures for gathering assessment and evaluation information have a natural fit with the formative purposes described in Chapter 1. As teachers seek to understand the language learning in their classrooms in response to curriculum innovations over the past two decades that have seen a shift towards learner-centred instruction and pair/small-group activities, formative assessment provides a principled and systematic way to get information that is directly linked to those teaching and learning activities. I do not mean to relegate interpretivist procedures to classroom-based assessment contexts alone, any more than I mean to relegate positivist measures to large-scale assessment contexts. In both contexts there is the possibility of defining the language ability that is being assessed (or the programme designed for that ability being evaluated) in ways that are indicative of one paradigm or the other. However, the most developed inquiry and thought about interpretivist assessment procedures has so far been framed within the classroom context and much of it in relation to formative assessment purposes (see, for example, Johnstone 2000; Rea-Dickins and Gardner 2000; Rea-Dickins 2001). On the other hand, some work is beginning to surface which links classroom-based language assessment to the larger policy arena (Brindley 1998; Teasdale and Leung 2000).

I also do not intend a limitation of interpretivist procedures to what can be called informal assessment. Rea-Dickins (2001: 457) defines 'informal assessment' as being embedded within instruction, and providing opportunities for learning. As she points out, this means that informal assessment may be essentially the same thing as good teaching practice. However, as she also points out, for informal assessment to serve a formative purpose (or any of the purposes outlined in Chapter 1), there must be an intake of that good teaching practice by the learners and evidence that learning has taken place. This chapter will present ways of gathering that evidence; the next chapter will discuss methods for analysing the information to make assessment and evaluation decisions. Although some of the formats or techniques may have been around for a long time, their use within interpretivist designs for language assessment and programme evaluation is relatively new. As Rea-Dickins (2001: 457–8) has reminded us, we still need to clarify what quality formative assessment (and other forms of interpretivist assessment) looks like and what constitutes evidence of learning within this perspective.

5.2 ASSESSMENT PROCEDURES

Although, in principle, all assessment formats are possible within an interpretivist design, in practice the focus is on the constructed response format discussed in Chapter 3. Since measurement, per se, is not a goal, formats whose main benefit is their ease of quantification (along with the concept of objectivity in scoring) lose their rationale. Instead, assessors and evaluators opt for procedures that provide the opportunity for the co-construction of meaning and understanding that underlies this perspective as a basic guiding principle (see, for example, Gattullo 2000: 280).

5.2.1 Portfolios

In almost any discussion of 'alternative assessment', or interpretivist assessment designs, the concept of the 'portfolio' will be central. This procedure, in general, involves the collection of samples of learner work (usually writing, but could include other forms of language ability such as oral proficiency or reading records), which allows for a longitudinal picture of student learning (Brandt 1998: 7–8). Portfolio assessment will generally include narrative descriptions or judgements from teachers, responses from parents, and suggestions for future work (Mabry 1999: 17).

What distinguishes portfolio assessment as an interpretivist procedure, however, can be found in the importance of shared control and collaboration in its collection, selection and reflection aspects. An interpretivist approach to portfolio assessment encourages the sharing of control between learners and teachers (and other stakeholders, depending on the context) over the specification of portfolio contents (collection and selection) as well as the criteria by which the portfolio will be judged (including reflection). One of the most important values of portfolio-based assessment is that it can act as a focus for community building within the instructional context and support curriculum innovation and development. As Hamp-Lyons and Condon (2000: 64) see it, 'the portfolio is a change agent, in and of itself', but they also remind us that the benefits of change will be realised most fully if the portfolio system is grounded in a coherent theory of writing (and, therefore, a clear and conscious choice about paradigm). This results in curriculum coherence, as discussed previously, which can be documented as evidence for programme evaluation.

In general, the portfolio procedure involves several stages. First, the basic parameters for selecting work to be included in the portfolio need to be negotiated between the learners and teachers. In certain contexts this might include other stakeholders, such as programme administrators or parents. Part of this negotiation will lead to the establishment of the criteria that will be used to judge the portfolio. In the next stage, the learner works towards creating the selection of items. To be a complete portfolio, there needs to be several selections of work and several drafts of each selection. To provide the kind of information needed by an interpretivist approach to assessment, there needs to be reflection and self as well as peer commentary on the drafts. In this stage of the portfolio process, we see the collaborative and co-constructed nature of the assessment. The various forms or commentary – self-reflection through journals, self-commentary and reaction to teacher and peer critique, notes of peer commentary and teacher reflection – will then be included as a part of the portfolio, along with the drafts and final versions. At the end of the process, the portfolio is assembled as a collection of evidence that provides a portrait of the individual learner within the learning community in relation to the language ability being worked on (note that terms like 'drafts', which apply mainly to writing, have been used, but that the basic procedure could be used with other language abilities as well). In the final stage, the portfolio is actually presented and judged. This can take a variety of forms; remember, however, that the criteria for judging need to be negotiated, with participation of the learners, at the beginning of the portfolio process.

5.2.2 Work samples

Portfolio assessment represents the accumulation of several instances of another type of assessment procedure, known as 'work samples'. With early childhood learners, in particular, it is useful to collect instances of language produced in the classroom or other language-use contexts (Wortham 1995: 185–6). Even when language skills are just emerging, such as with early literacy, work samples can be systematically collected from activities where children produce writing or pictures with writing (Turner 2002a, 2002b). Other procedures for recording work samples will be discussed below.

5.2.3 Performance tasks

A variety of tasks can be used to gather assessment information. The 'performance task' is one in which a problem or question requiring a solution is posed to the learners. This may be done individually or in small groups. Performance tasks are often designed to require evidence for planning, revision, organisation and evaluation of the solution constructed.

Most of the communicative tasks presented in Chapter 3 qualify as performance tasks of this sort. The task, whether it is labelled performance or communicative, is not inherently positivist or interpretivist. It is the overall assessment design, flowing from the choice of paradigm, that differentiates a positivist assessment measure from an interpretivist assessment procedure.

Let me try to illustrate this with two versions of the same task. In Chapter 3, I discussed the 'storyline test'. The task for the storyline test is actually a set of tasks united by a common theme, or story: writing a letter, writing notes, compiling a report, participating in a job interview, participating in a group discussion. In a positivist assessment design, these linked tasks would be carefully constructed and controlled by the teacher. Each individual would perform the tasks in a standardised way that is scripted by the teacher. Each individual would be given quantitative scores on each task and for the performance test overall. The scores would represent a measure of the individual's ability in reference to a language trait or traits that are presumed to exist independently of our attempts to assess them, like the individual's height or weight. In an interpretivist design using the same storyline format, the teacher and the learners would discuss the theme or story and jointly decide on what tasks might be relevant to pursue it further. The learners would plan, revise and organise their tasks, as well as establishing the criteria by which the performances will be judged with the teacher (in this way, the storyline approach can be seen as similar to a mini-portfolio). The performances on these tasks would be judged against the pre-negotiated criteria, and a summary would be written for each individual by the teacher, or perhaps by a combination of teacher, self and peers. The summary judgement would represent the individual's ability as a co-constructed interpretation.

5.2.4 Projects

Another assessment procedure that is similar to the performance task is the 'project'. This usually involves a task that is highly specialised, often requiring the integration of knowledge from different disciplines and, from a language perspective, involves the range of abilities and language modalities that the learners are in the process of developing. The projects are devised and carried out by students themselves (as individuals or in groups), and represent highly personalised goals and interactive uses of language.

As with portfolios and performance tasks, projects can span the formal-to-informal assessment continuum. In a curriculum that is designed to be project-based (Eyring 2001), projects as assessment can blend with instruction and appear more 'informal', as discussed previously. Projects can also be used in curricula that are not project-based, with the focus on assessment information, putting them at the more formal end of the assessment continuum.

An example of how projects can come into being is illustrated by Mabry (1999: 144) in the context of a high school with a special section that allowed students to receive credit towards graduation for individualised projects. Mabry tells the story of a student who was having trouble defining a school project that would relate to his interests, complaining that all he ever wanted to become was 'a heavy-equipment rental yard owner'. Of course, as soon as this admission left his mouth, his project was on the way to being defined! Teachers and fellow students worked with him on defining a project that included visiting heavy-equipment rental yards, interviewing owners and managers, researching business requirements, and talking with institutions such as banks to determine the necessary financial structure for planning such a business.

5.2.5 Simulations

Another type of procedure that is similar to the performance task is the 'simulation'. In this case, the procedure attempts to re-create, or simulate, the conditions and requirements for language use from practical or professional contexts outside the classroom. Simulations will vary in the mount of similarity to these extra-classroom contexts, and often make use of role-play techniques. With younger learners, the simulation and role play can sometimes effectively be done with puppets (see Zangl 2000).

Simulations overlap with performance tasks (and can also form a part of a project). An example of this is described by Stoller (1997), where the larger project involved researching local political issues through newspaper and magazine articles, writing letters to politicians and political organisations, and interviewing local political groups. The simulation was a political debate related to the local elections.

5.3 RECORDING ASSESSMENT PROCEDURES

I have emphasised the overlap and interconnection between assessment and teaching tasks and procedures. In the case of informal, formative assessment, the distinction between the two is particularly difficult to draw. However, one aspect of assessment will always occur, although it may not necessarily be present in a purely teaching activity, and that is the recording of the individual learner's response or performance. Some of the assessment procedures discussed above, such as performance tasks and simulations, could easily be seen as teaching only. What makes them assessment, in the way that I am discussing it, will be some sort of record of the task that will subsequently be analysed for the purposes of making a decision or judgement. Classroom instructional activities that focus on language and for which the teacher (or others) records individual responses or performances are examples of assessment in this sense. Rea-Dickins (2001) has provided us with a detailed description and analysis of this type of formative assessment, or 'assessment for learning'. This will be discussed further under Section 5.3.2 'Spontaneous speech sampling' below.

5.3.1 Recording classroom observations

One method for gathering information from interpretivist assessment procedures is to record the observation of the individuals participating in and performing these tasks in the classroom. Where resources allow, this can be done using videotape or audiotape recorders. In other contexts, or where recording devices would be too intrusive, pose ethical problems, or be practically unmanageable, the procedures can be recorded with notes taken by the teacher or other observers. In a performance task, for example, the teacher could take notes on individual students to characterise the language ability demonstrated in the completion of the task. The recording of classroom observation for evaluation purposes will also be discussed later in this chapter.

5.3.2 Spontaneous speech sampling

Classroom activities that are less complex than performance tasks or the other assessment procedures discussed above can also provide assessment information for recording. Rea-Dickins and Gardner (2000), for example, document examples of this type of assessment recording, where the instructional activity (a primary-school context with English as an Additional Language learners) is done in small groups with familiar objects (such as a potato, a lemon, a glass bottle) and the teacher circulating to ask questions of the students about the objects. The student answers are recorded by the teacher or the language coordinator as 'language samples' which become part of an ongoing assessment record. The samples are the words and phrases spoken by individual learners, such as 'it's hard on the outside and juicy inside', 'it grows on the ground', it's not waterproof', 'not natural X (error)' (Rea-Dickins and Gardner 2000: 233), and can become part of an ongoing profile for the learner (see the following section on 'Profiles').

In an example from Rea-Dickins (2001: 436), children in a similar school context to the one described above are in pairs, working on vocabulary items. The teacher circulates and asks for examples of antonyms for selected words, and the learners collaborate on the answers, which they write out on a small whiteboard. The teacher records their answers as part of the ongoing language-samples record. Note that in the case of group or pair work, individual learners' answers are socially mediated and co-constructed. This is in tune with the interpretivist perspective, but poses problems for recording: is the language co-constructed by pairs or groups recorded for individuals? This also has implications for our traditional notions of validity in assessment (which assumes the goal of measuring language ability as an independently existing, individual-internal trait).

5.3.3 Profiles

Another form of recording information from assessment procedures is the 'profile'. Unlike the language samples described above, the profile does not usually include specific examples of learner work or language, although as mentioned, these examples of learner language will inform the development of the profile. This record is written out by the teacher, learner, learner's peers, or a combination of the three. It represents a summary description of the language ability demonstrated in the assessment procedure. With further analysis (as discussed in the next chapter), the profile, or a set of profiles, can evolve into an assessment judgement.

5.3.4 Ethnographic assessment

Tarone (2001) has proposed an approach to recording assessment information that combines elements of genre analysis (Bhatia 1993) and ethnographic research techniques such as in-depth interviewing, observation and analysis of written texts and other language artifacts produced and used by the learner in the cultural context.

With this type of recording, it is assumed that the assessment procedure is an actual interaction between the learner and the cultural context of language use. In other words, the assessment is conducted outside the language-learning classroom. Examples given by Tarone come from studies conducted by teachers and teachers-in-development (Kuehn 1994; Mori 1991; Ranney 1992; Rimarcik 1996) in socio-cultural contexts such as medical offices, social-services agencies, and the use of automated voice-response systems (AVRSs). Each context involves the analysis of particular genres, such as the medical interview, the social-services intake interview, and listening and responding to AVRSs.

Of course, not all assessment contexts will be able to take advantage of the richness of the ethnographic approach to recording. Not all contexts will have access to extra-classroom tasks or interactions such as the ones mentioned above. Although the studies cited above were done by teachers and teachers-in-development, it appears that they were done as a part of supervised graduate-level coursework and research. Not all assessment contexts will be able to incorporate this type of research-and-practice synergy. However, the benefits seem clear enough to warrant mention and encouragement. Language teachers and applied linguistics departments need to be vigilant in finding such collaborative possibilities. It may also be possible to combine simulations (where the assessment procedure is carried out in the classroom) with elements of the ethnographic approach to record and analyse the assessment information (such as interviews with specialist informants from the context/genre being simulated).

5.4 INTERPRETIVIST EVALUATION PROCEDURES

Much of the information gathered from interpretivist assessment procedures can be aggregated to form a programme level set of evidence for evaluation purposes. For example, portfolios, work samples, performance tasks and projects can be summarised at the level of the classroom, or other group representing the programme. Procedures for recording assessment information can be extended for the purposes of evaluation. For example, observation and spontaneous speech sampling can shift from the individual learner to the classroom as the unit of analysis. Other forms of recording, such as profiles, can be drawn upon to construct the portrait of the programme that is necessary for interpretivist evaluation. And the ethnographic techniques mentioned in the preceding section are at the core of the interpretivist evaluation repertoire.

The following sections will focus on those ethnographic techniques for evaluation purposes: observation, interviewing, journal-keeping, logs and gathering documents from the setting. These are recognisable data-gathering methods for any sort of interpretivist research. Here, I will discuss them as procedures for gathering evaluation information.

5.4.1 Observation

An interpretivist approach to observation will differ from the observation procedure that I discussed in Chapter 3 in a formal and a substantive sense. In the formal sense, it will tend to be unstructured; that is, the evaluation team will not approach the setting (classroom, meeting hall, playground and so on) with a schedule or instrument that delineates the categories to be observed. The evaluation team will instead approach the observational setting as something to be explored, and the important categories for that setting will emerge from the act of observation rather than from a pre-existing list. In the substantive sense, it will view the 'object' of observation to be something that will be interpreted and constructed in the act of observation, rather than an object that exists independently of the observation that can be captured through the proper technique.

This is not to say that the evaluation team approaches the observational task as a blank slate, with no preconceived ideas or categories. By the time the information-gathering procedures begin, the team has established a sense of the evaluation audience, goals, context and themes. Indeed, this is what led to the evaluation design that makes use of the interpretivist procedures. The evaluation team has a sense of what is going on, what is at stake in the programme and with its evaluation, and these are a legitimate part of what shapes the lens through which they will observe. The interpretivist goal is, while acknowledging these pre-existing ideas and categories, to be open to discovering new ideas and allowing new categories to emerge from the observation process. These are no more (nor less) truthful or objective than the ones the team initially brings with it; being open to them is a key element of the interpretive and socially constructed nature of this approach to observation. They become part of the mix of information that the evaluation team will sort through among itself and with the programme participants and stakeholders as the interpretations become crafted into evaluation conclusions, recommendations and decisions.

Any interpretivist observation effort can still benefit from a guide, prepared in advance, as long as that guide does not become too rigid or constraining. I have presented such guides elsewhere (Lynch 1996: 109, 118–19); basically they involve the traditional journalistic who-what-where-when-how-and-why questions. In a classroom setting, for example, the guide would remind you to look for who the participants are, to try to identify roles for them, and to describe what they are doing (without jumping to an interpretation of the meaning of the actions). It would also remind you to note the physical characteristics of the setting, the time period(s), and to be on the lookout for changes in the pattern of events and interactions.

It is important to remember the interpretivist perspective, here, which means that there is no one, true, objective reality that the observer is trying to capture. The observer is interpreting and constructing (even when recording descriptions). As I will try to clarify below, the ways in which the observer records the observational period can incorporate a recognition of the choices being made about what to focus on and the relationship between description and interpretation, or judgement.

The procedure for recording the observation can include mechanical recording (video- and/or audiotaping) as well as field notes. The latter should probably always be used, even with mechanical recording, to provide context that the camera or recorder may miss and to ensure that mechanical failures do not result in a complete lack of data. Field notes for interpretivist observation can have multiple levels. In my own work and when teaching courses on evaluation and interpretivist methods, I have tended to emphasise the descriptive level of note-taking, which is reflected in the guide characteristic mentioned above: 'describe what they are doing (without jumping to an interpretation of the meaning of the actions)'. Implicit in this statement is the belief that we need to start with the descriptive before moving to the explanatory and judgemental. Of course, this may mask an essentially positivist characteristic: that there is something like an objective, neutral description possible in our observations. Rather than suggest a 'pure' description, I would prefer to see the goal as an openness to seeing the variety and complexity that any setting presents. This means being aware of the explanations and judgements that we naturally bring to our attempts to see and understand what we see. For example, compare the following pair of field-note excerpts.

1. The teacher has established a very good rapport with the students. The affective environment is very positive and supportive.
2. T asks S_1 about the homework assignment and jokes about her always being late for class. S_1 smiles and says that it was S_2's fault – he was asking her about the homework at the coffee shop before class. Most of the Ss laugh; T laughs and says, 'I knew this assignment was going to be confusing – let's go over it now and try to clear things up'.

In the first example, the field note-taker has jumped to an explanation and an implicit valuing or judging of what was being observed. The 'very good rapport' does this; the 'affective environment' is a pre-existing category that may have unconsciously guided what the note-taker looked for as well as what was seen, and 'very positive and supportive', like the 'very good rapport' may represent a variety of things that the participants in this setting may, or may not have, experienced. In the second example, the field note-taker is making the effort to describe what was observed. This does not mean there are no judgements or explanations mixing in with the description or influencing what the note-taker looked at, but it does represent an attempt to bring as much as possible into the record of the observation. It may be that, especially later, when analysis is the goal, the description of the 'T' and the 'Ss' will be summarised as 'very good rapport'. However, there may be other possible interpretations; in fact, the interpretivist approach would insist upon that possibility. Interpretivist observers, although not aiming for a supposedly neutral or objective view, attempt to keep their eyes wide open and to be as aware as possible of their move from description to judgement.

Interpretivist observers also attempt to document their own subjectivity and its interaction with the subjectivity of others in the observational setting. This can lead to another level for field notes, a reflexive level which can appear in a variety of ways in the observational record. For example, the notes from the second example above might include something like:

> My own teaching style tends to use humour a lot, and I feel predisposed to view the joking and laughter as a 'good' thing, and to assume this is somewhat conscious and intentional on the teacher's part. I'm also interpreting laughter on the part of the students as a sign of enjoyment.

This obviously moves away from the descriptive end of the description–evaluation continuum for field notes. However, the implicit evaluation behind some of the description is being made explicit, as a reminder to the observer and a probing of what is being seen and understood.

At another level, the field notes can include something on the order of 'memos to self', or quickly noted insights or ideas that arise during the observational period. Continuing the field-notes example above, the observer might record something like:

> [Memo to self: laughter may be signalling different things from some students: cultural differences? Follow-up informal interviews with several students and teacher?]

This type of memo will also be used during the analysis stages and will be discussed as 'analytic memos' in the next chapter.

5.4.2 Interviewing

As with observation, interpretivist interviewing is conducted in a less structured fashion than the survey-type interviewing presented in Chapter 3. It can also be done in ways that span a continuum from informal to formal. At the informal end are the casual conversations that can occur between the evaluation team and programme participants during the course of the evaluation. This type of evaluation information will typically be recorded as field notes, similar to those described for observation, as soon after the conversational interaction as is feasible. Of course, there are particular ethical concerns with using these types of interactions as information that becomes part of an evaluation or research report. The evaluation team needs to inform and receive prior consent from all participants for the types of data that will be collected and how it will be used and reported (including observational data as discussed above). The ethics of assessment and evaluation will be discussed in greater detail in Chapter 7.

At the formal end of the continuum is the interview that is explicitly set up with the participant or group of participants for the express purpose of collecting evaluation information. This formal interview can be conducted essentially in the same way that an informal conversation would occur, with no structured set of questions or pre-ordained agenda (other than to collect information of some sort for the evaluation). Of course, as with observation, the interviewers and the interviewees do not come to the interaction as blank slates. The interviewers may indeed have a pre-ordained agenda, or at least particular questions they are anxious to ask. The interviewees will have, most likely, some sort of script in their minds for the interview as a genre or event; they will have questions they assume will be asked, or even answers that they are anxious to give. A conversational approach to the formal interview means that no structure other than the typical structure that conversation, in general, and interview conversation (and expectations), in particular, places on the interaction.

Another approach at the formal end of the interview continuum is to use an interview guide, similar to that used for observation. Generally, the interview guide is a set of questions that the interviewers want to cover with the interviewees. For the most part, the questions come from the evaluation team's understanding of the context and themes that have surfaced in the programme, along with the goals for the evaluation. However, the questions are not asked in any particular order, some of the questions may not be asked at all, and other questions may be added as the interview proceeds. The interview retains a conversational flow, but the interviewers use the guide to begin the process, and to keep it going when the interviewees have nothing further to say, or are not generating topics of their own.

What will be most important for interpretivist interviewers is to establish rapport with the interviewees. This means genuinely valuing the interviewee's perspective, thoughts, opinions, feelings and knowledge. It also means being aware of the dynamics and power relations inherent in an interview. Typically this dynamic is characterised as one where the interviewer holds the power, and must find ways to share this power with the interviewee. However, as Scheurich (1995) has pointed out, this characterisation comes from a predominantly positivist view (or, as Scheurich labels it, 'modernist') of the interview and research. An interpretivist (or, in Scheurich's terms, 'postmodernist') view allows for there being different relations of power, relations of dominance, but also for resistance.

> Interviewees do not simply go along with the researcher's programme, even if it is structured rather than open. I find that interviewees carve out space of their own; that they can often control some or part of the interview; that they push against or resist my goals, my intentions, my questions, my meanings. Many times I have asked a question that the respondent has turned into a different question that she or he wants me to answer. While sometimes this may be an effect of misunder-standing, at other times, it is the interviewee asserting her or his own control over the interview. In other words, interviewees are not passive subjects; they are active participants in the interaction. In fact, they often use the interviewer as much as the interviewer is using them.
>
> (Scheurich 1995: 247)

Power relations and their role in determining the ethics of assessment and evaluation will be discussed further in Chapter 7. For the discussion here, I want to focus on the implications for the interview procedure. Basically, for the interpretivist interview, it is important to allow for an open sense of who controls the interview, to avoid the paternalistic notion that the interviewer has the sole ability to determine the agenda and must share, or give power and control to the interviewee. It is also important for the interviewer to consider the interviewee's perspective on the interview, to be aware of her or his own unspoken agendas, as well as the unspoken agendas of the interviewee, and to allow for a shifting between those agendas in the co-construction of the interview. This is not to say that the interview, from an interpretivist perspective, can be seen as a neat and tidy co-construction that, if conducted properly, will result in a clear set of words that can be interpreted unambiguously. Interviews contain more than the co-construction of meaning, including the possibility for resisting that co-construction, as mentioned above, and that this means the interview is 'ultimately indeterminable and indescribable' (Scheurich 1995: 244).

Although I allow for elements of indeterminism in the interview, as a recognition of the diversity and richness that will be part of any such process, my own position is that the interpretivist interview can ultimately be described, interpreted and used for evaluation purposes. The record of the interview, its transcript or other form of depiction, will be a co-construction that is perhaps inherently indeterminate (open to many interpretations), but its analysis, through procedures to be discussed in the next chapter, will move towards another level of co-construction of meaning for the purposes of the evaluation. This analysis will not result in some sense of ultimate truth about what the interviewee was trying to communicate in the interview, but will instead represent one possible construction of some of the vast array of meanings that occur in any interview.

Another issue related to the general notion of interview dynamics and power relations is who does the talking. In my own work and teaching about the interview, I have tended to propose that the best interview is one where the interviewee does most of the talking. The danger in this proposition is that it assumes that the role of the interviewer is to remain hidden, in the background. Scheurich (1995: 246) points out the positivist characteristics of this assumption. In the interpretivist interview, in order to recognise the dynamics discussed above, including the establishment of rapport, interviewers need to participate in the talking, respond to interviewee questions, and often share stories of their own. Of course, it would be less than genuine if the interviewer pretends that the primary purpose of the interview is something other than aimed at gathering information for the evaluation. As such, the focus needs to remain on listening to and understanding the interviewee's story, allowing for the possibility of the interviewee choosing to resist that focus (and this, in itself, becomes interesting and important information for the evaluation, to the extent that the interviewer can determine the motivations behind this resistance).

Recording the more formal end of the interview continuum includes the option of tape-recording. In general, this is something that needs to be negotiated with the interviewee, for basic ethical reasons, as well as for maintaining the interpretivist perspective. That is, the deciding factor in whether to record mechanically or not is what will facilitate the co-construction of meaning and the open sense of control in the interview as discussed above. Of course, part of this negotiation may be the interviewer's desire to be able to have as complete a record of what was said as possible, for the purposes of subsequent analysis. This, in the interpretivist per-spective, is just one of several competing desires present in the interview context. Even if the decision is not to record mechanically the interview, the interviewer will want to negotiate the taking of notes. Although most interviewees may expect this to happen, following the traditional script for interviews, it is important that the interviewer does not assume that note-taking will be unproblematic for the inter-viewee. It may also be problematic for the interviewer, in the sense that it disrupts the conversational flow, as well as emphasising the traditional power imbalances between interviewer and interviewee. The problem of note-taking disrupting the conversational interaction of the interview is probably more important than the somewhat superficial signal of power that the note-taking sends. The interviewee knows (or should know, if standard ethical consent procedures are followed) that the interviewer is going to use information from the interview – that is its explicit purpose. The lack of note-taking does not hide this purpose and the inherent power relations it represents. However, it does strengthen the interpretivist nature of the interview when these elements are discussed and negotiated up front; it may even be appropriate to ask interviewees if they would like to take notes as well (and to offer them a copy of the mechanically recorded interview).

5.4.3 Other procedures

Although observation and interviewing are the primary procedures for gathering interpretivist evaluation information, there are several others that deserve some mention. First of all, 'open-ended questionnaires' may be used when scheduling interview time becomes difficult. Basically, the types of questions suggested for inter-viewing above could be used as the items for this procedure. Often, a combination of interviewing and questionnaires works best. In my own work, I have done this in two ways. First, an open-ended questionnaire can be useful in generating some ideas to then pursue with individuals or groups in more depth using an interview. Second, the reverse can also be illuminating: the interviews can produce a set of questions to ask with an open-ended response questionnaire at a later date. In evaluation contexts where a prolonged engagement with the programme setting is possible, the evalu-ation team can also move back and forth between interviews and questionnaires. For example, an initial set of interviews may reveal several important questions that would be interesting to probe further. Time and scheduling constraints may make it useful to ask these questions with a questionnaire (allowing the participants some flexibility about when they answer, possibly even via email). Then, after beginning to analyse the questionnaires, it may be important to return to individual or group interviews to clarify aspects of the responses. This illustrates that with such an interpretivist design, the information-gathering as well as analysis stages will need to be iterative rather than linear.

Another procedure for gathering evaluation information is 'journal-keeping'. Journals can be kept by the evaluation team to record its emerging sense of the context and preliminary interpretations of evaluation goals. They can also serve as an auditing device that allows the team to trace the sources of various interpretations and conclusions. This can be useful in establishing validity, as will be discussed in Chapter 7. Where appropriate, participants can also be asked to keep journals that can be shared with the evaluation team, with other participants, or kept as a personal, dialogue journal with one evaluation-team member. Journals can range from a personal and unstructured format to a more structured response to topics or questions determined by the participants in advance (see Lynch 1996: 135–6).

An abbreviated version of a journal that can be useful in tracking major programme events as well as evaluation themes and interpretations is the 'log'. There is no set format, but the defining characteristics are dates of entry; dates of events (if different from entry dates); a listing of key elements such as participants, type of event, relationship to other events or themes; and a space for comments. Like the journal, the log is useful in helping the evaluation team to piece together different events, sources of information and interpretations in order to verify how it moved from the initial gathered information to the final conclusions drawn from that information. Like the journal, in addition to tracking the genesis of conclusions, it is a source of information in its own right, a place where the log keeper will record particular observations and insights that might otherwise get lost in the hectic evaluation process.

When the evaluation design is constrained in terms of time, making observations and interviews limited, the evaluation team can make use of 'retrospective narratives'. Asking programme participants to recall what the programme was like for them, after the experience has been over for some time, may be questionable in terms of positivist concepts of reliability. However, these recalled experiences may have a legitimate place in constructing an interpretivist account of the meaning of the programme. This can also be useful for getting background information about the programme prior to the time that the evaluation team was present in the setting. The benefits and controversy of using retrospective narratives are well documented in the work of Beretta (1990, 1992) and responses to it (Prabhu 1990).

Where time and resources allow, another interesting procedure is to have various programme participants take photographs (or make videos) of the programme setting. The idea here is to see what different participants will select as important or defining elements of the programme. It also allows them another medium for expressing their thoughts and feelings about the programme.

Gathering 'programme documents' is another useful procedure for interpretivist evaluation. These documents include official publicity flyers and booklets for the programme, published minutes from meetings, descriptions of the programme curriculum, correspondence (for example, between the evaluation team and programme stakeholders), and newspaper and other media accounts of the programme. Documents such as these represent multiple perspectives on the programme: the point of view of the programme administration, the original vision for the programme framed in the curriculum objectives, the ongoing articulation of programme goals and process by the staff, and the way the programme is understood by the surrounding community.

All of these procedures for gathering interpretivist evaluation information are important and useful. The ideal evaluation design will incorporate all of them; most evaluation contexts will dictate a design that includes only some. Whatever the constraints placed upon the design, it is useful for the evaluation team to be aware of the range of alternatives, and to continue to be open to the possibility of procedures that may present themselves as unexpected opportunities (a last-minute invitation to a programme meeting; a community forum on educational priorities; a poster in the school hallway) during the evaluation.

5.5 CONCLUSION

This chapter has presented a variety of procedures for doing assessment and evaluation from the interpretivist perspective. This perspective is still 'the new kid on the block' as far as applied linguistics is concerned. I say 'new kid on the block' not so much in terms of time of residence, but in terms of acceptance as *bona fide* research and practice. Although this is changing, the dominant paradigm and set of standards by which research and practice is judged remains essentially positivist. With assessment perhaps more than with evaluation, I agree with Rea-Dickins and Gardner (2000: 239) that we still don't know enough about how to develop and use these interpretivist procedures. It is my hope that this chapter will encourage you to use these procedures, when the audience–goals–context–design combination calls for them, in your own future work. This will make an important contribution towards gathering the full range of information we need to address assessment and evaluation concerns.

EXERCISES

1. Think of a classroom activity, involving some sort of task, performance, or project work, that you have experienced as a teacher or learner. What would you need to do in order to make this an interpretivist assessment?
2. Go to a public place, and spend 5–10 minutes writing down everything there is to observe. Next, choose three or four things from your list, and for 5–10 minutes take notes on what you observe in relation to those items. Were the items you selected observable in that period? Were there other things, not on your list, that occurred? Examine your notes carefully. Which things appear to be 'descriptive', which 'evaluative'?

SUGGESTIONS FOR FURTHER READING

1. Hamp-Lyons, L. and W. Condon (2000), *Assessing the Portfolio: Principles for Practice, Theory, and Research*, Cresskill, NJ: Hampton Press, Inc.
Hamp-Lyons and Condon present a complete account of portfolios and assessment. In particular they offer detailed descriptions of portfolio components and process, with examples from their own work.

2. Patton, M. Q. (1990), *Qualitative Evaluation and Research Methods* (2nd edn), Newbury Park, CA: Sage.

Patton's book is full of ideas for gathering qualitative evaluation data. The chapters on observation and interviewing are particularly helpful.

Chapter 6

Analysing interpretivist assessment and evaluation information

6.1 INTRODUCTION

The information gathered from interpretivist procedures presented in Chapter 5 is qualitative in form and can be analysed in essentially the same way, whether the purposes are assessment or evaluation. The methods of analysis come from the qualitative tradition in research (see, for example, Denzin and Lincoln 2000). What differs between assessment and evaluation is the decisions or judgements that are made once the information is analysed. For assessment, by the definition I am using here, the decisions and judgements are at the individual level and fulfil the types of purposes discussed in Chapters 1 and 2. For evaluation, the decisions and judgements are not focused on individuals, but on programmes (including, but not limited to, the individuals for which we may collect assessment information).

The variety of assessment procedures discussed in the previous chapter – portfolios, work samples, performance tasks, projects and simulations – and the additional procedures for gathering evaluation information – observation, interviewing, journals, logs, retrospective narratives, photos and programme document analysis – are recorded using a similar variety of procedures (profiles, observational field notes, audio- and videotaping). In the following sections of this chapter, I will illustrate a set of generalised steps for analysing this recorded information.

6.2 A GENERALISED FRAMEWORK FOR INTERPRETIVIST ANALYSIS

Whether interpretivist analysis is being done for assessment or for evaluation purposes, there is an overwhelming amount of information that cannot easily be summarised as with the use of quantitative techniques presented in Chapter 4. Instead, there is a labour and time-intensive process of getting familiar with the various sources and forms of data or information, sifting through in order to begin to find patterns, trying out different ways of looking at the patterned data, going back (many times) to the original information to check the emerging patterns and interpretations, and finally committing to a set of interpretations and conclusions.

Methods for interpretivist analysis have not tended to be articulated in as systematic a fashion as for positivist approaches to assessment and evaluation. This leaves those who choose an interpretivist design with a feeling of uncertainty, at times: 'Okay, now I have all of this information, what am I going to do with it? How am I going to make sense of it, and have something credible to say?' What seemed at first a necessary accumulation of data, which would provide depth and richness for the interpretations to be made, can suddenly seem like a curse, a sea of information in which the assessors or evaluators will ultimately drown.

The steps that I will outline in the following sections portray the analysis of the data (representing all the types of information gathered for assessment or evaluation purposes) as an interactive, iterative process involving collection, reduction, display and interpretations/conclusions with verification. Data reduction is the move from the huge mounds of data that interpretivist designs normally collect to a more manageable pile. This process includes selecting parts of the data to focus on, 'coding' or labelling the data with a set of important themes or concepts (either applied from theory or developed from the data itself), summarising and reorganising the data. This is part of analysis, not just preparing for it. Data display is the further organisation of the data into formats that help the researcher to see further patterning and begin to draw conclusions and make interpretations. This, too, is part of analysis. Deciding what the columns and rows should be for a matrix display, for example, involves making decisions about what the data mean. Forming interpretations, drawing conclusions and verifying them are steps that happen throughout the data-gathering and analysis process. To make interpretations about what the data mean, as noted above, necessitates finding regularities, patterns, explanations, as the data are reduced and displayed. Verification happens when you check back into the data to make sure that the display includes all the relevant information, when you check a preliminary explanation with the research participants, or when you ask several colleagues to code portions of the data to check against your own coding. Verification also involves looking for alternative explanations and counter examples, which means going back to the data again.

6.2.1 Step one: focusing

In the process of interpretivist information/data-gathering, you will begin to analyse the data in a preliminary fashion. Your original assessment or evaluation goals and questions may start to change, to be modified in certain ways based on what your interaction with the research setting is telling you. New goals and questions that you did not anticipate may also begin to surface. Even if your original goals remain essentially the same, you need to give yourself a way of starting, a focus for beginning to sort through the massive piles of data you're likely to have collected.

6.2.1.1 *Thematic frameworks*

One way of finding your focus is to develop a 'thematic framework'. Thematic frameworks come from an analysis of the themes that formed part of the earlier stages of designing the assessment or evaluation. Basically, a theme is an issue that has surfaced in the process of negotiating your entry to the setting and/or during the gathering of data. These themes represent a way of summarising what you know about your setting in relation to the assessment or evaluation goals, problems and questions. For example, you may have had a preliminary conversation with a school's headteacher in order to get permission to conduct aspects of an evaluation at a particular school site. As you explained your understanding of the evaluation goals, the headteacher may have raised an issue (for example, 'we expect a great deal from our students in terms of achievement') that seems important for understanding the setting and answering your questions. As you began to collect your data – for example, during interviews with the school teachers – another issue may have arisen (for example, 'the headteacher is out of touch with what's actually going on in the classroom'). These issues, as you begin to focus your research in the data-analysis stages, may become part of your thematic framework. For example, you may articulate the following themes: 'expectations for student achievement' and 'communication between administration and teachers' (or 'headteacher's understanding of the classroom'). By specifying the themes, you are beginning to analyse the data.

For assessment purposes, the thematic framework will often come from issues that the individual assessor or teacher has noticed in relation to the individual and her or his interaction with the curriculum. Rea-Dickins and Gardner (2000) provide examples of these types of themes and how they function as an informal thematic framework that the teachers use when analysing the spontaneous language samples they have collected for individual learners. Here is my reconstruction of what this type of thematic framework might look like, in part:

- areas of the curriculum that have language problems for the learners;
- the relationship between language-support coordinators (LSCs) and mainstream class teachers (CTs);
- differences in the way language is presented by LSCs and CTs;
- relationship of learning to the National Curriculum objectives;
- the use of different types of language (for example, imaginative, fantasy) by bilingual learners.

6.2.2 Step two: organising the data

Depending on your approach to data-gathering (and your personality type), this step may already be accomplished. It is always a good idea to take a second inventory, however, and make sure everything is where you think it is. Also, there will be particular requirements for organising the data, depending on the techniques for analysis you will be using. For example, if you are going to use computer-based data-analysis programmes (see Weitzman 2000), then you will need to get your data into the required electronic format. Regardless of whether you will be analysing the data with computer assistance or not, the following are important considerations.

6.2.2.1 Check for completeness

Make a list of all our data sources, by type of data-gathering and person or place gathered from (for example, Interview Transcripts: Teachers, Students, Other Staff) and then make certain that all of the things that you list are in fact there. Sometimes things you have assumed are in your files, on your desk, or other locations – for example, returned survey forms from all participants – have gone missing. It is also a good idea at this point to check that the individual instances of each data source are complete; for example, that a tape transcript covers the entire event (in my own work, I have discovered problems such as an interview transcript that had only one side of the interview tape transcribed).

6.2.2.2 Check for quality

Go through your data and make certain that all records (for example, handwritten notes for assessment, field notes, documents) are legible and that formats such as audiotapes are audible for transcription purposes. After transcription, check that the transcripts are legible and accurate (you will need to check against the tape-recordings). Note that not all tape-recorded data will necessarily need to be transcribed in order to be used in interpretivist analysis. For example, when the ideas being expressed are the focus, rather than the language used to express them, you may choose to work from the original recordings, transcribing only those portions to be used in reporting results. There are also a variety of levels and types of transcription that can be applied to the original recordings.

6.2.2.3 Create a system of files

It is a good idea to systematise your data into files in order to know where each piece is and to be able to retrieve any particular piece quickly and easily. As an example, in my evaluation of an EFL project (Lynch 1992, 1996), I had two major files: the 'ADMIN' file and the 'TREATMENT' file. The 'ADMIN' file had two subfiles: the 'Project Director's Log' and 'Meeting Notes. The 'TREATMENT' file had three subfiles: 'The Teacher Logs', 'Classroom Observations' and 'Student Interviews'. If you are using computer software such as NUD*IST or NVivo (QSR 1998, 2000), there are built-in organisation systems that keep your data in folders such as 'Commands' (mini-programs for doing analysis actions across the dataset), 'Database' (where the analysed data is stored), 'Rawfiles' (the transcripts and other data that will be analysed), and 'Reports' (results of analysis, saved in particular formats that you specify).

6.2.2.4 Make copies

Follow Davidson's (1996: 267) important laws for handling any sort of data: 'Law 1: Back it up; Law 2: Do it now'. There are countless horror stories concerning lost data. Davidson's laws use the language of computer-formatted and analysed data, but they apply to non-electronic forms as well. Have multiple copies of your data and store them in different locations (for example, one copy at home, the other copy at work or other non-home location).

6.2.3 Step three: coding the data

This step is where you make use of your thematic framework or start list to begin to 'reduce' the data to a more manageable size. 'Codes' are markers or labels that summarise how particular pieces of the data relate to larger ideas. It should be pointed out that some interpretivists and some forms of interpretivist analysis may argue against coding, or at least aspects of coding. Parkinson et al. (1998) present clear examples of where coding is useful and where it may be problematic for particular paradigms, purposes and designs. However, most arguments against formal coding apply to the data-collection stage, rather than the analysis stage. The problem with coding as a mechanism for collecting data, from an interpretivist perspective, is that it may shape and limit the information prematurely. With *a priori* codes determining what information you will use in your analysis, unanticipated aspects of the assessment or evaluation context will be lost. The interpretivist perspective does not want to isolate or constrain individual actions, words, or behaviours from their larger, dynamic social life, especially at the data-gathering stage. At the analysis stage, it is important to be aware that codes are tools for interpreting and understanding. They are not some sort of short hand for a presumed reality, against which the data are judged. The following procedure, then, can be used as a guide for the coding stage.

6.2.3.1 Review the data

To develop your codes, first read through all of your data, making notes about key issues, ideas and questions that you see in relation to your research questions. You will have a thematic framework or start list in mind, but stay open to new issues as well. Basically, this is the second phase of getting close to your data (the first phase is the actual data-gathering). One good source of these preliminary codes is any 'memos to self' that you may have recorded during the data-gathering stages. At this point as you go through the data, and as you develop codes and move to the next steps in the analysis process, you may also notice certain themes or ambiguities for the first time, and you may begin to form ideas for new codes or even potential interpretations of what you are beginning to see in the data. These should be recorded in a separate folder or space as 'analytic memos'. They are working ideas, which may or may not pan out in the fullness of your analysis. The articulation of these ideas can be more or less elaborate. Charmaz (2000: 517) gives examples of analytic memos that are several paragraphs long and are used to detail the fuller meaning subsumed by the emerging codes. Often the memos incorporate quotes from the original data, to keep the analysis closely linked to the source of its ideas. Sometimes they can be single sentences or phrases on the order of 'reminder to self'.

6.2.3.2 Decide on preliminary codes

The form of the code should combine brevity (that is, be short enough to serve the purpose of a time-saving data marker/label) and transparency (that is, be immediately interpretable and not be confused with other codes). From your notes that you take during your initial review of the data, and your existing thematic framework and/or start list, you can generate a list of abbreviated labels for the major themes and concepts that are relevant to your goals and questions. For example, some of the preliminary codes from the evaluation of the Project Oriented Computer Assisted Language Learning (PrOCALL) project (Debski 2000; Lynch 2000) were:

- 'COMPLIT' ('the importance of student computer literacy');
- 'SDISC' ('discourse generated by students');
- 'CREATIVE' ('fostering and enhancement of student creativity, communication and means of expression');
- 'IMPACT' ('impact of the project on teaching and departmental policy').

I should point out that there is no one form or type for coding. Some coding techniques use full phrases rather than words or shorthand abbreviations such as those given above. For example, in Charmaz (2000: 516) codes take the form of 'deciding to relinquish', 'accounting for costs', 'relinquishing identity' and 'making identify trade-offs'. Of course, these phrases could be abbreviated for use once the final coding scheme has been developed. There is value in elaborating the codes somewhat in the preliminary coding stages, to make certain that you are clear on what they are meant to mark in the data. For more on types of coding, see Strauss (1987) and Strauss and Corbin (1998).

6.2.3.3 Code (preliminary)

If you are using a computer application, your coding will be facilitated and you'll be able to keep the coded data separate from the original data. If you are coding without electronic assistance, you will want to make multiple copies of the original data before coding. You can also simulate what the computer applications do using simple word-processing applications. Whether using computers or not, what you are doing is tagging or labelling sections of your data in relation to your goals and questions. The nature of these sections may be fixed at first; for example, coding (marking via computer, or in the margins of a paper copy of the data) the text (transcript, notes, document) can be done line-by-line, assigning one or more codes to each line. As you get further into the preliminary coding, other segmentations may begin to make more sense; for example, in the case of interview transcripts, it may be more illuminating to code each turn in the interview conversation as a separate section. In any case, the goal is not to reduce each segment (line, conversational turn, or larger unit) to a single code, but to find all codes that apply. With the data marked in this way, you will then be able to locate all references to particular themes or concepts quickly and efficiently as you proceed with your analysis. With computer assistance, you can also quickly reorganise these tagged pieces of text, and match them with other coded pieces of text.

6.2.3.4 Get an external code check (if possible)

It is a good idea to have someone who has not been involved with the development of the preliminary codes, but who is familiar with the assessment or evaluation setting, to check your coding. One method is to give this person your list of codes, with brief explanations for each, along with a portion of your data (10–20 per cent will do). The purpose of this check, from the interpretivist perspective, is not to demonstrate the reliability of your coding. Remember that the codes are being used as tools of interpretation, and not as representations of an external reality. The coding check is a means of understanding your data more fully. Disagreements between your coding and the coding of your external checker will not necessarily be evidence of unreliability, at least from the interpretivist perspective. You may be disagreeing for all the right reasons. Where there are differences in the way the codes are being applied, this information can help you to revise your codes, to develop new codes, to arrive at multiple perspectives on the same event, or to uncover new questions that need to be addressed in your analysis.

6.2.3.5 Revise codes

In light of the external check, and any discoveries or new ideas that surface during the preliminary coding stage, the original codes will need to be revised. You don't necessarily need to complete coding all the data before you revise the codes. The following are examples of how some of the previously mentioned PrOCALL codes were revised.

- 'COMPLIT': understanding of this code was revised: ('the importance of student computer literacy (presence or deficit), in terms of its impact on multi-media task-oriented (PrOCALL) language teaching and learning');
- 'SDISC': this code was dropped (overlapped too much with another code, 'TL USE' – patterns of target language use);
- 'CREATIVE': understanding of this code was revised: ('fostering and enhancement of student creativity, communication and means of expression through PrOCALL; evidence of creating MM texts (beyond written essays)');
- 'StuLL': this code was added: ('student views on Language Learning (including differences with PrOCALL learning goals and philosophy)').

6.2.3.6 Code (iterative with code revision, return to previous coded data)

Once the codes have been revised, you need to go back to the data and recode all (if you have preliminarily coded the entire dataset) or that portion previously coded and then complete the coding of all data. It may be that in later stages of analysis, new themes or ideas emerge that are related to existing codes but somewhat different. Even in the preliminary coding stages, new ideas and themes suggest themselves. Using line-by-line coding, for example, Charmaz points out that the process 'keeps us thinking about what meanings we make of our data, asking ourselves questions of it, and pinpointing gaps and leads in it to focus on during subsequent data collection' (Charmaz 2000: 515). Thus, the iterative nature of interpretivist analysis means that the coding stage can send us back to the data-gathering stage, as well as back to the existing data. This is a principled revisiting of data-gathering, what Charmaz calls 'theoretical sampling' (p. 519), with the goal of filling in gaps that have been noticed during coding and extending our understanding of the 'theory', or construction, that is emerging in the analysis. In the later stages of data analysis, it may not be productive to recode the entire dataset, but simply use the existing codes as markers to find the relevant parts of the data that need to be reconsidered in light of the new themes and ideas that have surfaced during the coding and subsequent theoretical sampling.

6.2.4 Step four: classifying and reducing the data

After coding the data, you are in a position to sort it in various ways. For example, you can locate all the instances with a particular code and look at them. Or you can locate the intersection of two codes; for example, using the example codes above from the PrOCALL evaluation, you could look at all the instances in the data that were coded as both 'CREATIVE' and 'TLU'. You can also sort your data in a combination of codes and data sources; for example, you can look at all instances in the student-interview data that were coded 'TLU'.

In part, you are looking for ways of grouping, or classifying your data in order to begin to make sense of it. This is also a continuation of the data reduction that began in the coding stage. You are also attempting to find ways of accommodating the various perspectives, and voices, that exist in an assessment or evaluation context. Looking at the same issue or event from these different points of view, as represented in the data, is fundamental to this classification and reduction stage.

6.2.4.1 Experiment with various classification systems

Your thematic framework or start list can be helpful as it was with creating codes in the previous step. To create a classification system, you need to order your themes or codes from your framework or list in some systematic way. By grouping themes or codes together, you are creating meaningful categories for your analysis (and 'reducing' the data from a larger set of themes/codes to a smaller set). For example, in my evaluation of an EFL programme (Lynch 1992, 1996), I found there were three main categories in the thematic framework and coding:

- 'PROC' (= 'process': activities, practices, methodology);
- 'STRUCT' (= 'structure': setting, organisation, goals/objectives);

- 'RELATs' (= 'relations': social climate, attitudes, motivation, perceptions/ judgements).

Another approach to classifying is to develop a *typology*. For example, in her Ph.D. dissertation, Kathi Bailey (1982) classified the teaching assistants she was investigating into five types (with a category of 'others' for the few that did not fit any particular type). The following list summarises the characteristics of her typology:

- Active Unintelligible: (only non-native speakers) physically active, fast-talking, knowledgeable, but unintelligible;
- Mechanical Problem-Solver: competent in subject matter, able to solve and explain students' homework problems and conduct labs, but relatively passive and quiet;
- Knowledgeable Helpers/Casual Friends: competent, like Types I and II, but also demonstrated purposeful teaching behaviours (explanation, clarification, paraphrasing, demonstrating) with a helpful, friendly, but 'business-like' tone;
- Entertaining Allies: (only native-speakers) competent, like Types I–III, but used *humour* consistently and actively in the classroom;
- Inspiring Cheerleaders: (both taught 8.00 a.m. classes) skilful, competent and serious teaching with classrooms characterised by high level of positive affect, consistent and active use of students' names and 'bonding' behaviours (use of 'we', 'us'; praising, encouragement, valuing students as individuals).

6.2.4.2 Experiment with various data displays

In Miles and Huberman (1994), there are many examples of what they call 'data displays', or ways of organising to look for trends and patterns that will help you analyse your data and answer your assessment or evaluation questions. Some examples of data displays are the 'event listing' (Miles and Huberman 1994: 112), where you organise excerpts/paraphrases from the data by time periods. These time periods are usually displayed as columns in the matrix and can intersect with the perspectives of various participants or other sources of data, forming the rows.

Another example of a data display is the 'thematic conceptual matrix', where you organise excerpts/paraphrases from data by themes. This will be done after you've attempted to organise your initial themes into a classification system of some sort, and you have a clear understanding of how they can be displayed as a matrix of intersecting columns and rows. For example, in the PrOCALL evaluation, I created a theme-by-perspective display, using excerpts from the student interviews where they talk about the use of the target language, coded TLUse (see Table 6.1).

Using qualitative data-analysis computer applications such as NUD*IST, you can call up all references to a particular word or phrase (can be an important 'theme') for particular data sources. For example, in the PrOCALL evaluation, I was able to search for all references to 'learn' by students, in an effort to display the range of perspectives on what makes a successful language class (see Table 6.2). Note that these same displays could be used for individual assessment purposes as well.

Table 6.1   Theme-by-perspective matrix (partial): PrOCALL project evaluation

Language/Student	Target Language Use (TLUse)
German	
Annette	We contacted a few universities in Gemany and got them to send their opinions of the Green Party … and they responded, some in German…and we wrote back in German … If I'm just on the Internet or e-mailing I write what I think is German and I can only correct myself to a point because I don't get other people to review it … I write emails anyway to friends in Germany …
Donald	The whole class was in German. We used German 95% of the time … To talk with the tutor, you speak in German, you don't have to, but most of the time you do. With my partner, we discussed everything in German – which images we should use, what changes to this paragraph had to be made, which sites were good, what colour background, everything like that. All that was in German.
Japanese	
Kylie	When we were talking to the teacher we spoke in Japanese but when L. did the demonstrations all the explanations were in English … We might talk to our classmates more in English because we can communicate better in English than in Japanese and it's difficult explaining in Japanese. So most of the time we spoke English because we didn't want to lose any vital information talking in Japanese.
…	…

Table 6.2   Example string search (partial) for 'learn' by student: PrOCALL project evaluation

Kylie (Japanese): I think that the way I learn Japanese is through reading texts and learning phrases and, from the text, trying to read difficult kenjis and things like that, but for making a web page I used the skills I already had and was just writing from there and I wasn't reading anything new … I didn't really feel I gained a lot about [Kylie named a Japanese artist they were studying here] … well, maybe I know how to read someone's name, but I'd say that would be about it. I don't really think that it has played a significant role in my Japanese learning.

Kylie (Japanese): It may be that I don't recognise it [interesting work done in Japanese] myself because even when I was in Japan for a year and I came back my parents told me my Japanese had improved but I didn't really think that, so that might be the same case for this.

Annette (German): I learned very little language. You'd pick up some vocabulary to express yourself in computer language, but that could be done in a class, it doesn't require a whole semester course, although it is fun in learning how to use Claris Works. I was just really disappointed because I only have 5 hours contact with German, out of uni I don't unless I'm reading, and I'd like to utilise my hours to learn some German and have someone that obviously knows the language and I can talk to and communicate with and pick up bits but there was very little communication.

…

6.2.5 Stage five: interpreting the data

You will already have begun to interpret the data in the act of coding and classifying/ reducing the data. These initial interpretations about what is important, how themes and issues are related to each other, need to be looked at more carefully and systematically for the larger patterns and trends that they can suggest. This step, then, involves revisiting your classification systems and displays.

6.2.5.1 Review any classification system or typology that you've constructed

Are these the major relationships in your data? Have you adequately portrayed your data in your typology? Review the classification systems for patterns (for example, shared characteristics across types, interactions with types and other data categories); this may influence the structure or restructuring of data displays. In evaluation contexts, you can write profiles (or use existing ones from assessment recording) for your participants, or key individuals, based on your typology; these may be important for communicating your interpretations and answers to your research questions, in the sense of giving your audience a fuller understanding of the research participants.

In assessment contexts, you may already have recorded information for individual learners in the form of profiles. Where multiple profiles have been recorded, you can synthesise a master profile for the individual learner. If only one profile has been recorded for the learner in relation to the assessment goal or question, this profile can be elaborated or revised in relation to the learner typology that you are beginning to create for the classroom or group of learners as a whole.

6.2.5.2 Scan the data displays that you've constructed

Are there patterns (for example, similarities and differences across cells in matrix)? Are there mostly positive or negative references for particular themes, from particular participant categories? Do the references to particular themes change over time? Do particular participant categories use different ways of referring to particular themes? Look at how one column in your matrix may have commonalities (or differences) with another column. For example, in my evaluation of an EFL programme (Lynch 1992, 1996), when analysing a data display that tracked changes in the dynamics of the setting, I noticed that most of the entries in the matrix column representing 'change/resolution' were types of procedures, and that 'team teaching' was a common solution for many problems. This procedure was a repeated element in the matrix, at times becoming an entry in the 'problems' column. As a 'resolution' that led to other problems, it was identified as an important aspect of the programme's dynamics. Another repeated concept in the matrix was 'lack': lack of support, classrooms, attendance, language proficiency. This may seem like a predictable element for most programmes, but it became an important aspect of the interpretation and analysis of these data.

6.2.5.3 Formulate explanations for patterns

Using your growing understanding of the assessment or evaluation context, and growing familiarity with your data, you will begin to explain the patterns you have found in your review of the classification systems and data displays. Using the previous example of the repeated concept of 'lack': most of the 'lack' could be explained as a 'mismatch between expectations and reality'. The programme students were expecting a typical EFL class that taught the four skills (listening, reading, speaking and writing), rather than the curriculum's focus on specific-purpose reading skills; the programme teachers were expecting students with low-intermediate language proficiency, enough classrooms for small class sizes, and unconditional support from the host institution, none of which proved to be present for this context.

As another example, in the PrOCALL evaluation (Lynch 2000), several preliminary explanations or interpretations in relation to one of the general evaluation goals ('determining the appropriateness and likelihood of success in using PrOCALL for specific modern languages') were developed:

- There is a threshold level of computer skills that can lead to greater success (as indicated in the data by positive comments from students, teachers and administrators) for the PrOCALL approach.
- There may be a language-skills threshold necessary for successful use of PrOCALL (related to first interpretation). Furthermore, this may be different for different languages; for example, there may be a higher language-skills threshold necessary for character-based languages such as Japanese and Chinese.
- Many students are positively motivated by the 'dual benefits' of language and multi-media knowledge and experience provided by PrOCALL.
- The biggest obstacle to success in the PrOCALL approach may be its methodological differences with traditional, teacher-centred language pedagogy. This may interact with the second bullet point, above.
- There are technical problems associated with particular languages that need to be addressed in order for a PrOCALL-type approach to be successful. For example, technical requirements for character input on the Web argue against tasks that rely too heavily on text input, which may make the development of writing skills more difficult for these languages in the PrOCALL approach.

6.2.5.4 Validate/verify explanations

There are different frameworks that you will appeal to for establishing the validity of your findings from qualitative analysis, depending on the paradigm you are working within. Even within a positivist approach such things as the use of multiple sources (persons and data-collection types), searching for rival explanations, keeping a systematic log or 'audit' of how you moved from data to interpretations to conclusions are warranted. However, there are validity frameworks that have been established for interpretivist analysis in particular. I will discuss this in more detail in the next chapter.

6.2.5.5 *Formulate conclusions for reporting on goals or questions*

After validation efforts, you are faced with committing to a conclusion of some sort. This may be entirely your own conclusion, as assessor or evaluator, to make, or it may be made in collaboration with other participants and stakeholders. I will discuss these collaborative efforts at conclusion making further in the next chapter. The following are two examples of conclusions reached for the PrOCALL evaluation. They represent primarily my own conclusions (Lynch 2000), although I collaborated closely with other programme participants, in particular the project director (Debski 2000).

- Preparing students with basic computer skills and beginning at higher levels of language instruction/proficiency (especially Japanese and Chinese) may improve the success of the PrOCALL-type approach.
- PrOCALL provides students with a motivating and authentic language-learning environment, but a balance must be struck between activities that focus on the technology and ones that focus on language-learning opportunities.

6.3 CONCLUSION

The generalised set of steps for interpretivist analysis I have presented are, of course, only one way of approaching the task. Unlike the positivist procedures presented in Chapter 4, interpretivist approaches are more open-ended and capable of being adapted and modified in ways that suit different assessment and evaluation contexts. This open-endedness is both the strength and weakness of interpretivist analysis. It is a strength because it allows for creativity and responsiveness to context; it is a weakness because it lacks the clarity that would make us feel more certain and confident as we proceed through the analysis stage. Hopefully, the generalised steps of this chapter provide at least some clarity to guide your journey through the data en route to assessment and evaluation conclusions.

Within the interpretivist perspective as I have outlined it for this book, there are different levels of prescriptiveness concerning methods of analysis. The set of generalised steps used in this chapter represent a sort of middle ground, midway between seeing data as instantiations of a social reality that can be known (such as the constructivist-grounded theory approach defined by Charmaz 2000) and seeing data as indeterminate in relation to an unresolvably ambiguous social reality (such as the postmodernist approach as defined by Scheurich 1995). The tension between these two extremes underscores one of the fundamental problems posed by the interpretivist paradigm when being used for language assessment and evaluation purposes: how do we analyse information about something as dynamic and fluid as language (using language to do so) in such a way as to be true to its ambiguities and indeterminacies while at the same time being able to make a decision or judgement about it? How do we end up with something to say (with confidence)? One way of dealing with this tension is to see different dimensions to the assessment and evaluation activity. One dimension is understanding and explaining. In this dimension, the interpretivist paradigm encourages us to be open to ambiguity and indeterminacy. Another dimension is producing or reporting. In this dimension, even within the most radical interpretivist approaches, we have to commit ourselves to a decision or judgement (see, for comparison, Pearce 1995: 106).

EXERCISES

1. Using your notes from Chapter 5, Exercise 2 (or any set of observation notes, or other qualitative data that you can access), develop a set of codes. Code your notes and evaluate the degree to which they help you to reduce the data.
2. Using the results from Exercise 1, above, develop a 'data display'. What does this display suggest in the way of interpreting your data?

SUGGESTIONS FOR FURTHER READING

1. Moss, P. A., J. S. Beck, C. Ebbs, B. Matson, J. Muchmore, D. Steele, C. Taylor and R. Herter (1992), 'Portfolios, accountability, and an interpretive approach to validity', *Educational Measurement: Issues and Practice*, 11(3), 12–21.

This article describes the use of interpretivist assessment principles in relation to portfolios. In particular, it demonstrates an assessment coding system and its use in arriving at assessment interpretations.

2. Mitchell, R. (1992), 'The "independent" evaluation of bilingual primary education: a narrative account', in J. C. Alderson and A. Beretta (eds), *Evaluating Second Language Education*, Cambridge: Cambridge University Press, pp. 100–40.

The evaluation that Mitchell reports on begins as a primarily positivist design. However, the use of interpretivist procedures provide some interesting counterpoint to the quantitative results.

3. Miles, M. B. and A. M. Huberman (1994), *Qualitative Data Analysis: A Sourcebook of New Methods* (2nd edn), Thousand Oaks, CA: Sage.

This is an extensive collection of techniques for analysing qualitative data. There are dozens of examples of the data displays, guidelines for developing interpretations and a summary of existing computer programs for qualitative data analysis.

Chapter 7

Validity and ethics

7.1 INTRODUCTION

In order to reach assessment and evaluation conclusions and to have enough confidence in those conclusions to report them, we need to establish validity. A generic definition for validity would be the veracity of conclusions, or inferences; that is, we have validity to the degree that our inferences represent what we claim they represent. In the case of assessment, we have validity to the extent that we have assessed the skill or ability that we set out to assess. If we claim to be assessing the ability to negotiate meaning in an informal conversation, but our assessment procedure is actually focused on, or influenced by, some other skill or ability (such as the ability to decode written text, or the ability to compute simple mathematical problems), then our claims for validity are weakened. In the case of evaluation, we have validity to the extent that our evaluation findings provide credible answers and solutions for our evaluation questions and goals. If we claim to have provided evidence that the programme's students are achieving the program's objectives, but have overlooked information that suggests there are explanations for their achievement that have nothing to do with the programme, then our findings are lacking in validity.

When discussing definitions of validity, words like 'veracity', 'truth' and 'credibility' naturally come into play. The generic definition stated as 'the degree to which our conclusions, or inferences are true' works reasonably well within the positivist paradigm, where the knowledge to be pursued is an external truth that is 'out there', waiting to be captured, or at least partially captured, by our inquiry. Within the interpretivist framework, where this view of knowledge and inquiry is replaced by one that sees what can be known as constructed by the act of inquiry and allows for multiple truths, or realities, the generic definition of validity becomes more difficult. An interpretivist definition for validity tends to focus on the notion of credibility, or trustworthiness; it shifts from a correspondence with truth to establishing an argument that is convincing to us and to our audiences. As I will try to demonstrate in the following sections, the ways in which we establish validity – the rules for establishing a correspondence with truth or for establishing a credible argument – will differ between the two paradigms. This will be unsettling, or even unacceptable to some: how can there be different rules for establishing validity? If there isn't one set of rules, how do we decide between competing knowledge claims? Does this mean that interpretivists have to accept (or reject) positivist findings, and vice versa, simply because they play by different rules? These are difficult questions, and I will not pretend to be able to provide definitive answers. What I will try to do is lay out the different approaches for grappling with the problem of validity. Ultimately, for assessment and evaluation, we will come back to the combination of audiences, goals and context as determining a design that will commit to a particular (and paradigm-influenced) strategy for establishing validity.

Issues of ethics are usually discussed in terms of consent, deception, privacy and confidentiality (for example, Punch 1994). In this sense, ethics describes what is considered to be the appropriate relationship between the assessors or evaluators and those assessed or evaluated. The basic concerns of ethical practice, then, focus on the rights of people participating in assessment or evaluation not to be harmed (socially, psychologically, emotionally, physically) and to not be coerced or manipulated against their will. This places ethics within the notion of validity, as pointed out by Hamp-Lyons (1989). Whatever the paradigm, validity establishes what the relationship between assessor/evaluator and participant should be; what the participant can or should be asked to do; how the assessor/evaluator decides what counts as evidence for the validity argument. These validity issues influence the way the ethical questions are posed and answered. In one sense, ethical questions are independent of paradigm, as are the appropriate responses; no one believes that assessment or evaluation participants should be harmed or coerced. However, depending on the way validity is conceptualised, the harm and coercion that the assessor or evaluator is responsible for may be defined differently.

Throughout this book I have tried to demonstrate the connection between the research paradigm as a worldview and the choices that are made in the design and conduct of assessment and evaluation. I have also pointed out that assessment and evaluation are inherently social and political activities. In the discussion of validity and ethics, the social and political implications of these activities become all the more visible. What follows, then, are sections that describe the validity of assessment and evaluation from the two paradigm perspectives – positivist and interpretivist – as well as sections that develop the particularly ethical dimensions of validity. Social and political issues will be an integral part of the discussion in most of these sections.

7.2 THE VALIDITY OF ASSESSMENT

When examining the validity of assessment, it is important to remember that validity is a property of the conclusions, interpretations or inferences that we draw from the assessment instruments and procedures, not the instruments and procedures themselves. However, the validity of assessment is focused on what we can know using particular tests or other assessment procedures. In that sense, it is narrower in scope than the validity of evaluation, for which assessment procedures will usually be only one source of information for the conclusions and interpretations being drawn.

Accordingly, there have been frameworks and typologies developed for testing and assessment, related but separate from the typologies developed for research in general, and evaluation in particular.

7.2.1 Positivist validity typologies

Assessment validity has traditionally been discussed as a set of types, depending on the evidence that is used. Some of the terms used in these typologies have been controversial, and none more controversial than 'face validity'. This is the term used to refer to a judgement rendered by a person untrained in language testing. Those who object to its use find it, true to its name, superficial and without empirical basis. Typically, judgements of face validity have to do with judgements of content and format; for example, the judgement that a 'direct test', one that involves a performance that directly reveals the ability being tested (such as an essay exam to test writing ability) as having more face validity than an 'indirect test' (for example, using a multiple-choice test of ability to detect writing mistakes as a test of writing ability). If there is a legitimate place for face validity, it would be a concern with public credibility and the investigation of the social (and political) consequences of assessment. This type of evidence will be discussed further as consequential validity.

Criterion-related validity' refers to the relationship between the test we are trying to validate and some other relevant measure. This type of validity has two basic subtypes: 'predictive validity', where the relevant measure is some test or measure (presumed to be valid) of an ability we are trying to predict from the scores on our test. For example, we might wish to use a test of English language proficiency as a predictor of success at university. The evidence would come from a comparison (correlation) of scores on our English test with some measure of success (for example, university grade point average) as evidence of predictive validity for the English test. The other subtype is 'concurrent validity'. In this case the evidence would come from how well our test matches up against another test of the same ability (again, presumed to be valid). Of course, this puts criterion-related validity in a chicken-and-egg quandary: from where did the criterion get its validity? The answer would be that the very first test of a particular ability to be validated would have to depend on evidence other than this concurrent type.

Another way of thinking about validity is to examine the content of the test in relationship to its purpose and what we intend to measure. This is traditionally called 'content validity'. Evidence for this type of validity usually involves having people with expertise in the ability being tested make judgements about the degree of match between the test items and tasks and the ability to be tested. My colleague, Fred Davidson, and I (Davidson and Lynch 2002) also argue that the match found between test specifications, as discussed in Chapter 3, and items produced from those specs is evidence of content validity. Using Bachman's test method and communicative-language frameworks (Bachman 1990), language testers have also performed detailed content analyses in support of this type of validity evidence (Bachman et al. 1995a).

Perhaps the most important and certainly the most central type of validity is 'construct validity'. Basically, this type of validity asks the question: are we measuring the relevant underlying trait or construct? Here we are fundamentally interested in evidence that speaks to the relationship between test performance and criterion performance. When there is a gap, this signals lack of authenticity (the test method is not related to the test construct). One example of evidence for establishing construct validity would be correlating scores on the test to be validated with scores on tests of similar and different abilities using different test methods (the multi-trait, multi-method design; see Bachman 1990: 263–5). The scores on the test to be validated should correlate highly with scores on other tests, taken to be valid measures of the same ability (convergent validity), and should not correlate with scores on other tests, presumed to measure different abilities (divergent validity). There should also be higher correlations between tests of same ability using different testing methods than correlations between tests of different abilities using the same testing method (that is, if tests using the same method are correlating better than tests using different methods, there may be a 'method effect': we may be primarily measuring ability to do well on that particular format of test). We could also establish construct validity by correlating scores on tests to be validated with group member-ship (for example, 'native speakers' versus 'non-native speakers'), or we could analyse the test scores using statistical techniques such as factor analysis and/or structural equation modelling to see if the resulting statistical structure relates to our theoretical structure for the ability being measured. The relationship between construct validity and other types of validity is demonstrated in these forms of evidence: we are using various forms of criterion-related validity to establish the degree to which our measurements represent the underlying construct.

We can also use experimental evidence. Different forms of treatment, or inter-vention, can be given to experimental and comparison groups and the test to be validated given as the post-test measure. Here, unlike traditional experimental designs, we are testing the test, not the treatment. So, we need to use treatments that have known effects (see Bachman 1990: 267). For example, suppose we have identified a teaching method that works for improving conversational ability in a second language, and we have a test we've developed to measure conversational ability. Experimental evidence for the validity of our test could be gathered by selecting and assigning students (preferably on a 'random' basis) to two treatments: one that uses our known method of teaching conversational ability, and one that teaches, for example, essay-writing skills. If we give our test to these two groups at the end of the experimental period (for example, a semester's worth of instruction), then we would expect the conversation-treatment students to score higher on our test than the academic-writing students, if our test is measuring the construct we assume it is. Quasi-experimental evidence can also be gathered using intact groups such as educated native speakers of the language being tested. For example, we would hypothesise that educated native speakers would be able to achieve near-perfect scores on a test that claims to measure proficiency in that language (see, for example, Klein-Braley 1985). Other experimental and quasi-experimental evidence can be gathered by systematically varying the characteristics of the test (for example, changing the reading difficulty of the text prompt, or the scale and evaluative criteria used for scoring a performance, and hypothesising that test scores would be lower when the text prompt or evaluative criteria are more difficult).

Davies (1990) describes the different strengths that are associated with evidence of different validity types. He also points out the advantages of combining evidence from different approaches in order to arrive at an overall determination of validity. Bachman and Palmer (1996) discuss types of validity evidence within a framework of 'test usefulness'. This framework posits qualities of good tests that are seen as being complementary and in need of being balanced differently for assessment contexts. The qualities are reliability, construct validity, authenticity, interactiveness, impact and practicality. The assessment context will vary depending upon the specific purpose (type of decision, the use for which the test information will be put), the specific test takers, and the specific language-use domain (which they refer to as the *target language-use* (TLU) *domain*, from which TLU tasks are selected). Bachman and Palmer define tests as not having pedagogy, or teaching purposes, as their primary function. However, all of the test qualities except reliability and construct validity are shared directly with teaching and learning; reliability and validity are central to their positivist definition of testing as measurement.

What the language-assessment community appears to have agreed upon (Chapelle 1999) is that construct validity is central to all test validity. This notion was formalised in the work of Messick (1989, 1994, 1996). His framework for test validity also incorporated 'consequential validity', which has also been related to the notion of 'washback' (Messick 1996), especially in terms of the effect of tests on individuals and social institutions. Tests very often have an overriding influence on such things as what gets taught and how it gets taught (and, consequently, on such things as what teaching materials get produced and purchased). In this way, consequential validity is closely tied to issues of assessment reform (changing existing assessment procedures). McNamara (2000) discusses assessment reform as potentially problematic, such as when there is an attempt to measure more complex language performances through the use of ongoing assessment (for example, with portfolios and performance projects) that leads to the development of coaching programmes which are differentially available to students. In this case the consequential validity of the assessment procedures is threatened by unfair and unequal access to the resources that affect assessment performance.

It is important to remember that Messick's framework is intended for test, or measurement, validity and, as such, falls under the positivist perspective as I am using the term here. For example, Messick makes it clear that different test-score outcomes based on sex or ethnicity, or the adverse effect of negative social consequences, is not necessarily a test-validity issue:

> But whether the adverse impact is attributable to construct-relevant or construct-irrelevant test variance or to criterion-related or criterion-unrelated test variance are salient validity issues in appraising functional worth and in justifying test use.

If irrelevant sources of test and criterion variance are likely culprits in this regard, adverse impact through the use of the test is an issue of test *invalidity*. However, if the sex or ethnic score differences reflect valid properties of the construct tapped by the test, they contribute to score meaning and thus are an issue of test *validity*. That is, if sources of invalidity, especially construct-irrelevant variance or criterion contamination, are not plausible – or can be discounted as the cause – then the adverse impact is an issue of political or social *policy*, whether deliberate or de facto.

(Messick 1989: 85; original emphasis)

Here we see that Messick is making social consequences a concern for test validators, but is limiting the validity issue to properties of measurement. If the social consequences can be linked to interpretations of test scores that are irrelevant to the construct being measured or the criterion we wish to make inferences about – construct-irrelevant variance or criterion-unrelated variance – then this is evidence against validity. If the social consequences, however adverse they may be, are reflecting the construct and the criterion we are measuring and making inferences about, then the validity of the test is not threatened.

The question is: how far does the responsibility for the consequences of tests extend? If negative consequences are the result of otherwise valid test measurement (construct relevant test-score variance), is the test still valid? Is this the test developer's responsibility? Questions like these make the relationship between validity and ethics (as well as the social and political nature of both) all the more apparent. And the fact that Messick's framework raises these questions demonstrates its usefulness as a bridge between positivist validity typologies and interpretivist approaches to assessment validity, the subject of the next section.

7.2.2 Interpretivist approaches to assessment validity

Although still dominated by an essentially positivist perspective, there are signs that interpretivist inquiry is beginning to emerge in the field of language assessment (Hamp-Lyons and Lynch 1998; Lynch and Hamp-Lyons 1999). As I have argued elsewhere (Lynch 1997, 2001a), alternative assessment – what I am referring to here as interpretivist assessment – is particularly well suited for addressing the sorts of issues discussed above as value implications and social consequences. However, alternative assessment has been criticised for claiming to be automatically valid (Brown and Hudson 1998). That is not the claim I wish to make here. Any approach to assessment needs to establish evidence that can speak to the validity of the inferences or decisions being made. Even positivist approaches to validity require developing a validity argument (see Chapelle 1999). The question is whether or not there is a single, universal validity framework, regardless of the approach. My view is that different research paradigms such as positivism and interpretivism require different validity frameworks. Consider the question that Pamela Moss (1994) raised: 'Can there be validity without reliability?' From the positivist perspective, this question seemed either absurd or heretical. In all positivist validity frameworks, reliability defines how much of our measurement is without error – if there is no reliability, then everything we have measured is in error, and cannot be valid. Moss, however, argued that, with interpretivist assessment, reliability is not necessarily a precondition for validity. Assessors of portfolios, for example, may disagree (resulting in a lack of reliability, in measurement terms), but their disagreement may provide valuable information for making valid inferences about the individual's portfolio. Disagreement may indicate differing but equally important and valid views on the individual's ability (also see Moss 1996).

In order to examine the validity of the interpretations of individual language ability, we need some sort of criteria. As Rea-Dickins and Gardner point out, to develop these criteria we need to complement the existing theoretical base for language assessment with a base that draws on teacher knowledge: 'In addition, we need a richer experiential base; in other words, a theory of praxis' (2000: 239). In a similar vein, McKay (2000) points out the need for validity criteria (in this case, as articulated in bandscale descriptors) that consider the local context of assessment: learner characteristics (for example, age and background knowledge) and classroom context (for example, type of assessment task, degree of preparation and support).

Ultimately, establishing validity from an interpretivist perspective involves achieving consensus across multiple audiences and sources of evidence. Peter Shaw and I (Lynch 2001b; Lynch and Shaw 1998) have proposed a one possible set of such validity criteria, modifying the work of Guba and Lincoln (1989) and Foucault (1982, 1990, 1997). This framework integrates validity with ethical considerations, especially in terms of consciously addressing the power relations that are at play in the assessment context. The framework is based on a close interconnection of validity with ethics, which will be discussed in the final section of this chapter, and is similar to the 'authenticity criteria' which will be presented in the section on interpretivist approaches to valuation validity.

7.3 THE VALIDITY OF EVALUATION

Like assessment validity, the validity of evaluation is a property of the inferences we draw from the evaluation information; it is not an inherent property of our design, the instruments we use to gather that information, or the techniques we use to analyse the information. Since evaluation will usually make use of some sort of assessment information, positivist or interpretivist, the validity of inferences drawn from those assessments will form part of the validity of the overall evaluation inferences. However, because the conclusions that we draw for evaluation purposes will go beyond conclusions about individual language ability (the focus of assessment validity), separate typologies have been developed for addressing the validity of evaluation.

7.3.1 Positivist approaches to evaluation validity

The traditional formulation of validity is: the degree to which we establish the truth of our findings. 'Truth' depends on the 'logic of justification' we use. Underlying the positivist logic of justification are the assumptions of an independently existing reality, and the belief that the universe is defined by causal relationships. Furthermore, if we can come to understanding them, we can manipulate the environment, including the social environment, to our advantage, and evolve (Cook and Campbell 1979: 29).

Validity, then, is a check on how well we have captured the independently existing reality and its causal relationships. The classic typology for this task, formulated by Campbell and Stanley (1966) and revised by Cook and Campbell (1979), divides validity into 'statistical conclusion validity', 'internal validity', 'construct validity', and 'external validity'. 'Statistical conclusion validity' refers to the degree of certainty with which we can infer that the variables being observed are related. Are the independent variable (the programme) and the dependent variable (the outcome measure) related? This relationship is expressed statistically as covariation, or how strongly variation in one variable goes along with variation in the other variable. For example, does the variation in the outcome measure (for example, scores on a test of language proficiency) go along with the variation in the independent variable (for example, whether the students were participating in the programme being evaluated or a comparison group)? 'Internal validity' focuses on whether or not the observed relationship between the independent and dependent variables is causal (for example, can the programme be taken to cause the observed gains in language proficiency?).

'Construct validity' looks for evidence concerning how well we can use our research findings to make generalisations about the constructs that underlie the variables we are investigating. Constructs, in this sense, can be thought of as the labels that assign meaning to the things we are measuring, which ultimately come from a theoretical framework. For example, our construct for the independent variable, or programme, may come from current theoretical work in such areas as English for Specific Purposes, or task-based approaches to second-language teaching. The construct for the dependent variable, or language ability, may come from current work in second-language acquisition and be influenced by socio-cultural theory. 'External validity' refers to evidence that allows us to generalise our evaluation findings to other persons, settings and times. For example, if we find a causal relationship between the programme we are evaluating and significant improvement in language ability, can we expect to find this relationship if the programme is used with other participants in another setting?

7.3.2 Threats to positivist validity

After defining the components of validity, we need a way of knowing when we have the necessary evidence for claiming validity for our evaluation interpretations. In the positivist paradigm, validity is demonstrated by ruling out, or providing evidence against, a set of threats to validity. These threats have been discussed in detail elsewhere (Cook and Campbell 1979; Lynch 1996). In general, the threats that have to do with the appropriate use of quantitative measurement techniques, the differences between the programme group and the comparison group that are not controlled for in our evaluation design, the theoretical frameworks that are used to define the programme and its objectives, particular aspects of the setting in combination with the programme, and particular events occurring external to the programme at a particular time. Threats that cannot be ruled out by the appropriate use of statistical procedures or the appropriate evaluation design need to be ruled out with documentation of the evaluation process and the programme context and, where possible, gathering information from multiple programme sites.

7.3.3 Interpretivist approaches to evaluation validity

Although they deny the existence of a universal framework that can serve as a foundation for judging the validity of our evaluation interpretations, interpretivist approaches still confront issues of validity, but do not link it to knowledge itself, but to applications of knowledge. For example, does the evaluation and the knowledge it brings serve to liberate people; does it lead to some action that results in social or educational reform; does it lead to a new understanding on the part of the evaluation participants (of themselves and others)? It may seem that adopting an interpretivist perspective means we are forced into a situation where our knowledge claims are reduced to purely aesthetic judgements or matters of opinion. My sense is that even with extreme relativists such as Smith (1988, 1990) there is still a central place for reason and rationality in our approach to validity. Validity evidence, from this perspective, is the construction of an argument that will unavoidably reflect our particular theoretical, social, political and personal interests and purposes. This is what is meant by 'value-laden theory' and 'interested knowledge'. There is no separation of 'facts' from 'values', but this is not the same thing as rejecting rationality. The dilemma for interpretivist evaluation is that it rejects prescribed notions of validity, but evaluation audiences demand methodological quality assurances. The solution that most interpretivist evaluators opt for is to view methodological concerns as choices that are made and need to be justified, to view evaluation procedures not as guarantors of validity, but as heuristics or metaphors, and to be open to validity criteria that emerge and evolve out of the evaluation (Greene 2000: 537).

There have been efforts to spell out actual criteria, to allow the interpretivist evaluator to make greater or lesser claims to validity depending on the degree to which these criteria have been fulfilled. These criteria are sometimes referred to as 'trustworthiness' (Guba and Lincoln 1989) or 'goodness' (Peshkin 1993) criteria; they can also be seen as 'parallel' to validity criteria for positivist evaluation. When using these criteria, it is not a question of how many of the criteria have been met, or how many techniques for meeting these criteria that you use, but the degree to which the criteria you discuss build a convincing argument for the credibility and trustworthiness of your findings. Interpretivist validity of this sort has to do with the clarity and thoroughness in using, and reporting your use of, the techniques that enhance validity.

One of the most useful of these 'parallel criteria' typologies is Guba and Lincoln's (1989) 'trustworthiness criteria'. There are four components to their typology: 'credibility' (which is the interpretivist translation of internal validity), 'transferability' (which is the interpretivist translation of external validity), 'dependability' (which is the interpretivist counterpart to measurement reliability) and 'confirmability' (which addresses the positivist concern for objectivity). Each of these components are then addressed with techniques (such as long-term engagement with the evaluation setting, checking with programme participants as interpretations develop) that enhance the evaluation team's ability to provide evidence in support of validity (see Lynch 1996: 55–63 for a detailed discussion of these criteria).

It can, perhaps, be argued that the process of doing interpretivist evaluation provides its own quality control; the interpretations and conclusions are arrived at through an iterative process of going back and forth between the data and the analysis of the data. However, this appeal to the method of doing the research, with validity being implicit, will not satisfy many people. Evaluation audiences expect explicit evidence in support of validity. However, some interpretivists have criticised the trustworthiness criteria as being overly methodological and dependent upon positivist validity typologies.

To counteract these deficiencies, Guba and Lincoln (1989) developed the 'authenticity criteria'. The first authenticity criterion is 'fairness', which refers to making certain that the range of stakeholders and participants in a particular evaluaton setting have all been taken into account, their perspectives and constructions of meaning represented in the evaluation. 'Ontological authenticity' is the degree to which these same stakeholders and participants are able to gain and use information as a result of the evaluation process, that they are able to improve 'their conscious experiencing of the world' (Guba and Lincoln 1989: 248). 'Educative authenticity' is closely related to ontological authenticity, but adds the requirement that stakeholders and participants gain an understanding of the perspectives and meaning constructions of those outside their own group (for example, teachers coming to understand the perspective of students). 'Catalytic authenticity' refers to the degree to which something is actually done as a result of the evaluation. Building upon this criterion, tactical authenticity refers to how well the stakeholders and participants are actually empowered to take the action that the evaluation sets in motion.

The evidence that is necessary for validity under these criteria comes from documenting discussions and testimony from the stakeholders and participants, conducting negotiation sessions concerning the developing interpretations and evaluation findings, and systematic follow-up sessions as the evaluation findings are translated into actions.

7.4 ETHICS AND THE CONDUCT OF ASSESSMENT AND EVALUATION

The embeddedness of ethics within validity has already been discussed in the preceding sections. Ethics is also defined, in its own right, in relation to the conduct of assessment and evaluation. By determining what is ethical, we are establishing roles for the assessor, the evaluator, the assessed and the evaluated. And these roles are defined in terms of what is acceptable, or good, practice. Ethics in assessment and evaluation, like ethics in research, is primarily concerned with protecting the individuals who are being assessed and evaluated. The ethical review boards associated with university research, for example, examine whether researchers have properly informed their participants about the nature of the research, the potential risks (and benefits), and have secured their voluntary and uncoerced consent prior to beginning the research. The ethical review board advocates for the research participant, and researchers must examine their proposed project through the eyes of the participant. At Portland State University, for example, the researcher must provide a description of how the research will take place – from selection, to consent, to conducting the research – writing in the first person, from the point of view of the participant.

In viewing assessment from the point of view of the participant, the issue of consent does not usually occur in the manner described for research. Individuals being assessed rarely have a choice in the matter. The notion of fully informed consent is relevant, however, and suggests that even when assessment is mandatory, those being assessed should be told that they are being assessed, what they are being assessed for, and how the assessment results will be used. This raises particular problems for informal assessment, such as the spontaneous speech samples discussed in Chapter 5, when the assessment is embedded within normal teaching and learning activities. However, the ethical issue of central importance remains a concern for avoiding harm and manipulation against the individual's will. The teacher-assessor establishes ethical practice through the understanding and rapport she or he develops with the students-assessees and the degree to which there is clear communication about teaching, learning and assessment goals and practices. This is an ongoing communication, in need of constant rearticulation and renegotiation.

The assessment relationship also comes up against the problems of 'deception' and 'privacy' or 'confidentiality'. As mentioned above, part of being fully informed prior to giving consent is knowing that assessment is taking place and why. This concern can be extended to the use of assessment formats that are unfamiliar to the individuals being assessed, as well as individual questions or tasks that may be intentionally 'tricky'. The focus here is on the potential for such practice to cause emotional or psychological harm to the individual, as well as to violate the basic rights that are implicit in an ethical relationship between assessor and assessee (rather than on the issue of deception resulting in invalid assessment, which is also important and related to ethics). To provide privacy and confidentiality in the assessment relationship can be much more problematic than in the general evaluation context. Since assessment results are often used for decisions that become public, it is difficult to ensure complete privacy or confidentiality. Even in a classroom-assessment context, the grades may be kept confidential, but the consequences (for example, advancing to the next level of study) will be visible and identify the individuals. Furthermore, certain assessment procedures, such as performance assessments of various types, are by their very nature public events. There are no formulaic answers for the range of ethical problems that assessment presents, but a constant awareness and evaluation of the potential for harm form the core of an ethical perspective.

Evaluation, focusing more on groups of individuals and the programme level of language teaching and learning, can respond to ethical issues in ways similar to those devised for general research. Obtaining fully informed consent, avoiding deception and providing privacy or confidentiality can be pursued without some of the problems mentioned for assessment. For both assessment and evaluation, ethics can be viewed as a relationship between assessor-evaluator and participants. It can also be viewed as a professional code. In the following sections I will discuss both views.

7.4.1 The assessment relationship: fairness and power relations

One of the criteria in the approach to interpretivist assessment validity described earlier is 'fairness'. In the traditional approach to assessment, fairness essentially means giving everyone the same treatment, from the administration of the test to the analysis of the results. Messick's (1989) validity framework can be seen to extend this notion of fairness to include a consideration of the consequences of assessment, as well as the value implications of our interpretations and use of assessment. The act of being fair (or unfair) implies relations of power. There are choices to be made about how the assessment will be handled, about what will happen to those being assessed, and power has to do with who makes those choices (Heron 1988). In the field of language assessment, Shohamy (2001) has provided a thorough investigation of the relationship of power to the assessment process. As she has done, my own analysis of power in the assessment relationship draws upon the work of Foucault (1979, 1982, 1990), as well as that of my brother, Dennis Lynch, and his colleague Stephen Jukuri (Lynch and Jukuri 1998).

Foucault describes the examination (in the sense of positivist testing, as I am using the term here) as being 'at the centre of the procedures that constitute the individual as effect and object of power, as effect and object of knowledge' (1979: 192). The power that makes the individual its effect or object comes in three basic forms: domination, exploitation and subjection (Foucault 1982). Foucault's way of discussing power at times (1982, 1990) seems to allow for relations that resist the basic forms of power: as reversible and reciprocal relations (Lynch and Jukuri 1998). Whether this is an overly optimistic reading of Foucault or not, a consideration of power relations would seem important in order to uncover potentially unethical relationships that might otherwise remain hidden. It may also open up a space for considering the potential for responses to unethical assessment procedures.

7.4.2 Critical language testing

In order to address the range of ethical issues that is raised by the assessment relationship, Shohamy (2001: 131–3) has articulated a set of principles for 'critical testing'. These principles derive from a consideration of the role of power relations in language assessment, and they argue for understanding assessment as a process shaped by political and social forces. Because of this, critical testing argues for an inclusion of multiple voices and perspectives in the assessment process. It views tests and other forms of assessment as potential instruments for ideological domination and control. Within this perspective, Shohamy discusses the responsibilities of those involved in assessment, and the rights of those who are assessed.

The critical perspective on language assessment implies sharing the authority of assessment with multiple perspectives, and therefore the responsibilities of assessment are shared as well. Shohamy's role for language assessors (defined as all those who are involved with the development and administration of assessment procedures) is defined as: 'The responsibility of testers then, is to admit the limitations of their profession and construct knowledge in a responsible way, by working together with a number of groups of users who accumulate evidence of the knowledge that is being assessed' (2001: 148). The type of evidence that is needed, according to Shohamy, includes the full range of information about validity discussed above, depending on the assessment audiences and their goals. Assessors need to communicate the assessment information and its validity evidence in a variety of ways, and to be explicit about the intended use of the assessment, the rationale for its use, and to predict as many consequences from the assessment as possible.

The rights of those being assessed are embodied in many of Shohamy's critical testing principles, such as 'Critical testing encourages test takers to develop a critical view of tests as well as to act on it by questioning tests and critiquing the value which is inherent in them' (2001: 131). The basic ethical principles that I outlined previously – concerning consent, deception, and privacy/confidentiality – form the basis for Shohamy's specific listing of test-taker rights:

> With regard to consent, a test taker should be given the right to be tested and the right to refuse to be tested. There should also be honesty with regard to the purpose of the test, its practice and methods. Next, a test taker should be granted the possibility of being assessed by an alternative method other than the traditional 'test-only' system. Such information can be used as counter evidence based on tests only. In addition ... there is a need for sharing the power of tests by training the public in testing methods, in the testing process and in the rights of test takers. Testing cannot remain a field that belongs only to testers but rather test takers and the public at large need to be part of the discussion.
>
> (Shohamy 2001: 158)

7.4.3 Codes of ethics, codes of practice

One way of articulating the ethical requirements for assessment is in a professional code. As Davies (1997) has discussed it, there are three levels of morality, or ethical concern: the professional, the public and the individual. As he sees it, professional ethics is established as a contract between these three levels. This contract is embodied in a code of practice for the profession. Interestingly, the International Language Testing Association (ILTA) decided first to establish a code of ethics before attempting a code of practice (ILTA 2000). In its preamble, it is described as:

> a set of principles which draws upon moral philosophy and serves to guide professional conduct. It is neither a statute nor a regulation and it does not provide guidelines for practice, but it is intended to offer a benchmark of satisfactory ethical behavior by all language testers.

There are nine principles, each with several 'annotations' designed to elaborate the general principle. For example, Principle 1 reads: 'Language testers shall have respect for the humanity and dignity of each of their test takers. They shall provide them with the best possible professional consideration and shall respect all persons' needs, values and cultures in the provision of their language testing service'. One of its annotations is: 'Where possible, test takers should be consulted on all matters concerning their interests'.

At the present time, ILTA is working on the companion code of practice, but not without difficulty. A central issue is whether or not one code of practice is possible for all assessment contexts, especially across different languages and cultures. If it is possible to articulate one universal code, might it not be too generalised to be of use in the local practice of language assessment?

7.4.4 Ethics in evaluation

The basic issues concerning the ethics of evaluation are the same as for assessment: consent and deception, privacy and confidentiality, and avoiding harm. These issues describe what is considered to be the appropriate relationship between the evaluation team and the evaluation participants.

The issue of avoiding deception and gaining consent is addressed by examining the degree to which the evaluation team is being open and honest with the participants. It is important to remember that 'consent' is formulated as 'informed consent'. Have the evaluation participants been clearly told what the evaluation will involve, including what they will be asked to do and what will be done with the evaluation findings?

In positivist approaches to research in general, and evaluation in particular, there is sometimes the need for a certain amount of deception, in order to accomplish the experiment and avoid threats to internal validity. This is sometimes described as a 'tilt toward deception' (Lincoln and Guba 2000: 170). When this deception is deemed necessary, there are ways of ensuring that the overall effect and process of the evaluation is still reasonably ethical. The participants can be given a partial, or even somewhat misleading, description of what the evaluation is focusing on. For example, if the evaluation is using a quasi-experimental design, and has a particular focus on comparing the effect of the programme's use of background music during classroom activities (versus a comparison group with no background music), you could tell all participants (programme and comparison groups) that the evaluation was investigating teacher and student attitudes towards language learning. Whenever deception is used, participants should ultimately be informed about the real purpose and goals of the research. One way of doing this is through a 'debriefing' session, in which the participants are given a full account of the research and allowed to discuss the issue of deception and how they felt about participating in the evaluation.

Consent needs to be thought of as an ongoing negotiation process throughout the life of the evaluation. Circumstances may change, and it is important to reassess participants' willingness and comfort with the evaluation periodically.

The issue of privacy and confidentiality is addressed by ensuring that the evaluation participants' involvement in the research does not identify them individually in some form of the data that may be available to others. In some cases participants may want to be identified in the documentation and reporting of the evaluation. The ethical requirement for the evaluation team is to consider how being identified may affect the individual participants, especially in relation to the next basic issue, the potential for harm.

Avoiding harm includes physical, emotional, psychological harm and damage to reputation or loss of time and resources as a result of participation. Harm can occur at the individual level or at the community level.

7.4.4.1 Steps in making evaluation ethical

The first step in addressing ethical concerns in evaluation comes when the evaluation is being designed. Most often, evaluation activities will require some sort of ethical review and approval by a committee. Ethics should be considered an integral part of the evaluation design, rather than an *ex-post-facto* hurdle or obstacle to getting the evaluation approved.

Before your evaluation can be ethically conducted, the evaluation team needs to obtain fully informed consent (one of the basic ethical issues outlined above) from all participants. Initially, consent is generally obtained by providing all participants with a 'Plain Language Statement', which describes, in simple, easy-to-understand language (free from technical jargon) what the evaluation goals are (subject to requirements for deception, mentioned above), what the participants will be asked to do, and what will happen to the evaluation data gathered. Along with the information statement, participants are usually asked to sign a written consent form (this form may need to be signed by a guardian or parent if the participant is under eighteen years of age).

In certain cases, written information statements may not be appropriate (for example, where literacy is questionable) and requesting written consent may be culturally inappropriate or otherwise problematic (for example, where the participants are in a vulnerable social or political situation, such as political refugees). For these situations, consent may be recorded by having a witness provide documentation of the process of consent (for example, a third party, who in writing or on a tape-recording, testifies to the process by which consent was obtained for each participant); by a verbally tape-recorded consent from the participant; or by a signed 'evaluation team statement' that details the process (step by step) by which fully informed consent was obtained and the reasons why written consent was inappropriate. However, the particulars of what is acceptable documentation of informed consent need to be checked carefully with the responsible ethical review committee.

In evaluation that uses voluntary, anonymous questionnaires, consent can be taken to be explicit when the questionnaire is returned and where there has been no pressure to do so. When the evaluation participants are seen to be in a more powerful position than the evaluation team (for example, politicians, or other public figures), the granting of an interview can be seen as explicit consent for participation in the evaluation (assuming the purposes of the evaluation and uses for the data collected have been explained in advance). Again, this is the general case, and needs to be checked for each specific ethical review context.

7.4.5 Codes of practice for evaluation

As discussed for assessment, ethics in evaluation can be approached as a professional issue. The Joint Committee on Standards for Education Evaluation (1994) created a set of standards for programme evaluation that acts as a code of practice. It sets out four sets of attributes for evaluation: utility, feasibility, propriety and accuracy. In particular, the 'proprietary standards' articulate important ethical principles for the profession.

7.5 CONCLUSION

In this chapter I have discussed validity and ethics as being interconnected. In some ways, ethics can be seen as embedded within all questions of validity. Or, following Davies (1997: 335), we can see validity as included within ethics, or at least consider its scope, within assessment, as being a question we are still working on. What I have argued here is that both validity and ethics will be approached differently, depending upon the paradigm that guides the design of assessment or evaluation.

In some ways, limiting assessment and evaluation to a concern for the technical issues of measurement instruments and evaluation procedures makes the task of defining validity and considering ethical problems more manageable. I take Davies' point when he says:

> An ethical perspective for a language tester is, I have argued, necessary. But I have also argued the need in all professional statements of morality for a limit on what

is achievable or even perhaps desirable. In my view, therefore, the apparent open-ended offer of consequential validity goes too far. I maintain that it is not possible for a tester as a member of a profession to take account of all possible social consequences. (Whether the tester as an individual does so is a matter for his or her conscience although I would propose that such complete openness is impossible to uphold.)

(Davies 1997: 335–6)

This position is reasonable and is at the heart of the attempts by ILTA, described earlier, to create a code of ethics and a code of practice for the language-assessment profession. It allows for a guided response to the myriad of social consequences that may present themselves in any particular assessment context, without being over-whelmed or making commitments to solve impossible situations. Also, it allows a definition of ethics (and validity) to include more than a concern with the technical properties of the assessment instruments that are being used.

Questions that remain include how we determine the manageable set of social consequences for which the profession can take responsibility. In approaching this task, I think that Shohamy's 'critical language testing' perspective will be important. The discussion about which consequences language assessors take responsibility for, since it will include an examination of the range of potential consequences, needs to include the widest range of assessment stakeholders. That discussion will be inherently social, political and cultural, and universal answers may be impossible to find.

These questions for the language-assessment community have parallel questions for the language-programme-evaluation community. The interaction of evaluation audiences, goals and context will lead to interpretivist designs and interpretations that cannot be adequately judged using positivist validity typologies. And with a shift in approach to validity comes a different perspective on ethical issues, such as the scope of consequences for which the evaluator (or the assessor) is responsible. These shifts between paradigms, even if they are movements along a continuum of perspectives, need to be acknowledged and discussed. What this means in practice is that applied linguists engaging in assessment and evaluation work need to be aware of the range of choices and the associated assumptions for what will count as evidence and what will constitute an ethical and valid argument for interpreting assessment and evaluation results. The authenticity criteria, for example, call for evidence that something has taken place as a result of the evaluation (catalytic authenticity) and that the evaluation participants become capable of carrying out that action (tactical authenticity). This gives the interpretivist approach to evaluation validity a strong advocacy and activist role. The positivist perspective on valid evaluation would see this as an unwarranted and undesirable loss of objectivity and neutrality on the part of the evaluator.

It would make this chapter, and this book, much easier to write if there were one universal paradigm, one validity framework and one set of ethical principles. However, such a portrait would oversimplify our work and the knowledge that we pursue to help guide that work. As applied linguists, we need to keep a dialogue going, first with ourselves (teachers and students in the field of applied linguistics), and also with our assessment and evaluation stakeholders.

EXERCISES

1. Using your examples of teaching and assessment activities from Chapter 2, Exercise 3, and Chapter 5, Exercise 1, decide what sorts of evidence you would need to establish a validity argument. Do this separately for 'tests' and 'interpretivist assessments', if you have both. How do the two compare?
2. Consider the 'authenticity criteria' and the 'positivist validity typology'. What do you find attractive about each perspective? What do you find troublesome?
3. Obtain a copy of the International Language Testing Association's Code of Ethics (available online: http://www.surrey.ac.uk/ELI/ilta/code.pdf; and in Shohamy 2001: Appendix A). Select one or two of the principles, and determine how you would use them to guide your language assessment practice. Think of a particular assessment context and problem; for example, use one of your activities from Exercise 1, above.

SUGGESTIONS FOR FURTHER READING

1. Chapelle, C. A. (1999), 'Validity in language assessment', *Annual Review of Applied Linguistics*, 19: 254–72.
This article provides a complete overview of the issue of validity in language assessment, including some discussion of interpretivist approaches.

2. Shohamy, E. (2001), *The Power of Tests: A Critical Perspective on the Uses of Language Tests*, London: Longman/Pearson Education.
I hope that my brief summary will encourage you to read this book in its entirety. Shohamy articulates an important perspective on ethics and validity for the language-assessment community.

3. McNamara, T. F. (1997), 'Policy and social considerations in language assessment', *Annual Review of Applied Linguistics*, 18: 304–19.
This review article covers important topics in relation to the political and social consequences of language assessment.

References

Alderson, J. C. (1979), 'The cloze procedure and proficiency in English as a foreign language', *TESOL Quarterly*, 13: 219–27.

Alderson, J. C. (2000), *Assessing Reading*, Cambridge: Cambridge University Press.

Alderson, J. C. and M. Scott (1992), 'Insiders, outsiders and participatory evaluation', in C. Alderson and A. Beretta (eds), *Evaluating Second Language Education*, Cambridge: Cambridge University Press, pp. 25–57.

Alderson, J. C., C. Clapham and D. Wall (1995), *Language Test Construction and Evaluation*, Cambridge: Cambridge University Press.

American Council for the Teaching of Foreign Languages (ACTFL) (1985), *ACTFL Proficiency Guidelines* (rev. edn), Hastings-on-Hudson, NY: ACTFL Materials Center. Available online: http://www.sil.org.lingualinks/languagelearning/otherresources/actflproficiencyguidelines/actflguidelinesspeaking.htm

Angoff, W. H. (1971), 'Scales, norms, and equivalent scores', in R. L. Thorndike (ed.), *Educational Measurement* (2nd edn), Washington, DC: American Council on Education, pp. 508–600.

Auerbach, E. (1994), 'Participatory action research', *TESOL Quarterly*, 28(4): 679–82.

Bachman, L. F. (1985), 'Performance on the cloze test with fixed-ratio and rational deletions', *TESOL Quarterly*, 19(3): 535–56.

Bachman, L. F. (1989), 'The development and use of criterion-referenced tests of language ability in language programme evaluation', in R. K. Johnson (ed.), *The Second Language Curriculum*, Cambridge: Cambridge University Press, pp. 242–58.

Bachman, L. F. (1990), *Fundamental Considerations in Language Testing*, Oxford: Oxford University Press.

Bachman, L. F. and A. S. Palmer (1996), *Language Testing in Practice*, Oxford: Oxford University Press.

Bachman, L. F., F. Davidson, K. Ryan and I. Choi (1995a), *An Investigation into the Comparability of Two Tests of English as a Foreign Language: The Cambridge–TOEFL Comparability Study*, Cambridge: University of Cambridge Examinations Syndicate and Cambridge University Press.

Bachman, L. F., B. K. Lynch and M. Mason (1995b), 'Investigating variability in tasks and rater judgements in a performance test of foreign language speaking', *Language Testing*, 12(2), 238–57.

Bailey, K. M. (1982), *Teaching in a Second Language: The Communicative Competence of Non-native Speaking Teaching Assistants*, unpublished Ph.D. dissertation: Applied Linguistics, University of California, Los Angeles.

Bentler, P. M. (1995), *EQS Structural Equations Program Manual*, Los Angeles, CA: BMDP Statistical Software, Inc.

Bentler, P. M. and E. C. Wu (1995), *EQS for Macintosh User's Guide*, Encion, CA: Multivariate Software, Inc.

Berk, R. A. (1986), 'A consumer's guide to setting performance standards on criterion-referenced tests', *Review of Educational Research*, 56, 137–72.

Beretta, A. (1986), 'Program fair language teaching programme evaluation', *TESOL Quarterly*, 20(3): 431–44.

Beretta, A. (1990), 'Implementation of the Bangalore Project', *Applied Linguistics*, 11(4): 321–37.

Beretta, A. (1992), 'What can be learned from the Bangalore evaluation', in C. Alderson and A. Beretta (eds), *Evaluating Second Language Education*, Cambridge: Cambridge University Press, pp. 250–73.

Bhatia, V. (1993), *Analysing Genre: Language Use in Professional Settings*, London: Longman.

Birenbaum, M. (1996), 'Assessment 2000: towards a pluralistic approach to assessment', in M. Birenbaum and F. J. R. C. Dochy (eds), *Alternatives in Assessment of Achievements, Learning Processes, and Prior Knowledge*, Dordrecht, Netherlands: Kluwer Academic Publishers Group, pp. 3–29.

Block, D. (1996), 'Not so fast: some thoughts on theory culling, relativism, accepted feelings and the heart and soul of SLA', *Applied Linguistics*, 17: 63–83.

Brandt, R. (1998), 'Introduction', in R. Brandt (ed.), *Assessing Student Learning: New Rules, New Realities*, Arlington, VA: Educational Research Service, pp. 1–16.

Brennan, R. L. (1992), *Elements of Generalizability Theory* (rev. edn), Iowa City, IA: American College Testing.

Brennan, R. L. (2001), *Generalizability Theory*, New York: Springer-Verlag.

Brindley, G. (1989), *Assessing Achievement in the Learner-centered Curriculum*, Sydney: National Centre for English Language Teaching and Research, Macquarie University.

Brindley, G. (1998), 'Outcomes-based assessment and reporting in language learning programmes: a review of the issues', *Language Testing*, 15(1): 45–85.

Brown, J. D. (1980), 'Relative merits of four methods for scoring cloze tests', *Modern Language Journal*, 64: 311–17.

Brown, J. D. (1983), 'A closer look at cloze: validity and reliability', in J. W. Oller, Jr (ed.), *Issues in Language Testing Research*, Rowley, MA: Newbury House, pp. 237–50.

Brown, J. D. (1988), *Understanding Research in Second Language Learning: A Teacher's Guide to Statistics and Research Design*, Cambridge: Cambridge University Press.

Brown, J. D. (1989), 'Language programme evaluation: a synthesis of possibilities', in R. K. Johnson (ed.), *The Second Language Curriculum*, Cambridge: Cambridge University Press, pp. 259–69.

Brown, J. D. (2001), *Using Surveys in Language Programs*, Cambridge: Cambridge University Press.

Brown, J. D. and T. Hudson (1998), 'The alternatives in language assessment', *TESOL Quarterly*, 32(4): 653–75.

Brown, J. D. and T. Hudson (2002), *Criterion-referenced Language Testing*, Cambridge: Cambridge University Press.

Bryk, A. S. and S. W. Raudenbush (1992), *Hierarchical Linear Models: Applications and Data Analysis Methods*, Newbury Park, CA: Sage.

Buck, G. (1997), 'The testing of L2 listening', in C. Clapham and D. Corson (eds), *Encyclopedia of Language and Education, Vol. 7: Language Testing and Assessment*, Dordrecht: Kluwer Academic Publishers, pp. 65–74.

Campbell, D. T. and J. C. Stanley (1966), *Experimental and Quasi-experimental Designs for Research*, Chicago: Rand McNally.

Caporaso, J. A. and L. L. Roos (1973), *Quasi-experimental Approaches: Testing Theory and Evaluating Policy*, Evanston, IL: Northwestern University Press.

Carroll, J. B. (1961 [1972]), 'Fundamental considerations in testing for English language proficiency in foreign students', in H. B. Allen and R. N. Campbell (eds) (1972), *Teaching English as a Second Language: A Book of Readings* (2nd edn), New York: McGraw-Hill, pp. 313–21.

Chapelle, C. A. (1999), 'Validity in language assessment', *Annual Review of Applied Linguistics*, 19, 254–72.

Charmaz, K. (2000), 'Grounded theory: objectivist and constructivist methods', in N. K. Denzin and Y. S. Lincoln (eds), *The Handbook of Qualitative Research* (2nd edn), Thousand Oaks, CA: PineForge (Sage), pp. 509–35.

Clapham, C. and D. Corson (eds) (1997), *Encyclopedia of Language and Education, Vol. 7: Language Testing and Assessment*, Dordrecht: Kluwer Academic Publishers.

Clark, J. L. (1985), 'Curriculum renewal in second language learning: an overview', *Canadian Modern Language Review*, 42(2): 342–60.

Coady, J. (1979), 'A psycholinguistic model of the ESL reader', in R. Mackay, B. Barkman and R.R. Jordan (eds), *Reading in a Second Language*, Rowley, MA: Newbury House, pp. 5–12.

Cohen, A. D. (1994), *Assessing Language Ability in the Classroom*, Boston, MA: Heinle and Heinle.

Cook, T. D. and D. T. Campbell (1979), *Quasi-experimentation: Design and Analysis Issues for Field Settings*, Boston, MA: Houghton Mifflin.

Council of Europe (2002), *A Common European Framework of Reference: Learning, Teaching, Assessment*, Strasbourg, France: Language Policy Division, Council of Europe. Retrieved online, 4 September 2002: http://culture2.coe.int/portfolio//documents/0521803136txt.pdf

Davidson, F. (1996), *Principles of Statistical Data Handling*, Thousand Oaks, CA: Sage.

Davidson, F. and B. K. Lynch (2002), *Testcraft: A Teacher's Guide to Writing and Using Language Test Specifications*, New Haven: Yale University Press.

Davies, A. (1990), *Principles of Language Testing*, Oxford: Basil Blackwell.

Davies, A. (1997), 'Demands of being professional in language testing', *Language Testing*, 14(3), 328–39.

Davies, A. (2000), *An Introduction to Applied Linguistics: From Theory to Practice*, Edinburgh: Edinburgh University Press.

Davies, A., A. Brown, C. Elder, K. Hill, T. Lumley and T. McNamara (1999), *Dictionary of Language Testing*, Cambridge: University of Cambridge Local Examinations Syndicate and Cambridge University Press.

Debski, R. (2000), 'Exploring the recreation of a CALL innovation', *Computer Assisted Language Learning*, 13(4–5): 307–32.

Denzin, N. K. and Y. S. Lincoln (eds) (2000), *The Handbook of Qualitative Research* (2nd edn), Thousand Oaks, CA: PineForge (Sage).

Doughty, C. (1991), 'Second language instruction does make a difference: evidence from an empirical study of SL relativisation', *Applied Linguistics*, 13(4): 431–69.

Douglas, D. (2000), *Assessing Languages for Specific Purposes*, Cambridge: Cambridge University Press.

Douglas, D. and L. Selinker (1991), *SPEAK and CHEMSPEAK: Measuring the English Speaking Ability of International Teaching Assistants in Chemistry*, Ames, IA: Department of English, Iowa State University.

Educational Testing Service (ETS) (1985), *The Speaking English Assessment Kit (SPEAK): Examinee Handbook and Sample Questions*, Princeton, NJ: ETS.

Eisner, E. W. (1991), *The Enlightened Eye: Qualitative inquiry and the enhancement of educational practice*, New York: Macmillan Publishing Company.

Elbow, P. (1973), *Writing without teachers*, Oxford: Oxford University Press.

Eyring, J. L. (2001), 'Experiential and negotiated language learning', in M. Celce-Murcia (ed.), *Teaching English as a Second or Foreign Language* (3rd edn), Boston, MA: Heinle and Heinle/Thomson Learning, pp. 333–44.

Excel (2000), *Excel for Windows*, Redmond, WA: Microsoft.

Fotos, S. S. (1994), 'Integrating grammar instruction and communicative language use through grammar consciousness-raising tasks', *TESOL Quarterly*, 28(2): 323–51.

Foucault, M. (1979), *Discipline and Punish: The Birth of the Prison* (translated from the French by A. Sheridan), New York: Vintage Books/Random House, Inc.

Foucault, M. (1982), 'The subject and power', in H. L. Dreyfus and P. Rabinow (eds), *Michel Foucault: Beyond Structuralism and Hermeneutics* (pp. 208–16 written in English by Michel Foucault; pp. 216–26 translated from the French by L. Sawyer), Brighton, UK: The Harvester Press, pp. 208–26.

Foucault, M. (1990), *The History of Sexuality: Volume 3: The Care of the Self* (translated from the French by R. Hurley), New York: Vintage Books/Random House, Inc.

Foucault, M. (1997), *Michel Foucault, Ethics: Subjectivity and Truth (The Essential Works of Michel Foucault, 1954–1984, Vol. 1)*, ed. P. Rabinow, London: Allen Lane/The Penguin Press.

Gadamer, H-G. (1989), *Truth and Method*, translated by J. Weinsheimer and D. Marshall, New York, NY: Continuum.

Gattullo, F. (2000), 'Formative assessment in ELT primary (elementary) classrooms: an Italian case study', *Language Testing*, 17(2): 278–88.

Goodman, K. S. (1967), 'Reading: a psycholinguistic guessing game', *Journal of the Reading Specialist*, 6(1): 126–35.

Goodwin, J. (1990), *Speaking Performance Scale for UCLA Oral Proficiency Test for Non-Native Teaching Assistants*, Los Angeles, CA: Department of TESL and Applied Linguistics, UCLA.

Gough, P. B. (1972), 'One second of reading', in J. F. Kavanagh and I. G. Mattingly (eds), *Language by Ear and Eye*, Cambridge, MA: MIT Press.

Gregg, K.R. (1984), 'Krashen's monitor and Occam's razor', *Applied Linguistics*, 5(1): 79–100.

Gregg, K. R., M. H. Long, G. Jordan and A. Beretta (1997), 'Rationality and its discontents in SLA', *Applied Linguistics*, 18(4): 538–58.

Greene, J. C. (2000), 'Understanding social programs through evaluation', in N. K. Denzin and Y. S. Lincoln (eds), *The Handbook of Qualitative Research* (2nd edn), Thousand Oaks, CA: PineForge (Sage), pp. 981–99.

Guba, E. G. (ed.) (1990), *The Paradigm Dialog*, Newbury Park, CA: Sage.

Guba, E. G. and Y. S. Lincoln (1989), *Fourth Generation Evaluation*, Newbury Park, CA: Sage.

Hambleton, R. K., H. Swaminathan and H. J. Rogers (1991), *Fundamentals of Item Response Theory*, Newbury Park, CA: Sage.

Hamp-Lyons, L. (1989), 'Language testing and ethics', *Prospect*, 5(1): 7–15.

Hamp-Lyons, L. (1990), 'Second language writing: assessment issues', in B. Kroll (ed.), *Second Language Writing: Research Insights for the Classroom*, Cambridge: Cambridge University Press, pp. 69–87.

Hamp-Lyons, L. (ed.) (1991), *Assessing Second Language Writing in Academic Contexts*, Norwood, NJ: Ablex.

Hamp-Lyons, L. and W. Condon (2000), *Assessing the Portfolio: Principles for Practice, Theory, and Research*, Cresskill, NJ: Hampton Press, Inc.

Hamp-Lyons, L. and B. K. Lynch (1998), 'Perspectives on validity: a historical analysis of language testing conference abstracts', in A. J. Kunnan (ed.), *Validation in Language Assessment*, Mahwah, NJ: Lawrence Erlbaum, pp. 253–76.

Hatch, E. and A. Lazaraton (1991), *The Research Manual: Design and Statistics for Applied Linguistics*, New York: Newbury House.

Hawkins, B. (1988), *Scaffolded Classroom Interaction and its Relation to Second Language Acquisition for Language Minority Children*, Ph.D. dissertation, University of California, Los Angeles.

Henerson, M. E., L. L. Morris and C. T. Fitz-Gibbon (1987), *How to Measure Attitudes*, Newbury Park, CA: Sage.

Henning, G., T. Hudson and J. Turner (1985), 'Item response theory and the assumption of unidimensionality', *Language Testing*, 2(2): 229–34.

Henning, G. (1987), *A Guide to Language Testing*, Cambridge, MA: Newbury House Publishers.

Henning, G. (1988), 'The influence of test and sample dimensionality on latent trait person ability and item difficulty calibrations'. *Language Testing*, 5(1): 83–99.

Heron, J. (1988), 'Assessment revisited', in D. Boud (ed.), *Developing student autonomy in learning*, London: Kogan Page, pp. 55–68.

Hess, G. A. (1999), 'Understanding achievement (and other) changes under Chicago school reform', *Educational Evaluation and Policy Analysis*, 21(1): 67–83.

Hudson, T. (1989), 'Mastery decisions in program evaluation', in R. K. Johnson (ed.), *The Second Language Curriculum*, Cambridge: Cambridge University Press, pp. 259–69.

Hughes, A. (1989), *Testing for Language Teachers*, Cambridge: Cambridge University Press.

ILTA (2000), *International Language Testing Association Code of ethics*. Available online: http://www.surrey.ac.uk/ELI/ilta/code.pdf

Jacobs, H. L., S. A. Zinkgraf, D. R. Wormuth, V. F. Hartfiel and J. B. Hughey (1981), *Testing ESL Composition*, Rowley, MA: Newbury House.

Johnstone, R. (2000), 'Context-sensitive assessment of modern languages in primary (elementary) and early secondary education: Scotland and the European experience', *Language Testing*, 17(2): 123–43.

Joint Committee on Standards for Education Evaluation (1994), *The Program Evaluation Standards* (2nd edn), Thousand Oaks, CA: Sage.

Judd, C. M. and D. A. Kenny (1981), *Estimating the Effects of Social Interventions*, Cambridge: Cambridge University Press.

Kane, M. (1994), 'Validating the performance standards associated with passing scores', *Review of Educational Research*, 64(3): 425–61.

Kincheloe, J. L. and P. McLaren (2000), 'Rethinking critical theory and qualitative research', in N. K. Denzin and Y. S. Lincoln (eds), *The Handbook of Qualitative Research* (2nd edn), Thousand Oaks, CA: PineForge (Sage), pp. 279–313.

Klein-Braley, C. (1985), 'A cloze-up on the c-test: a study in the construct validation of authentic tests', *Language Testing*, 2(1): 76–104.

Kramsch, C. (2000), 'Social discursive constructions of self in L2 learning', in J. P. Lantolf (ed.), *Sociocultural Theory and Second Language Learning*, Oxford: Oxford University Press, pp. 133–53.

Kuehn, K. (1994), 'Form-structured discourse: a script of a welfare office intake interview for ESL learners', unpublished M.A. Qualifying Paper: University of Minnesota.

Lazaraton, A. (1991), 'A conversation analysis of structure and interaction in the language interview', unpublished Ph.D. dissertation, UCLA, Los Angeles CA.

Lazaraton, A. (1996), 'Interlocutor support in oral proficiency interviews: the case of CASE', *Language Testing*, 13: 151–72.

Linacre, J. M. (1988), *Facets: A Computer Program for Many-facet Rasch Measurement*, Chicago, IL: Mesa Press.

Lincoln, Y. S. (1990), 'The making of a constructivist: A remembrance of transformations past', in E. G. Guba (ed.), *The Paradigm Dialog*, Newbury Park, CA: Sage, pp. 67–87.

Lincoln, Y. S. and E. G. Guba (2000), 'Paradigmatic controversies, contradictons, and emerging confluences', in N. K. Denzin and Y. S. Lincoln (eds), *The Handbook of Qualitative Research* (2nd edn), Thousand Oaks, CA: PineForge (Sage), pp. 163–88.

Lloyd-Jones, R. (1977), 'Primay Trait Scoring', in C. R. Cooper and L. Odell (eds), *Evaluating Writing*, NY: National Council of Teachers of English, pp. 33–69.

Long, M. H. (1984), 'Native speaker/non-native speaker conversation and the negotiation of comprehensible input', *Applied Linguistics*, 4(2): 126–41.

Long, M. H. (1998), 'SLA: Breaking the siege', plenary address to the third Pacific Second Language Research Forum (PacSLRF), Aoyama Gakuin University, Tokyo, Japan, 26–29 March 1998.

Longino, H. (1993), 'Subjects, power, and knowledge: description and prescription in feminist philosophies of science', in L. Alcoff and E. Potter (eds), *Feminist Epistemologies*, New York: Routledge, pp. 101–20.

Lumley, T. (1993), 'The notion of subskills in reading comprehension tests: an EAP example',

Language Testing, 10(3): 211–34.

Lumley, T. (2002), 'Assessment criteria in a large-scale writing test: what do they really mean to the raters?' *Language Testing*, 19(3): 246–76.

Lumley, T. and A. Brown (1996), 'Specific purpose language performance tests: task and interaction', in G. Wigglesworth and C. Elder (eds), *The Language Testing Cycle: From Inception to Washback: Australian Review of Applied Linguistics Series S*, 13: 105–36.

Lumley, T. and T. McNamara (1995), 'Rater characteristics and rater bias: implications for training', *Language Testing*, 12(1): 54–71.

Lumley, T., B. K. Lynch and T. McNamara (1994), 'A new approach to standard-setting in language assessment', *Melbourne Papers in Language Testing*, 3(2): 19–40.

Lynch, B. K. (1992), 'Evaluating a program inside and out', in C. Alderson and A. Beretta (eds), *Evaluating Second Language Education,* Cambridge: Cambridge University Press, pp. 61–99.

Lynch, B. K. (1996), *Language Programme Evaluation: Theory and Practice*, Cambridge: Cambridge University Press.

Lynch, B. K. (1997), 'In search of the ethical test', *Language Testing*, 14(3): 315–27.

Lynch, B. K. (2000), 'Evaluating a project-oriented CALL innovation', *Computer Assisted Language Learning*, 13(4–5): 417–40.

Lynch, B. K. (2001a), 'The ethical potential of alternative assessment', in C. Elder, A. Brown, E. Grove, K. Hill, N. Iwashita, T. Lumley, T. McNamara and K. O'Loughlin (eds), *Experimenting with Uncertainty: Essays in Honour of Alan Davies* (Studies in Language Testing Vol. 11), Cambridge: University of Cambridge Local Examinations Syndicate and Cambridge University Press, pp. 228–39.

Lynch, B. K. (2001b), 'Rethinking assessment from a critical perspective', *Language Testing*, 18(4): 351–72.

Lynch, B. K. and T. F. McNamara (1998), 'Using G-theory and Many-Facet Rasch measurement in the development of performance assessments of the ESL speaking skills of immigrants', *Language Testing*, 15(2): 158–80.

Lynch, B. K. and L. Hamp-Lyons (1999), 'Perspectives on research paradigms and validity: tales from the Language Testing Research Colloquium', *Melbourne Papers in Language Testing*, 8(1): 57–93.

Lynch, B. K. and P. A. Shaw (1998), 'Portfolios, Power and Ethics', paper presented at the 32nd Annual TESOL Convention; Seattle, Washington.

Lynch, D. A. and S. D. Jukuri (1998), 'Beyond master and slave: reconciling our fears of power in the writing classroom', *Rhetoric Review*, 16(2): 270–88.

Mabry, L. (1999), *Portfolios Plus: A Critical Guide to Alternative Assessment*, Thousand Oaks, CA: Corwin Press, Inc./Sage Publications Ltd.

McDonnell, L. M. (1995), 'Opportunity to learn as a research concept and a policy instrument', *Educational Evaluation and Policy Analysis*, 17(3): 305–22.

McGrath, J. E., H. Martin and R. A. Kulka (1982), 'Some quasi-rules for making judgement calls in research', in J. E. McGrath, H. Martin and R. A. Kulka (eds), *Judgement Calls in Research*, Beverly Hills, CA: Sage, pp. 103–18.

McKay, P. (2000), 'On ESL standards for school-age learners', *Language Testing*, 17(2): 185–214.

McNamara, T. F. (1990), 'Item Response Theory and the validation of an ESP test for health professionals', *Language Testing*, 7(1): 52–75.

McNamara, T. F. (1996), *Measuring Second Language Performance*, London: Longman.

McNamara, T. F. (1997), 'Policy and social considerations in language assessment', *Annual Review of Applied Linguistics*, 18: 304–19.

McNamara, T. F. (2000), *Language Testing*, Oxford: Oxford University Press.

McNamara, T. F. and T. Lumley (1997), 'The effect of interlocutor and assessment mode variables in offshore assessments of speaking skills in occupational settings', *Language Testing*, 14(2): 140–56.

Maruyama, G. M. (1998), *Basics of Structural Equation Modeling*, Thousand Oaks, CA: Sage.

Mellow, J. D., K. Reeder and E. Forster, (1996), 'Using time-series research designs to investigate the effects of instruction on SLA', *Studies in Second Language Acquisition*, 18: 325–50.

Messick, S. (1989), 'Validity', in R. L. Linn (ed.), *Educational Measurement* (3rd edn), Washington, DC: The American Council on Education and the National Council on Measurement in Education, pp. 13–103.

Messick, S. (1994), 'The interplay of evidence and consequences in the validation of performance assessments', *Educational Researcher*, 23(2): 13–23.

Messick, S. (1996), 'Validity and washback in language testing', *Language Testing*, 13: 241–56.

Miles, M. B. and A. M. Huberman (1994), *Qualitative Data Analysis: A Sourcebook of New Methods* (2nd edn), Thousand Oaks, CA: Sage.

Mitchell, R. (1992), 'The "independent" evaluation of bilingual primary education: a narrative account', in J. C. Alderson and A. Beretta (eds), *Evaluating Second Language Education*, Cambridge: Cambridge University Press, pp. 100–40.

Mori, M. (1991), 'Script for the medical consultation: comparison of the expectations between a Japanese and American', unpublished Course Paper: University of Minnesota.

Moss, P. A. (1994), 'Can there be validity without reliability?', *Educational Researcher*, 23(2): 5–12.

Moss, P. A. (1996), 'Enlarging the dialogue in educational measurement: voices from interpretive research traditions', *Educational Researcher*, 25(1): 20–8.

Moss, P. A., J. S. Beck, C. Ebbs, B. Matson, J. Muchmore, D. Steele, C. Taylor and R. Herter (1992), 'Portfolios, accountability, and an interpretive approach to validity', *Educational Measurement: Issues and Practice*, 11(3): 12–21.

Muthén, B. and L. Muthén (1998), *Mplus: Statistical Analysis with Latent Variables*, Los Angeles, CA: Muthén and Muthén.

Newmann, F. M., B. Smith, E. Allensworth and A. S. Bryk (2001), 'Instructional program coherence: what it is and why it should guide school improvement policy', *Educational Evaluation and Policy Analysis*, 23(4): 297–321.

Norris, J. M., J. D. Brown, T. Hudson and J. Yoshioka (1998), *Designing Second Language Performance Assessments*, Honolulu, HI: Second Language Teaching and Curriculum Center, University of Hawai'i Press.

North, B. (2000), *The Development of a Common Framework Scale of Language Proficiency*, New York: Peter Lang.

Oller, J. W., Jr (1979), *Language Tests at School*, London: Longman.

Outeiriño, E., R. Rich, A. Roberts, C. Silventoinen and T. West (2002), 'Responding to employment ads via voicemail', class assignment for Applied Linguistics 439/539, Language Testing, Portland State University.

Parkinson, B., P. Sandhu, M. Lacorte and L. Gourlay (1998), 'To code or not to code?' *Edinburgh Working Papers in Applied Linguistics*, 9: 86–103.

Parlett, M. and D. Hamilton (1976), 'Evaluation as illumination: a new approach to the study of innovatory programs', in G. V. Glass (ed.), *Evaluation Studies Annual Review, Vol. 1*, Beverly Hills, CA: Sage, pp. 140–57.

Patton, M. Q. (1990), *Qualitative Evaluation and Research Methods* (2nd edn), Newbury Park, CA: Sage.

Pavlenko, A. and J. P. Lantolf (2000), 'Second language learning as participation and the (re)construction of selves', in J. P. Lantolf (ed.), *Sociocultural Theory and Second Language Learning*, Oxford: Oxford University Press, pp. 155–77.

Pearce, W. B. (1995), 'A sailing guide for social constructionists', in W. Leed-Hurwitz (ed.), *Social Approaches to Communication*, New York, NY: The Guilford Press, pp. 88–113.

Pellegrino, J. W., L. R. Jones and K. J. Mitchell (eds) (1999), *Grading the Nation's Report Card: Evaluating NAEP and Transforming the Assessment of Educational Progress*, Washington, DC: National Academy Press.

Pennycook, A. (1989), 'The Concept of Method, interested knowledge and the politics of language education', *TESOL Quarterly*, 23(4), 589–618.

Pennycook, A. (2001), *Critical Applied Linguistics: A Critical Introduction*, Mahway, NJ: Lawrence Erlbaum.

Peregoy, S. and O. Boyle (1997), *Reading, Writing, and Learning in ESL* (2nd edn), New York: Longman.

Perrett, G. (1990), 'The language testing interview: a reappraisal', in J. H. A. L. de Jong and D. K. Stevenson (eds), *Individualizing the Assessment of Language Abilities*, Clevedon, England: Multilingual Matters, pp. 225–38.

Peshkin, A. (1993), 'The goodness of qualitative research', *Educational Researcher*, 22(2): 23–7.

Phillips, D. C. (1990), 'Postpositivistic science: myths and realities', in E. G. Guba (ed.), *The Paradigm Dialog*, Newbury Park, CA: Sage, pp. 31–45.

Popham, W. J. (1978), *Criterion-referenced Measurement*, Englewood Cliffs, NJ: Prentice Hall.

Popham, W. J. (1990), *Modern Educational Measurement* (2nd edn), Englewood Cliffs, NJ: Prentice Hall.

Popham, W. J. (1994), 'The instructional consequences of criterion-referenced clarity', *Educational Measurement: Issues and Practice*, 13: 15–18, 30.

Popham, W. J. (1997), 'What's wrong – and what's right – with rubrics', *Educational Leadership, 55*(2), Retrieved online, May 2002:
http://www.ascd.org.readingroom/edlead/9710/popham.html

Prabhu, N. S. (1990), 'Comments on Alan Beretta's paper "Implementation of the Bangalore Project"', *Applied Linguistics*, 11(4): 337–40.

Punch, M. (1994), 'Politics and ethics in qualitative research', in N. K. Denzin and Y. S. Lincoln (eds), *Handbook of Qualitative Research*, Thousand Oaks, CA: Sage, pp. 83–97.

Purpura, J. E. (1999), *Learner Strategy Use and Performance on Language Tests: A Structural Equation Modeling Approach* (Studies in Language Testing Vol. 8), Cambridge: University of Cambridge Local Examinations Syndicate and Cambridge University Press.

QSR (1998), *NUD*IST, N4 (Non-numerical Unstructured Data Indexing Searching and Theorizing) qualitative data analysis program*, Melbourne, Australia: QSR International Pty Ltd.

QSR (2000), *NVivo qualitative data analysis program, Version 1.3*, Melbourne, Australia: QSR International Pty Ltd.

Rampton, B. (1995), 'Politics and change in research in applied linguistics', *Applied Linguistics*, 16, 2: 233–56.

Ranney, S. (1992), 'Learning a new script: an exploration of sociolinguistic competence', *Applied Linguistics*, 13: 25–49.

Raudenbush, S., A. S. Bryk, Y. F. Cheong and R. Congdon (2000), *HLM5: Hierarchical Linear and Nonlinear Modeling*, Lincolnwood, IL: Scientific Software.

Rea-Dickins, P. (2001), 'Mirror, mirror on the wall: identifying processes of classroom assessment', *Language Testing*, 18(4): 429–62.

Rea-Dickins, P. and K. Germaine (1992), *Evaluation*, Oxford: Oxford University Press.

Rea-Dickins, P. and S. Gardner (2000), 'Snares or silver bullets: disentangling the construct of formative assessment', *Language Testing*, 17(2): 215–43.

Rimarcik, J. (1996), 'Automated voice response system (AVRS) telephone messages: reality of the nightmare for international students', unpublished M.A. Qualifying Paper: University of Minnesota.

Ross, S. J. (forthcoming), 'A diachronic coherence model for language programme evaluation', *Language Learning*, 53 (1).

Rumelhart, D. (1977), 'Toward an interactive model of reading', in S. Dornic (ed.), *Attention and Performance, Vol. 6*, New York: Academic Press, pp. 573–603.

Scheurich, J. J. (1995), 'A postmodernist critique of research interviewing', *Qualitative Studies in Education*, 8(3): 239–52.

Schwandt, T. D. (2000), 'Three epistemological stances for qualitative inquiry: interpretivism, hermeneutics, and social constructionism', in N. K. Denzin and Y. S. Lincoln (eds), *The Handbook of Qualitative Research* (2nd edn), Thousand Oaks, CA: PineForge (Sage), pp. 189–213.

Scriven, M. (1967), 'The methodology of evaluation', in R. W. Tyler, R. M. Gagne and M. Scriven (eds), *Perspectives of Curriculum Evaluation, AERA Monograph Series on Curriuclum Evaluation, No. 1*, Chicago, IL: Rand McNally, pp. 39–83.

Shepard, L. A. (1984), 'Setting performance standards', in R. A. Berk (eds), *A Guide to Criteriion-referenced Test Construction*, Baltimore, MD: Johns Hopkins University Press, pp. 169–98.

Shohamy, E. (2001), *The Power of Tests: A Critical Perspective on the Uses of Language Tests*, London: Longman/Pearson Education.

Smith, F. (1971), *Understanding Reading: A Psycholinguistic Analysis of Reading and Learning to Read*, New York: Holt, Rinehart and Winston.

Smith, J. K. (1988), 'The evaluator/researcher as person vs. the person as evaluator/researcher', *Educational Researcher*, 17(2): 18–23.

Smith, J. K. (1990), 'Alternative research paradigms and the problem of criteria', in E. G. Guba (ed.), *The Paradigm Dialog*, Newbury Park, CA: Sage, pp. 167–87.

Spada, N. and M. Frohlich (1995), *COLT Observation Scheme, Coding Conventions and Applications*, Sydney: National Centre for English Language Teaching and Research, Macquarie University.

SPSS (2002), *SPSS Base 11.0 User's Guide Package (SPSS for Windows, Release 11.0.1.)*, Chicago, IL: SPSS, Inc.

Stake, R. E. (1975), *Evaluating the Arts in Education*, Columbus, OH: Charles E. Merrill.

Stansfield, C. W., D. M. Kenyon, F. Doyle, R. Paiva, I. Ulsh and M. A. Cowles (1988), *Portuguese Speaking Test: Official Test Manual*, Washington, DC: Center for Applied Linguistics.

Steffenson, M. S., C. Joag-dev and R. C. Anderson (1979), 'A cross-cultural perspective on reading comprehension', *Reading Research Quarterly*, 15(1): 10–29.

Stoller, F. L. (1997), 'Project work: a means to promote language content', *English Teaching Forum*, 35(4): 2–9, 37.

Strauss, A. L. (1987), *Qualitative Analysis for Social Scientists*, New York: Cambridge University Press.

Strauss, A. L. and J. Corbin (1998), *Basics of Qualitative Research: Techniques and Procedures for Developing Grounded Theory* (2nd edn), Thousand Oaks, CA: Sage.

Swain, M. (1984), 'Large-scale communicative language testing: a case study', in S. J. Savignon and M. S. Berns (eds), *Initiatives in Communicative Language Teaching*, Reading, MA: Addison-Wesley, pp. 185–201.

Swain, M. (2000), 'The output hypothesis and beyond: mediating acquisition through collaborative dialogue', in J. P. Lantolf (ed.), *Sociocultural Theory and Second Language Learning*, Oxford: Oxford University Press, pp. 97–114.

Tarone, E. (2001), 'Assessing language skills for specific purposes: describing and analysing the "behaviour domain"', in C. Elder, A. Brown, E. Grove, K. Hill, N. Iwashita, T. Lumley, T. McNamara and K. O'Loughlin (eds), *Experimenting with Uncertainty: Essays in Honour of Alan Davies* (Studies in Language Testing Vol. 11), Cambridge: University of Cambridge Local Examinations Syndicate and Cambridge University Press, pp. 53–60.

Teasdale, A. and C. Leung (2000), 'Teacher assessment and psychometric theory: a case of paradigm crossing', *Language Testing*, 17(2): 163–84.

Turner, L. (2000a), 'Learning to write with a little help from my friends: the social construction of self and mind', *New Zealand Studies in Applied Linguistics*, 8: 21–44.

Turner, L. (2000b), 'Belonging, being friends and learning to write a second language: the social construction of self and mind', unpublished Ph.D. dissertation: Applied Linguistics, The University of Melbourne.

University of California, Los Angeles (UCLA) (2001), *Heritage Language Research Priorities Conference Report*, Los Angeles, CA: Author. Available: www.cal.org/heritage

University of Cambridge Local Examinations Syndicate (UCLES) (1987), *English as a Foreign Language: General Handbook*, Cambridge: University of Cambridge Local Examinations Syndicate.

Valencia, S. and P. D. Pearson (1987), 'Reading assessment: time for a change', *The Reading Teacher*, 40: 726–32.

Weigle, S. (1994), 'Effects of training on raters of ESL compositions', *Language Testing*, 11(2): 197–223.

Weigle, S. (2002), *Assessing Writing*, Cambridge: Cambridge University Press.

Weir, C. (1997), 'The testing of second language reading', in C. Clapham and D. Corson (eds), *Encyclopedia of Language and Education, Volume 7 (Language Testing and Assessment)*, Dordrecht: Kluwer Academic Publishers, pp. 39–49.

Weir, C. and J. Roberts (1994), *Evaluation in ELT*, Oxford: Blackwell Publishers.

Weitzman, E. A. (2000), 'Software and qualitative research', in N. K. Denzin and Y. S. Lincoln (eds), *The Handbook of Qualitative Research* (2nd edn), Thousand Oaks, CA: PineForge (Sage), pp. 803–20.

Widdowson, H. G. (1978), *Teaching Language as Communication*, Oxford: Oxford University Press.

Wolf, D., J. Bixby, J. Glenn III and H. Gardener (1991), 'To use their minds well: Investigating new forms of student assessment', *Review of Research in Education*, 17: 31–74.

Wolf, R. L. (1975), 'Trial by jury: a new evaluation method', *Phi Delta Kappan*, 57(3): 185–7.

Wortham, S. C. (1995), *Measurement and Evaluation in Early Childhood Education*, Englewood Cliffs, NJ: Prentice-Hall, Inc.

Wu, M. L., R. J. Adams and M. R. Wilson (1996), *Conquest: Generalised Item Response Modelling Software*, Camberwell, Victoria: Australian Council for Educational Research.

Zangl, R. (2000), 'Monitoring language skills in Austrian primary (elementary) schools: a case study', *Language Testing*, 17(2): 250–60.

Index